THIEF OF THIEVES ™

CREATED BY ROBERT KIRKMAN

ANDY DIGGLE
WRITER

SHAWN MARTINBROUGH
ARTIST

ADRIANO LUCAS
COLORIST

RUS WOOTON
LETTERER

SEAN MACKIEWICZ
EDITOR

SHAWN MARTINBROUGH
ADRIANO LUCAS
COVER

THIEF OF THIEVES, VOL. 4: "THE HIT LIST."
ISBN: 978-1-63215-037-0
PRINTED IN U.S.A.
First Printing

Published by Image Comics, Inc. Office of publication: 2001 Center Street, 6th Floor, Berkeley, California 94704. Image and its logos are ® and © 2014 Image Comics Inc. All rights reserved. Originally published in single magazine form as THIEF OF THIEVES #20-25. THIEF OF THIEVES and all character likenesses are ™ and © 2014, Robert Kirkman, LLC. All rights reserved. All names, characters, events and locales in this publication are entirely fictional. Any resemblance to actual persons (living or dead), events or places, without satiric intent, is coincidental. No part of this publication may be reproduced or transmitted, in any form or by any means (except for short excerpts for review purposes) without the express written permission of the copyright holder.

For information regarding the CPSIA on this printed material call: 203-595-3636 and provide reference # RICH - 595028.

IMAGE COMICS, INC.
Robert Kirkman – Chief Operating Officer
Erik Larsen – Chief Financial Officer
Todd McFarlane – President
Marc Silvestri – Chief Executive Officer
Jim Valentino – Vice-President

Eric Stephenson – Publisher
Ron Richards – Director of Business Development
Jennifer de Guzman – Director of Trade Book Sales
Kat Salazar – Director of PR & Marketing
Corey Murphy – Director of Retail Sales
Jeremy Sullivan – Director of Digital Sales
Emilio Bautista – Sales Assistant
Branwyn Bigglestone – Senior Accounts Manager
Emily Miller – Accounts Manager
Jessica Ambriz – Administrative Assistant
Tyler Shainline – Events Coordinator
David Brothers – Content Manager
Jonathan Chan – Production Manager
Drew Gill – Art Director
Meredith Wallace – Print Manager
Monica Garcia – Senior Production Artist
Addison Duke – Production Artist
Tricia Ramos – Production Assistant
IMAGECOMICS.COM

For SKYBOUND ENTERTAINMENT

Robert Kirkman - CEO
Sean Mackiewicz - Editorial Director
Shawn Kirkham - Director of Business Development
Brian Huntington - Online Editorial Director
June Alian - Publicity Director
Rachel Skidmore - Director of Media Development
Helen Leigh - Assistant Editor
Dan Petersen - Operations Manager
Sarah Effinger - Office Manager
Nick Palmer - Operations Coordinator
Lizzy Iverson - Administrative Assistant
Stephan Murillo - Administrative Assistant

International inquiries: foreign@skybound.com
Licensing inquiries: contact@skybound.com

WWW.SKYBOUND.COM

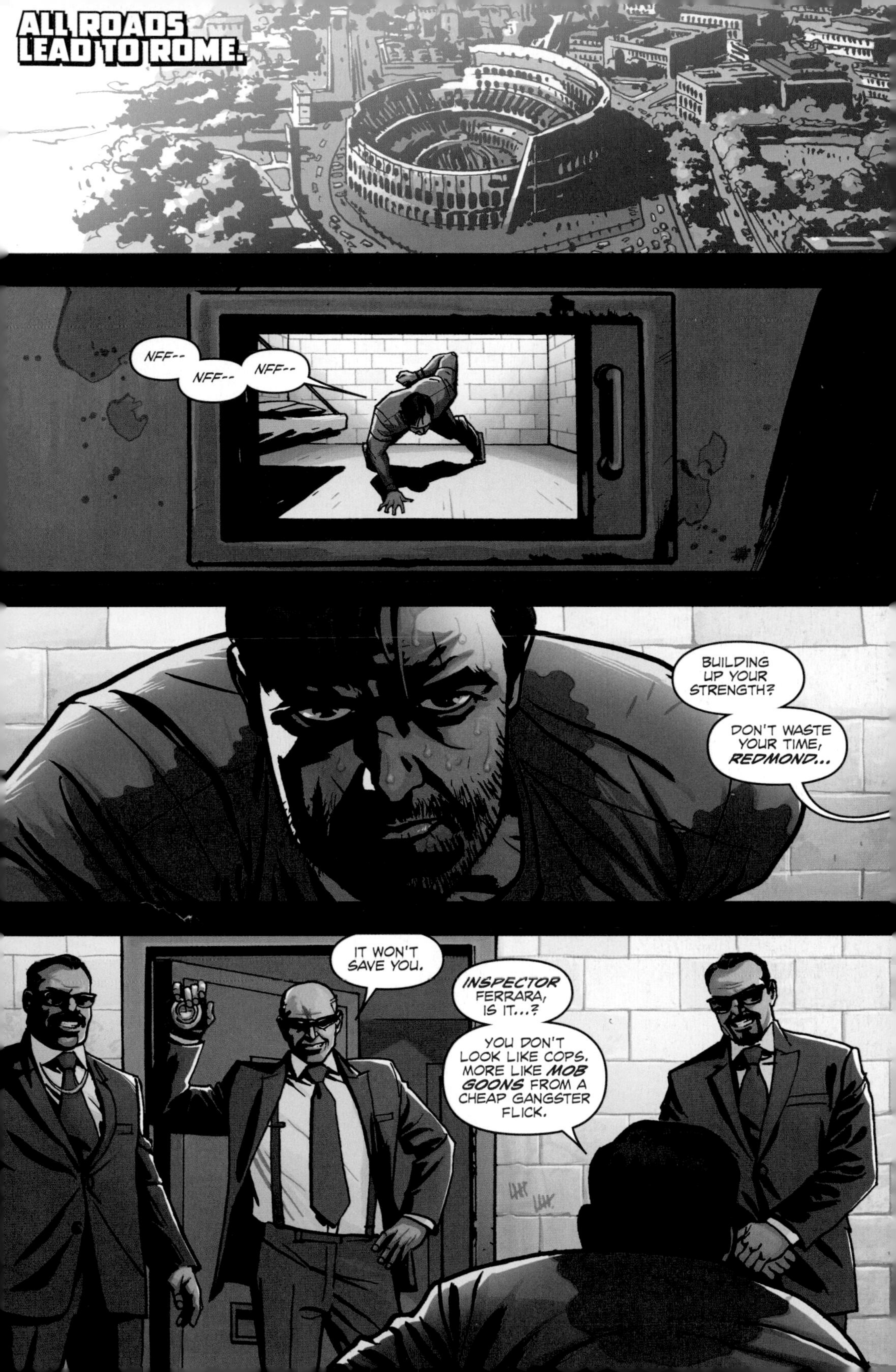
ALL ROADS LEAD TO ROME.
NFF--
NFF--
NFF--
BUILDING UP YOUR STRENGTH?
DON'T WASTE YOUR TIME, REDMOND...
IT WON'T SAVE YOU.
INSPECTOR FERRARA, IS IT...?
YOU DON'T LOOK LIKE COPS. MORE LIKE MOB GOONS FROM A CHEAP GANGSTER FLICK.

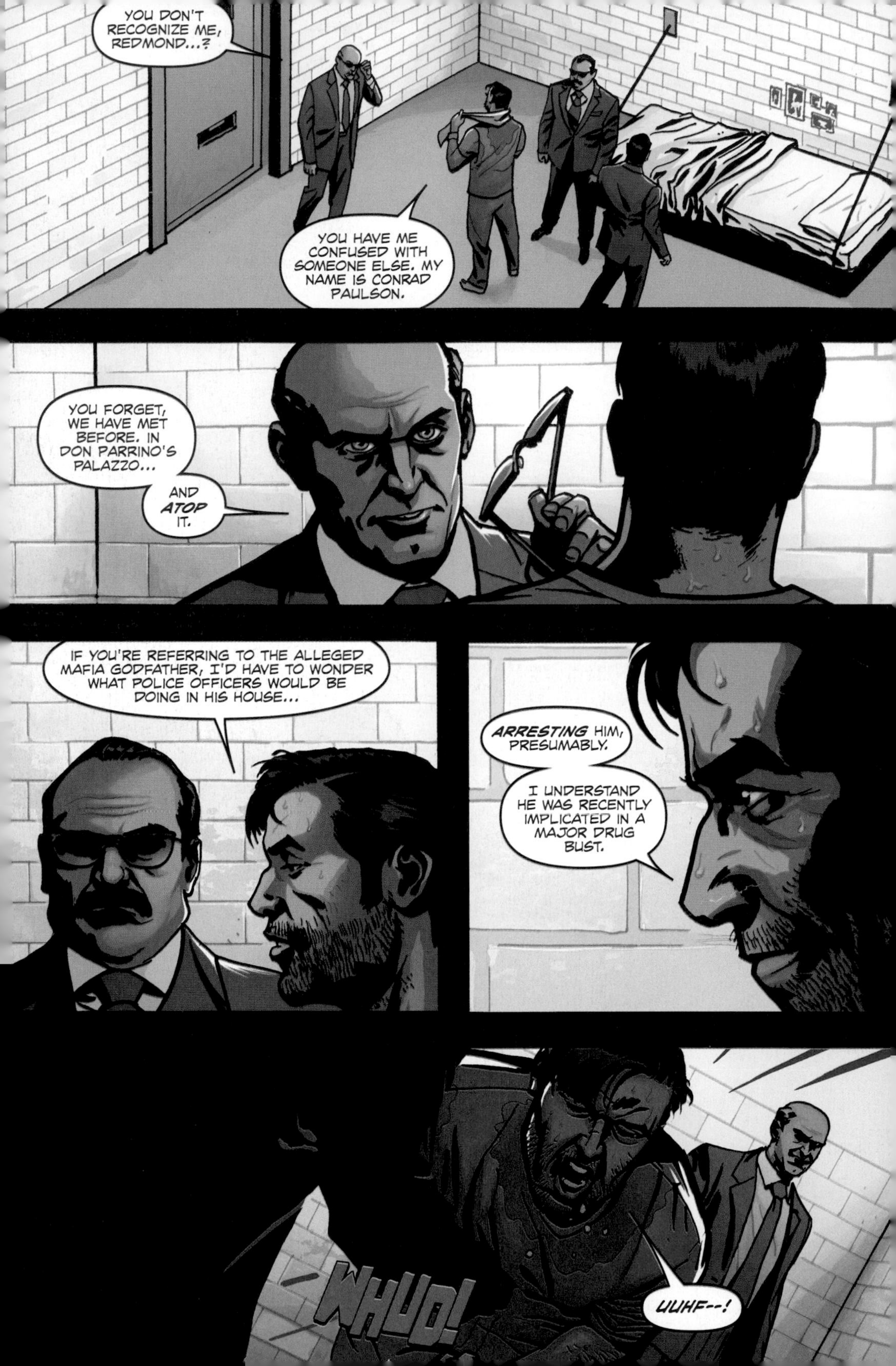
YOU DON'T RECOGNIZE ME, REDMOND...?
YOU HAVE ME CONFUSED WITH SOMEONE ELSE. MY NAME IS CONRAD PAULSON.
YOU FORGET, WE HAVE MET BEFORE. IN DON PARRINO'S PALAZZO...
AND *ATOP* IT.
IF YOU'RE REFERRING TO THE ALLEGED MAFIA GODFATHER, I'D HAVE TO WONDER WHAT POLICE OFFICERS WOULD BE DOING IN HIS HOUSE...
ARRESTING HIM, PRESUMABLY.
I UNDERSTAND HE WAS RECENTLY IMPLICATED IN A MAJOR DRUG BUST.
WHUD!
UUHF--!

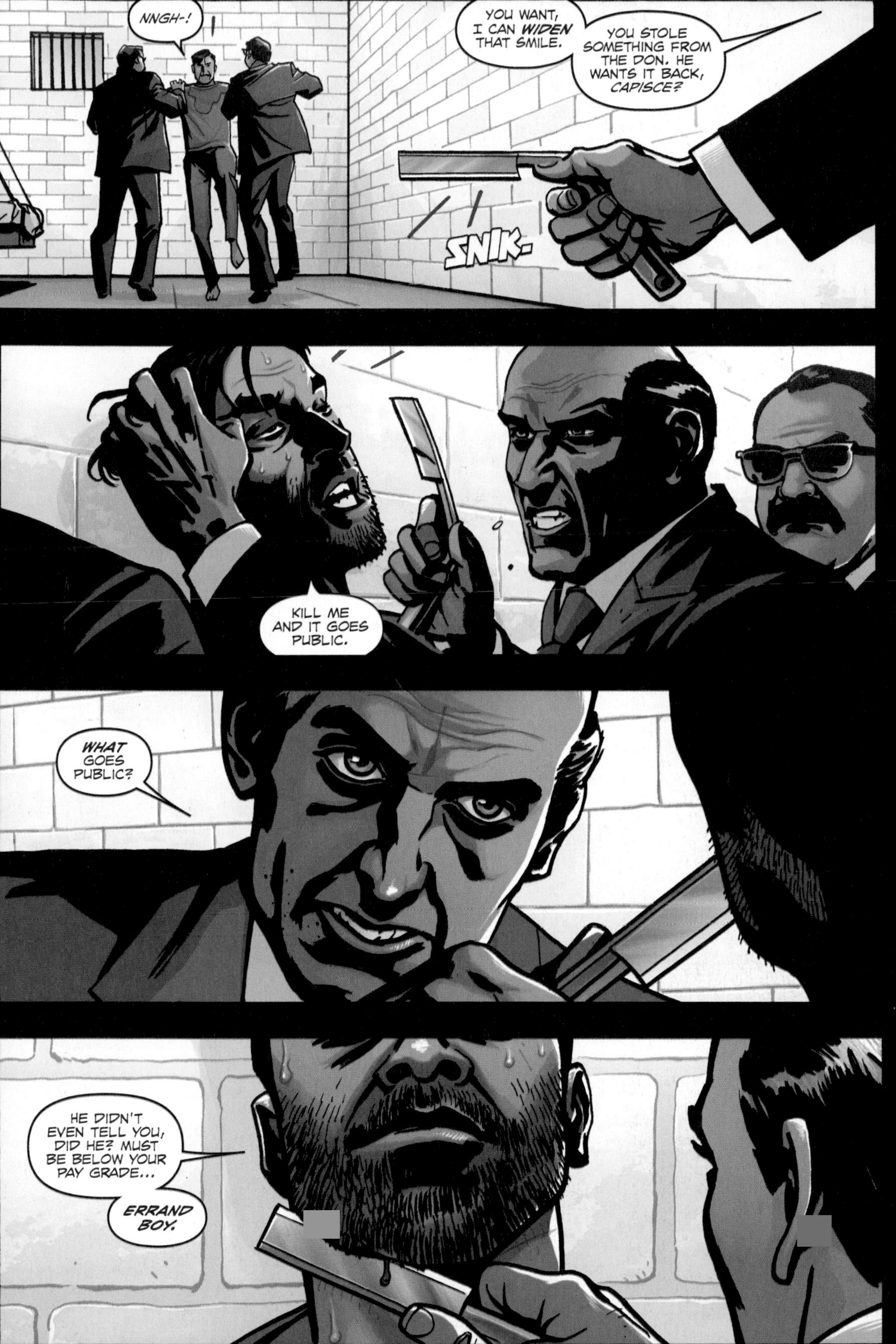
NNGH-!
YOU WANT, I CAN WIDEN THAT SMILE.
YOU STOLE SOMETHING FROM THE DON. HE WANTS IT BACK, CAPISCE?
SNIK-
KILL ME AND IT GOES PUBLIC.
WHAT GOES PUBLIC?
HE DIDN'T EVEN TELL YOU, DID HE? MUST BE BELOW YOUR PAY GRADE...
ERRAND BOY.

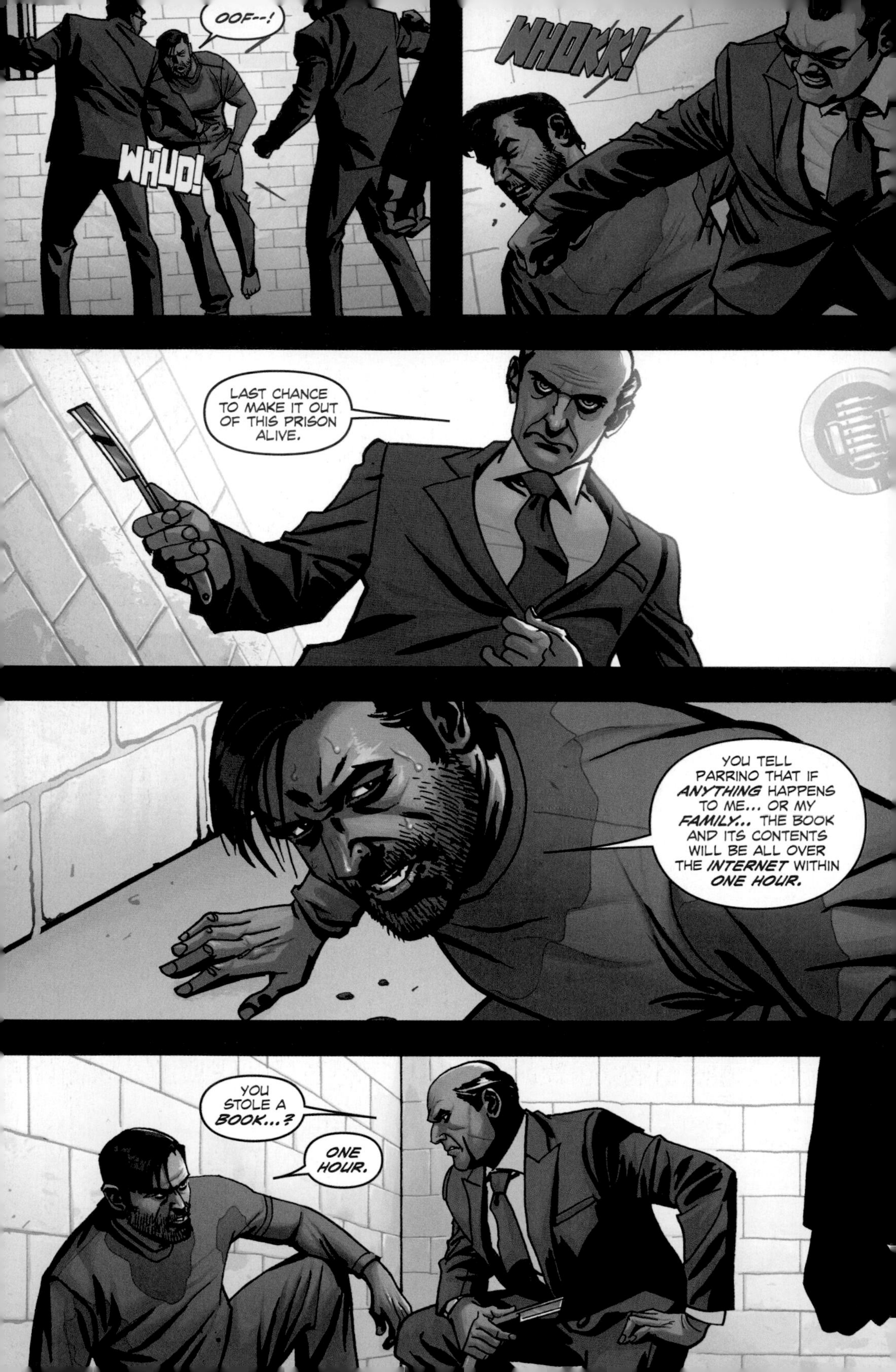
OOF--!
WHUD!
WHOKK!
LAST CHANCE TO MAKE IT OUT OF THIS PRISON ALIVE.
YOU TELL PARRINO THAT IF ANYTHING HAPPENS TO ME... OR MY FAMILY... THE BOOK AND ITS CONTENTS WILL BE ALL OVER THE INTERNET WITHIN ONE HOUR.
YOU STOLE A BOOK...?
ONE HOUR.

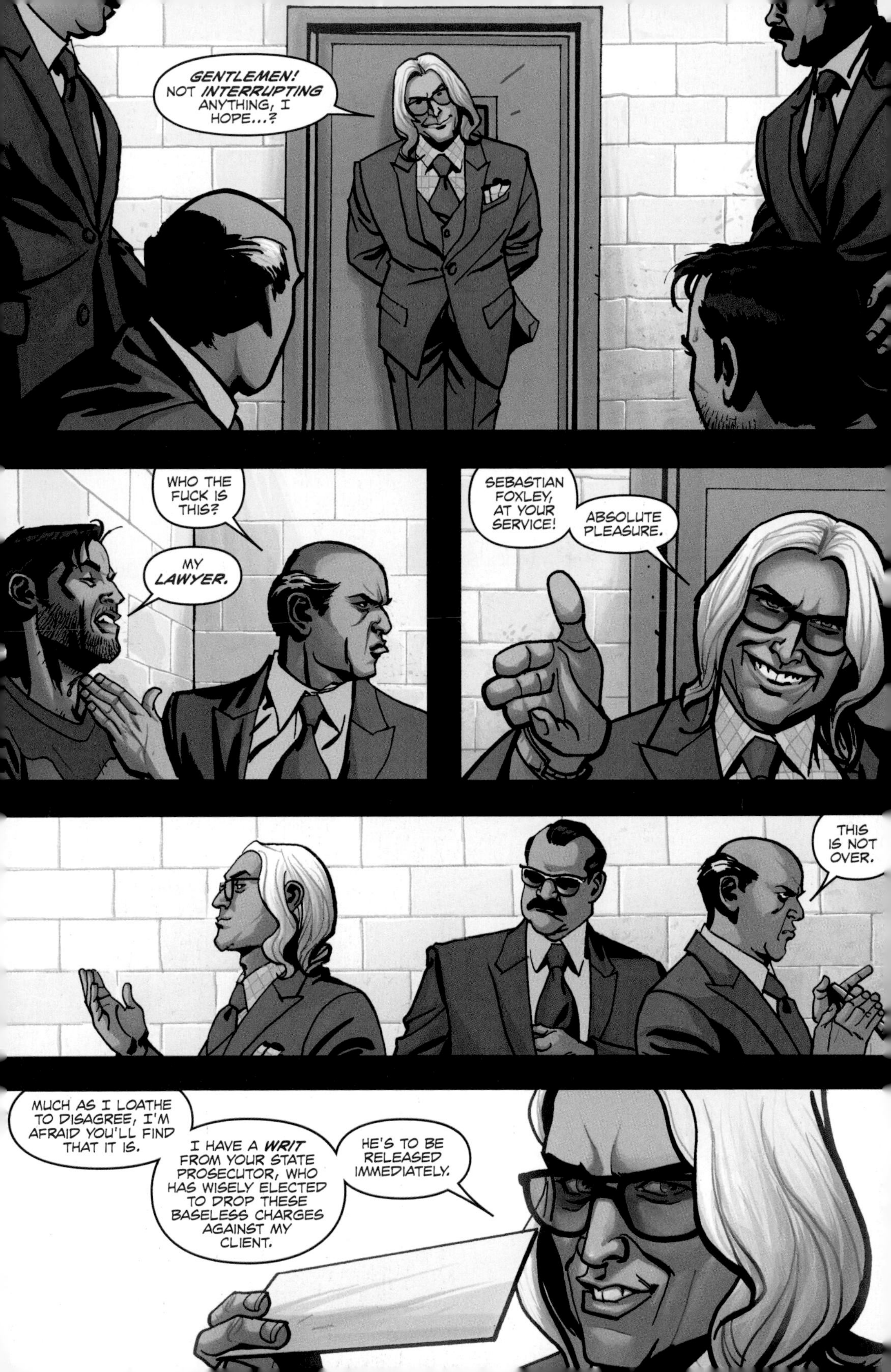
GENTLEMEN! NOT INTERRUPTING ANYTHING, I HOPE...?
WHO THE FUCK IS THIS?
MY LAWYER.
SEBASTIAN FOXLEY, AT YOUR SERVICE!
ABSOLUTE PLEASURE.
THIS IS NOT OVER.
MUCH AS I LOATHE TO DISAGREE, I'M AFRAID YOU'LL FIND THAT IT IS.
I HAVE A WRIT FROM YOUR STATE PROSECUTOR, WHO HAS WISELY ELECTED TO DROP THESE BASELESS CHARGES AGAINST MY CLIENT.
HE'S TO BE RELEASED IMMEDIATELY.

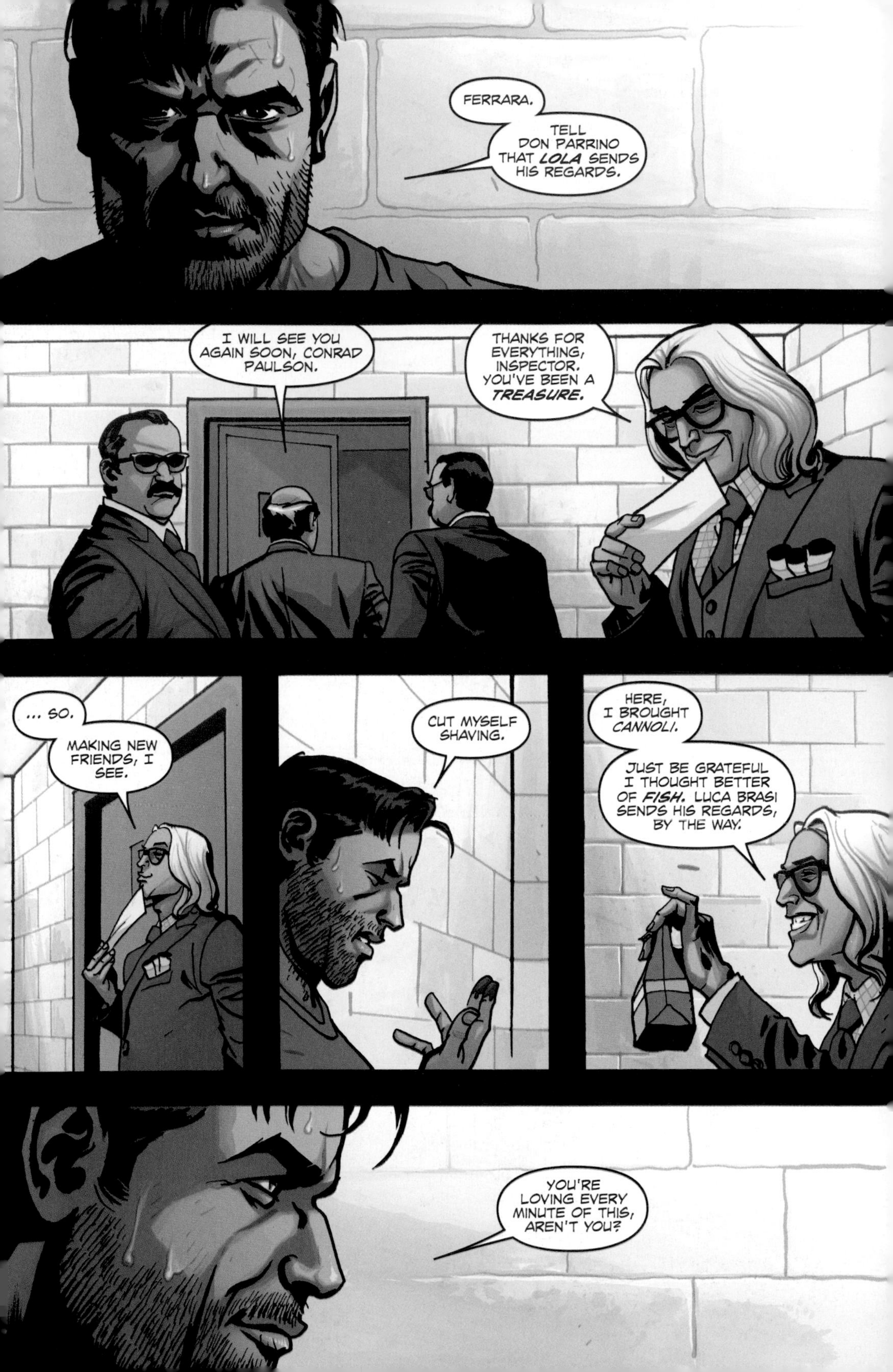
FERRARA.
TELL DON PARRINO THAT LOLA SENDS HIS REGARDS.
I WILL SEE YOU AGAIN SOON, CONRAD PAULSON.
THANKS FOR EVERYTHING, INSPECTOR. YOU'VE BEEN A TREASURE.
... SO.
MAKING NEW FRIENDS, I SEE.
CUT MYSELF SHAVING.
HERE, I BROUGHT CANNOLI.
JUST BE GRATEFUL I THOUGHT BETTER OF FISH. LUCA BRASI SENDS HIS REGARDS, BY THE WAY.
YOU'RE LOVING EVERY MINUTE OF THIS, AREN'T YOU?

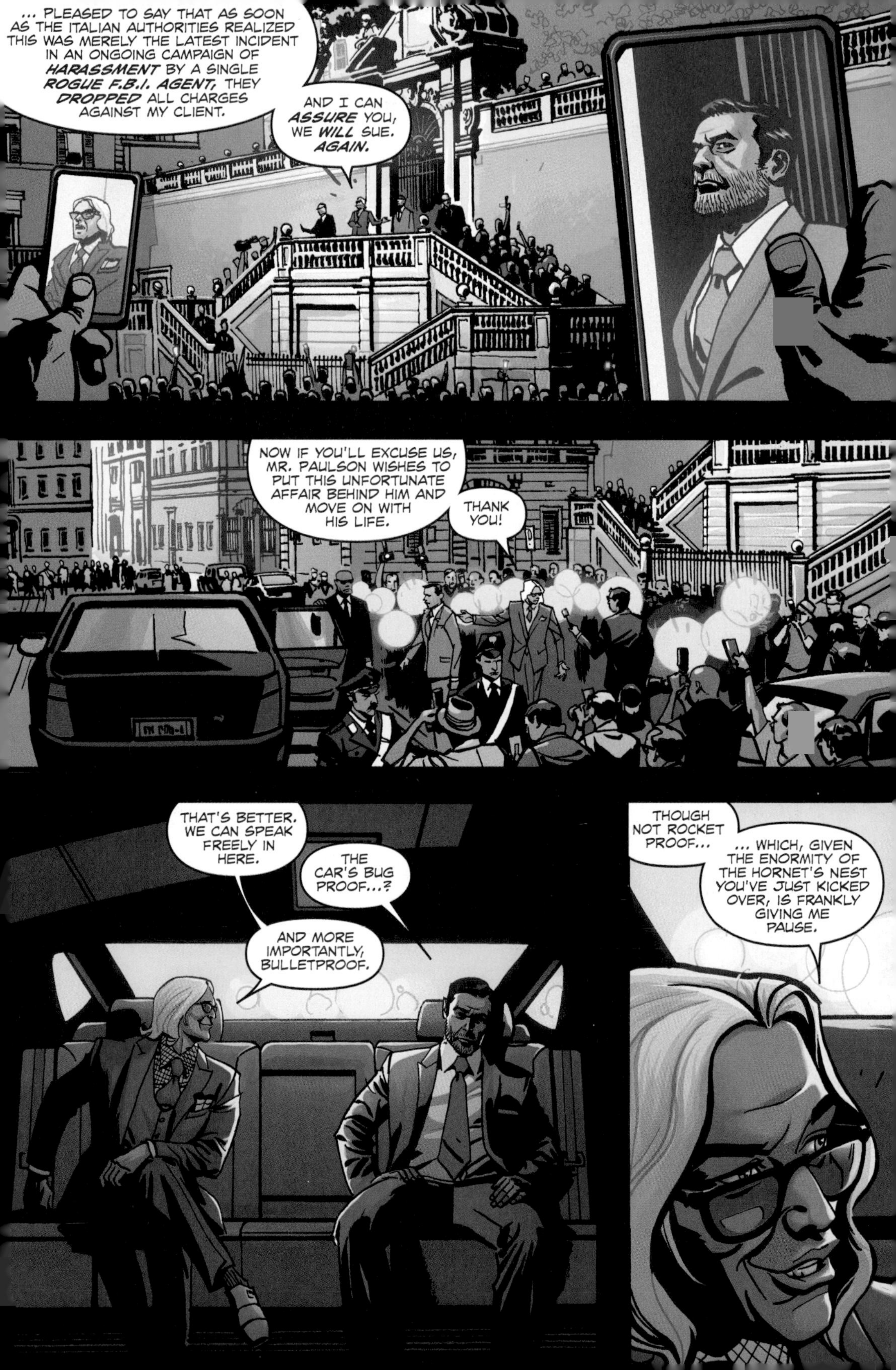
... PLEASED TO SAY THAT AS SOON AS THE ITALIAN AUTHORITIES REALIZED THIS WAS MERELY THE LATEST INCIDENT IN AN ONGOING CAMPAIGN OF HARASSMENT BY A SINGLE ROGUE F.B.I. AGENT, THEY DROPPED ALL CHARGES AGAINST MY CLIENT.
AND I CAN ASSURE YOU, WE WILL SUE. AGAIN.
NOW IF YOU'LL EXCUSE US, MR. PAULSON WISHES TO PUT THIS UNFORTUNATE AFFAIR BEHIND HIM AND MOVE ON WITH HIS LIFE.
THANK YOU!
THAT'S BETTER. WE CAN SPEAK FREELY IN HERE.
THE CAR'S BUG PROOF...?
AND MORE IMPORTANTLY, BULLETPROOF.
THOUGH NOT ROCKET PROOF...
... WHICH, GIVEN THE ENORMITY OF THE HORNET'S NEST YOU'VE JUST KICKED OVER, IS FRANKLY GIVING ME PAUSE.

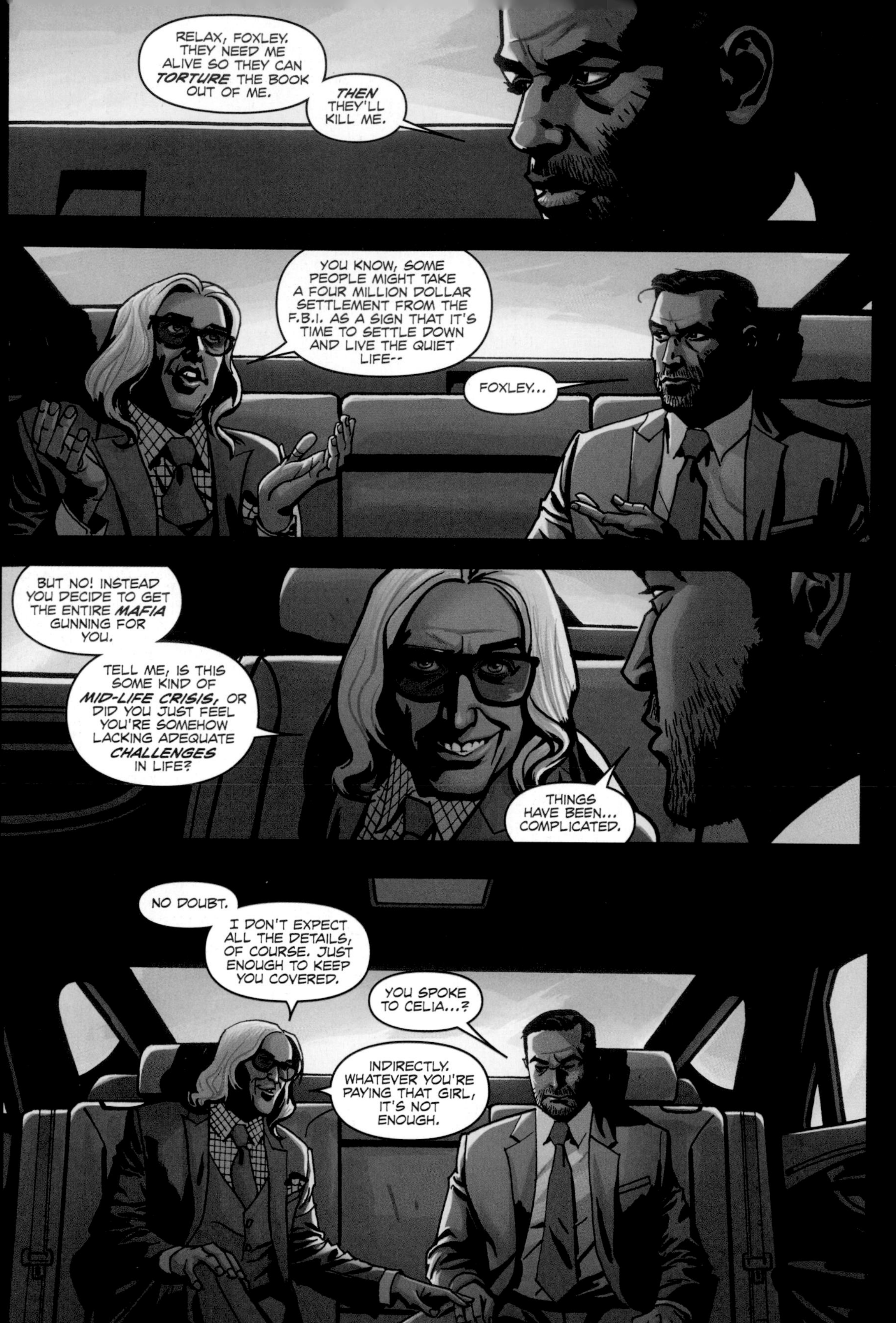
RELAX, FOXLEY. THEY NEED ME ALIVE SO THEY CAN TORTURE THE BOOK OUT OF ME.
THEN THEY'LL KILL ME.
YOU KNOW, SOME PEOPLE MIGHT TAKE A FOUR MILLION DOLLAR SETTLEMENT FROM THE F.B.I. AS A SIGN THAT IT'S TIME TO SETTLE DOWN AND LIVE THE QUIET LIFE--
FOXLEY...
BUT NO! INSTEAD YOU DECIDE TO GET THE ENTIRE MAFIA GUNNING FOR YOU.
TELL ME, IS THIS SOME KIND OF MID-LIFE CRISIS, OR DID YOU JUST FEEL YOU'RE SOMEHOW LACKING ADEQUATE CHALLENGES IN LIFE?
THINGS HAVE BEEN... COMPLICATED.
NO DOUBT.
I DON'T EXPECT ALL THE DETAILS, OF COURSE. JUST ENOUGH TO KEEP YOU COVERED.
YOU SPOKE TO CELIA...?
INDIRECTLY. WHATEVER YOU'RE PAYING THAT GIRL, IT'S NOT ENOUGH.

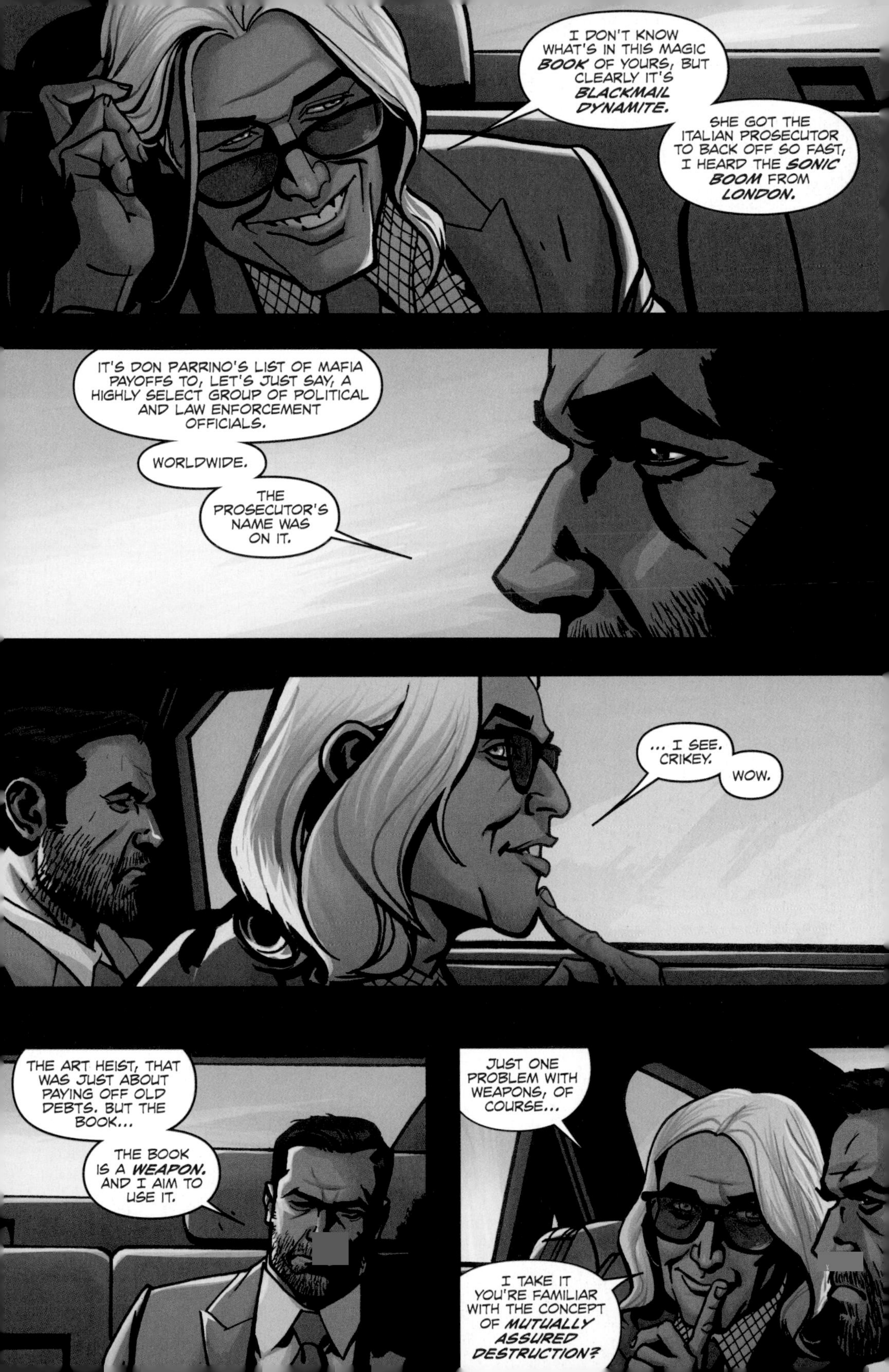
I DON'T KNOW WHAT'S IN THIS MAGIC *BOOK* OF YOURS, BUT CLEARLY IT'S *BLACKMAIL DYNAMITE.*
SHE GOT THE ITALIAN PROSECUTOR TO BACK OFF SO FAST, I HEARD THE *SONIC BOOM* FROM *LONDON.*
IT'S DON PARRINO'S LIST OF MAFIA PAYOFFS TO, LET'S JUST SAY, A HIGHLY SELECT GROUP OF POLITICAL AND LAW ENFORCEMENT OFFICIALS.
WORLDWIDE.
THE PROSECUTOR'S NAME WAS ON IT.
... I SEE. CRIKEY.
WOW.
THE ART HEIST, THAT WAS JUST ABOUT PAYING OFF OLD DEBTS. BUT THE BOOK...
THE BOOK IS A *WEAPON.* AND I AIM TO USE IT.
JUST ONE PROBLEM WITH WEAPONS, OF COURSE...
I TAKE IT YOU'RE FAMILIAR WITH THE CONCEPT OF *MUTUALLY ASSURED DESTRUCTION?*

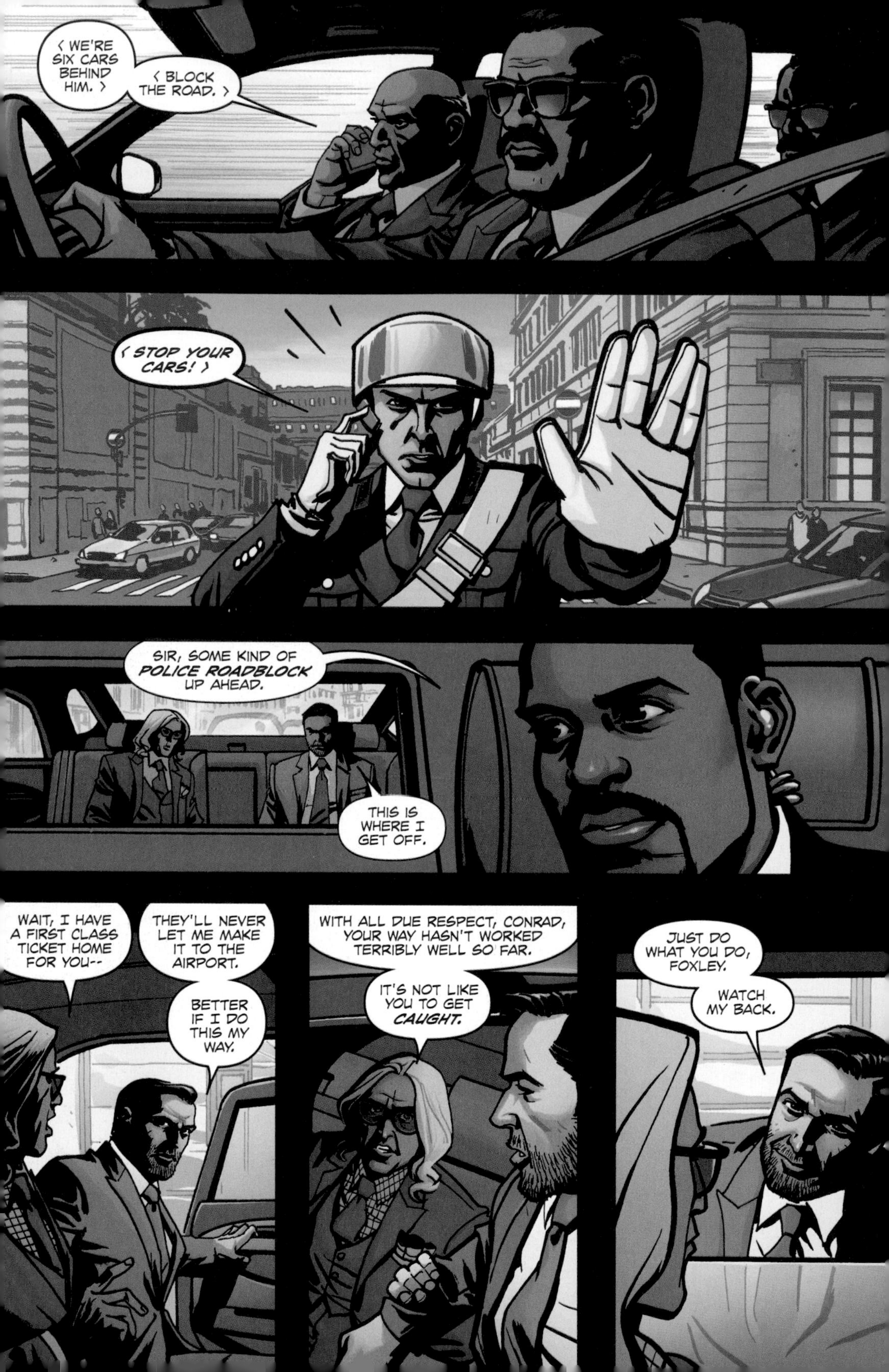

‹ WE'RE SIX CARS BEHIND HIM. ›
‹ BLOCK THE ROAD. ›
‹ STOP YOUR CARS! ›
SIR, SOME KIND OF *POLICE ROADBLOCK* UP AHEAD.
THIS IS WHERE I GET OFF.
WAIT, I HAVE A FIRST CLASS TICKET HOME FOR YOU--
THEY'LL NEVER LET ME MAKE IT TO THE AIRPORT.
BETTER IF I DO THIS MY WAY.
WITH ALL DUE RESPECT, CONRAD, YOUR WAY HASN'T WORKED TERRIBLY WELL SO FAR.
IT'S NOT LIKE YOU TO GET *CAUGHT.*
JUST DO WHAT YOU DO, FOXLEY.
WATCH MY BACK.

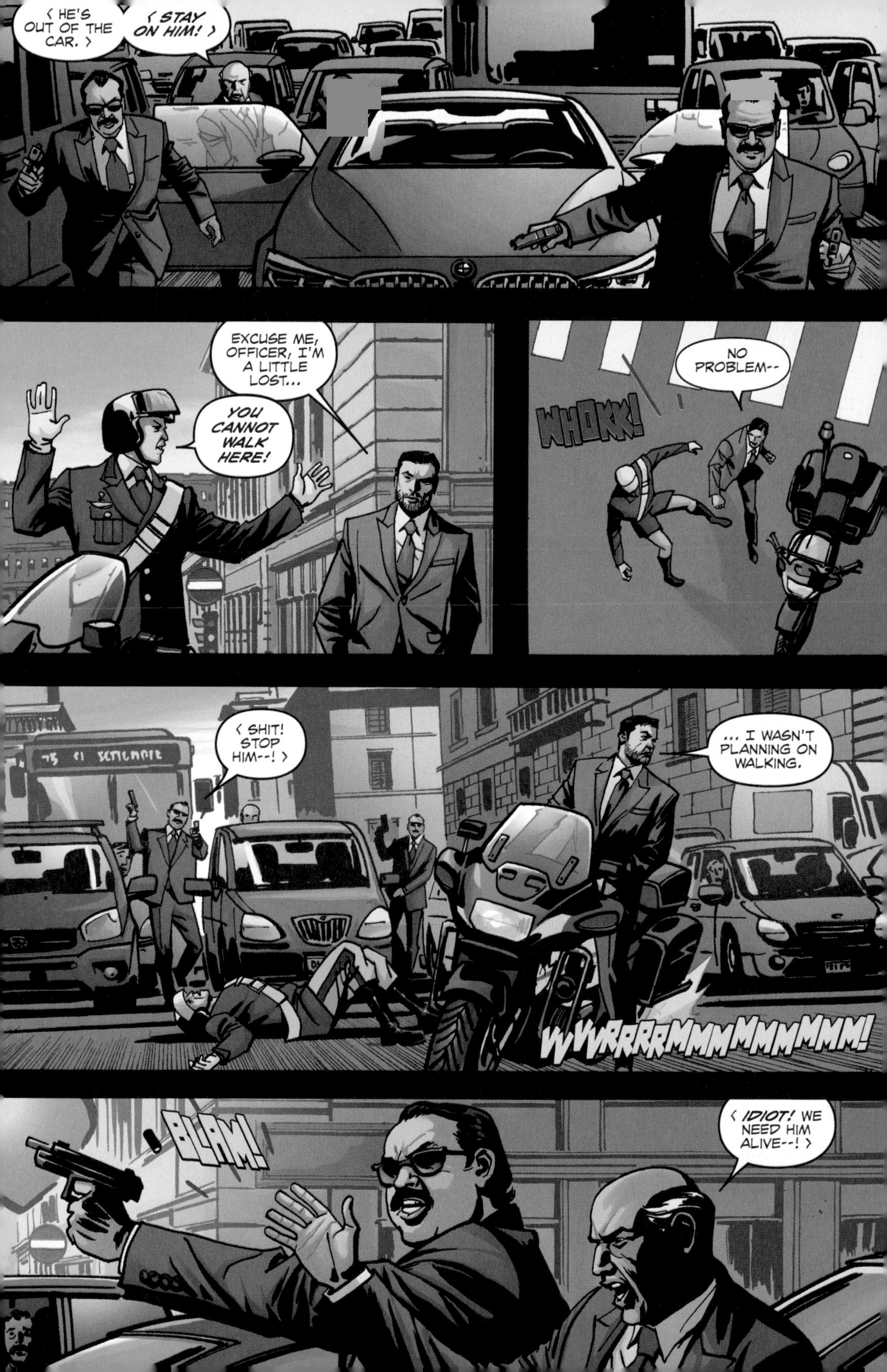

< HE'S OUT OF THE CAR. >
< *STAY ON HIM!* >
EXCUSE ME, OFFICER, I'M A LITTLE LOST...
YOU CANNOT WALK HERE!
WHOKK!
NO PROBLEM--
< SHIT! STOP HIM--! >
... I WASN'T PLANNING ON WALKING.
WVVRRRRMMMMMMMMM!
BLAM!
< *IDIOT!* WE NEED HIM ALIVE--! >

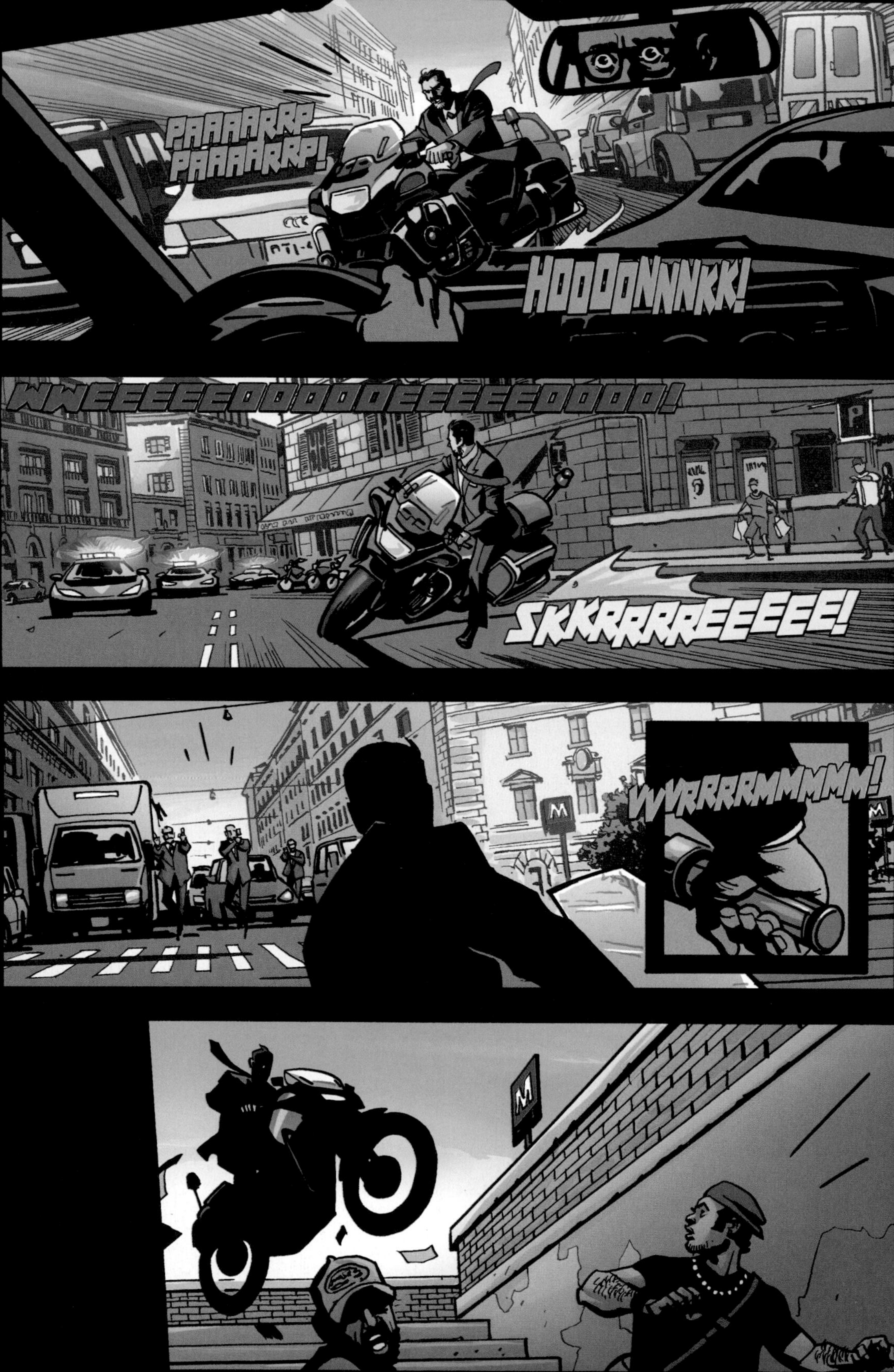

PAAAARRP
PAAAARRP!
HOOOONNNKK!
WWEEEEEOOOOOEEEEEOOOO!
SKKRRRREEEEEE!
VVRRRRMMMMM!

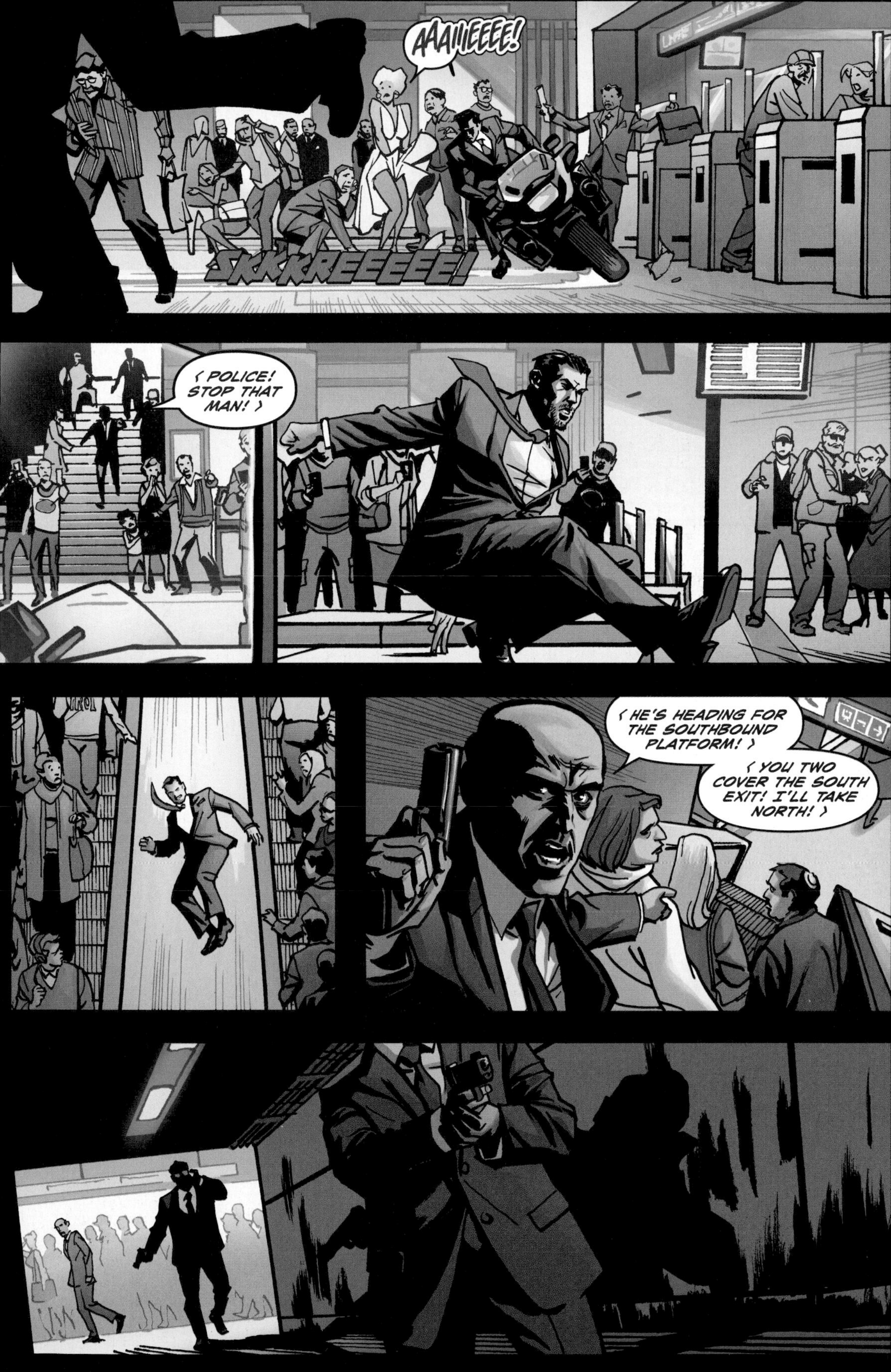
AAAIIIEEEE!
SKKKREEEEEE!
‹ POLICE! STOP THAT MAN! ›
‹ HE'S HEADING FOR THE SOUTHBOUND PLATFORM! ›
‹ YOU TWO COVER THE SOUTH EXIT! I'LL TAKE NORTH! ›

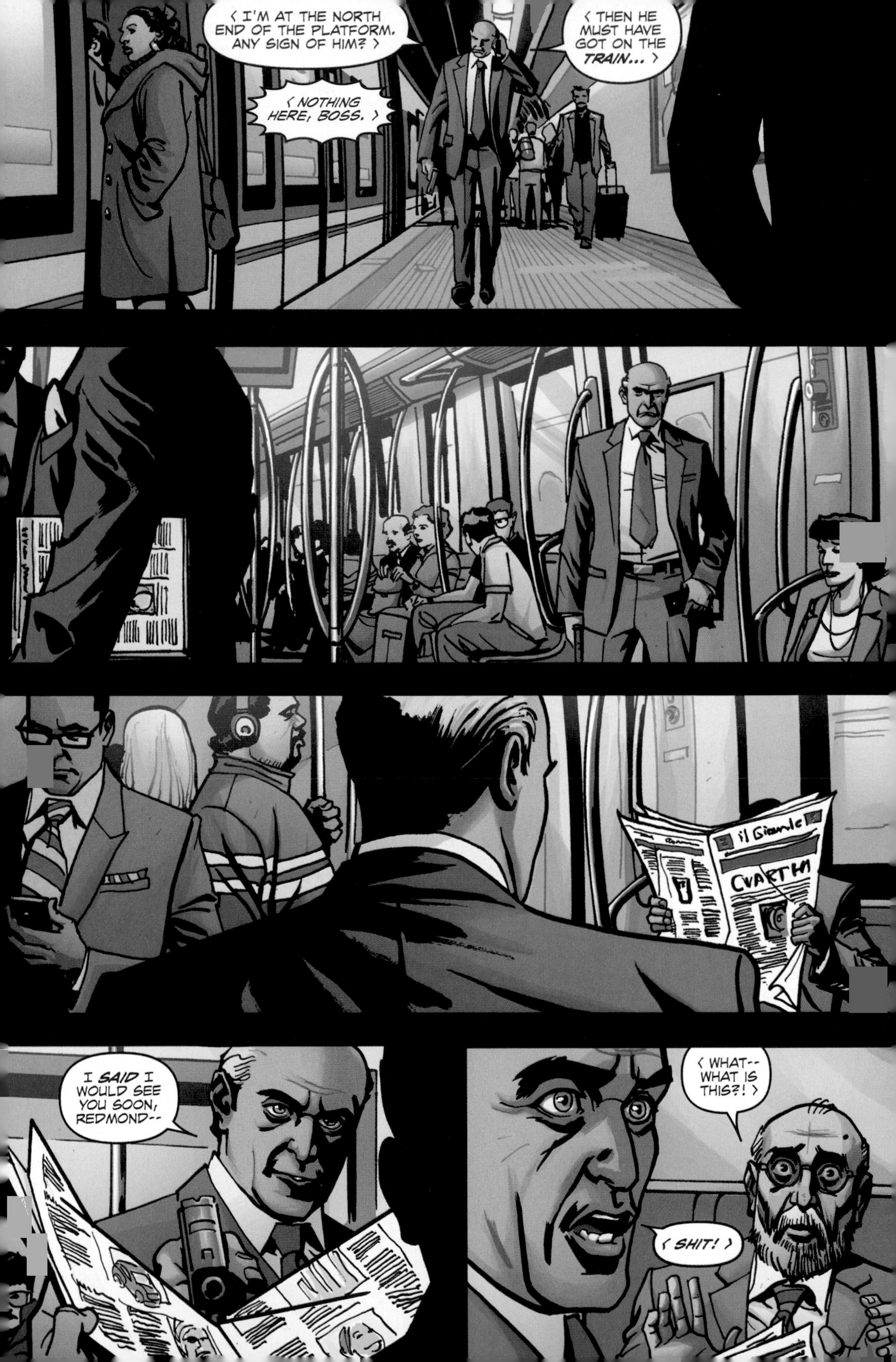

< I'M AT THE NORTH END OF THE PLATFORM. ANY SIGN OF HIM? >
< NOTHING HERE, BOSS. >
< THEN HE MUST HAVE GOT ON THE *TRAIN...* >
I *SAID* I WOULD SEE YOU SOON, REDMOND--
< WHAT-- WHAT IS THIS?! >
< *SHIT!* >

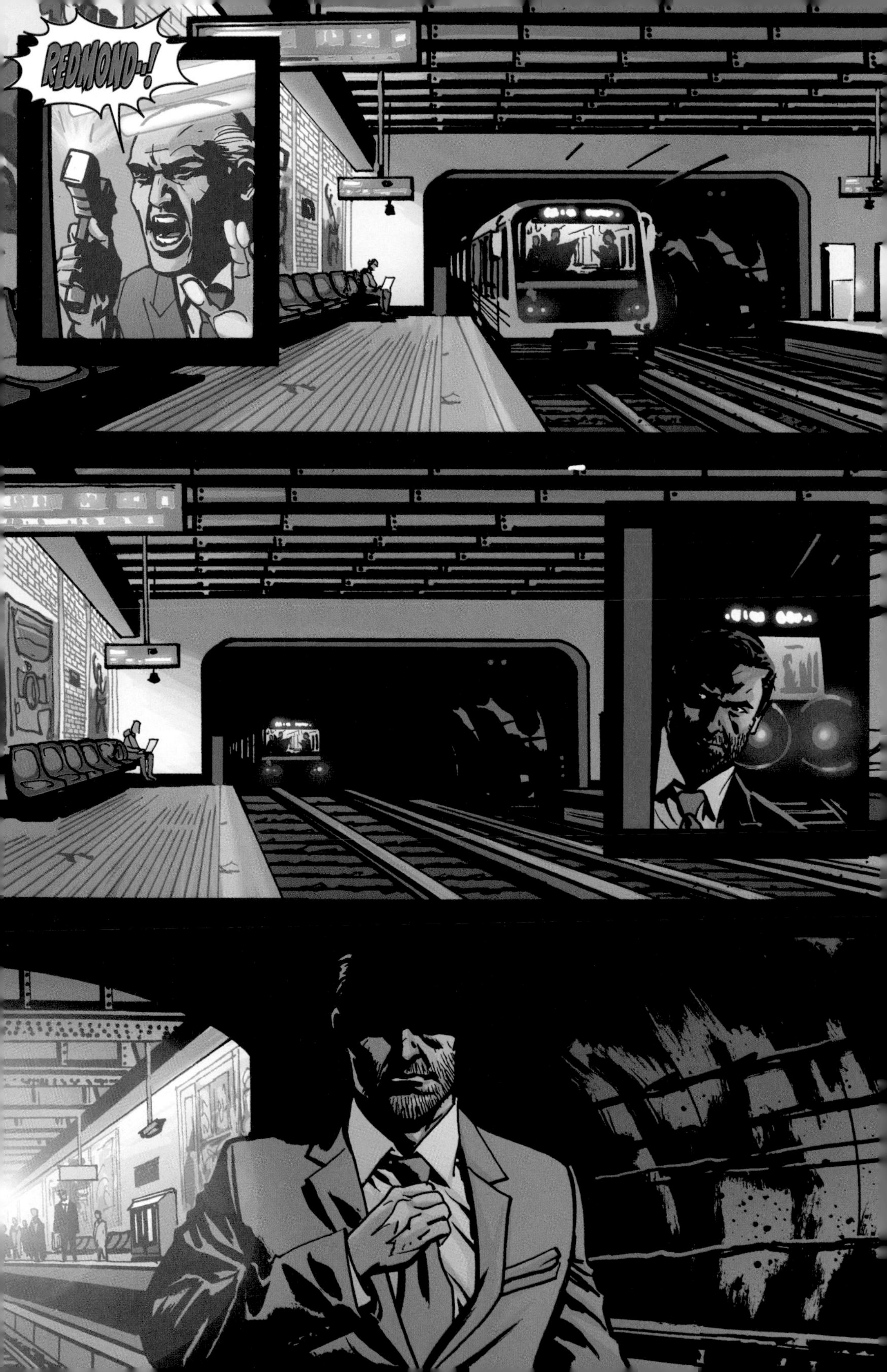
REDMOND-!

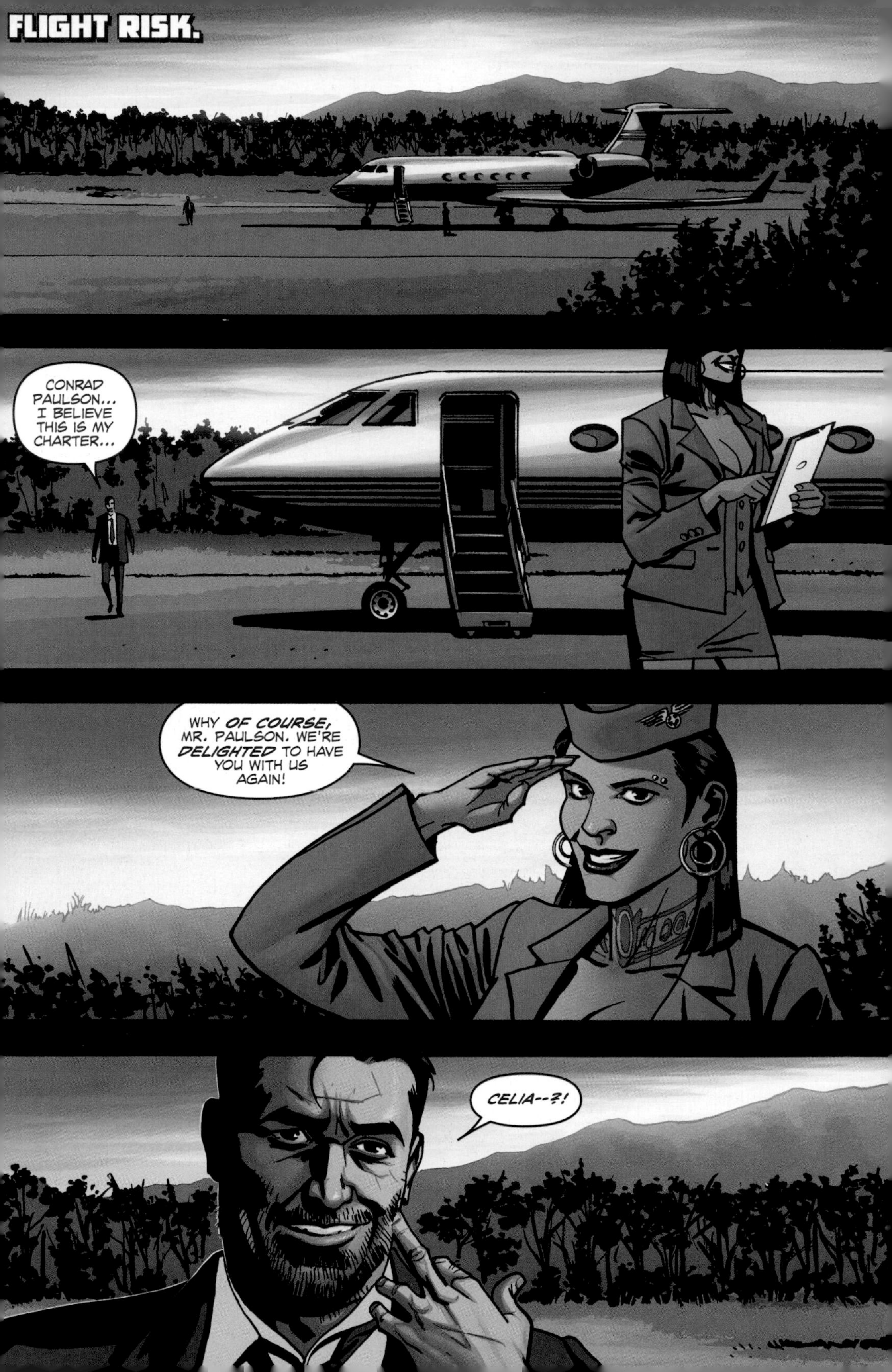
FLIGHT RISK.
CONRAD PAULSON... I BELIEVE THIS IS MY CHARTER...
WHY OF COURSE, MR. PAULSON. WE'RE DELIGHTED TO HAVE YOU WITH US AGAIN!
CELIA--?!

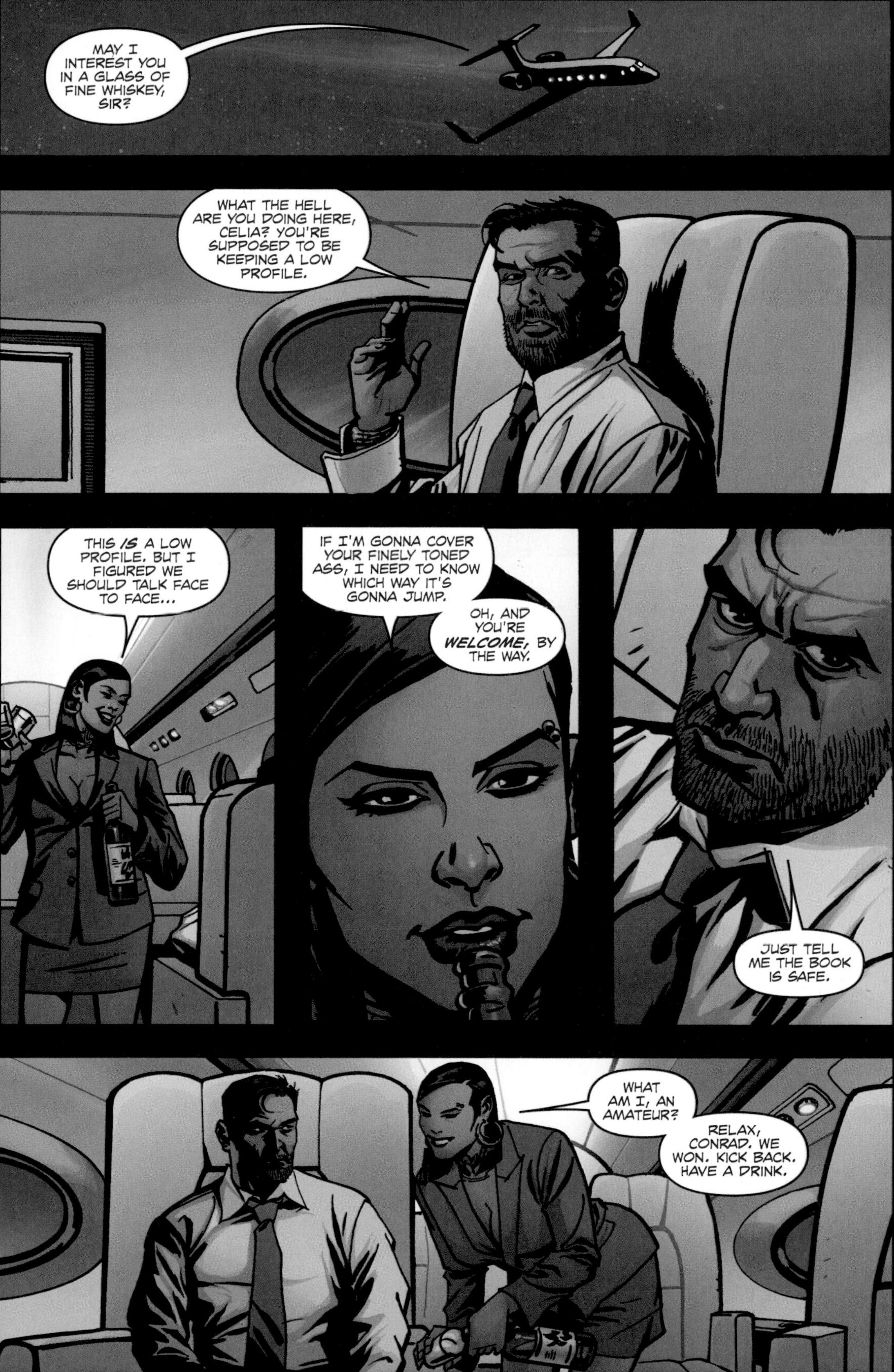
MAY I INTEREST YOU IN A GLASS OF FINE WHISKEY, SIR?
WHAT THE HELL ARE YOU DOING HERE, CELIA? YOU'RE SUPPOSED TO BE KEEPING A LOW PROFILE.
THIS *IS* A LOW PROFILE. BUT I FIGURED WE SHOULD TALK FACE TO FACE...
IF I'M GONNA COVER YOUR FINELY TONED ASS, I NEED TO KNOW WHICH WAY IT'S GONNA JUMP.
OH, AND YOU'RE ***WELCOME,*** BY THE WAY.
JUST TELL ME THE BOOK IS SAFE.
WHAT AM I, AN AMATEUR?
RELAX, CONRAD. WE WON. KICK BACK. HAVE A DRINK.

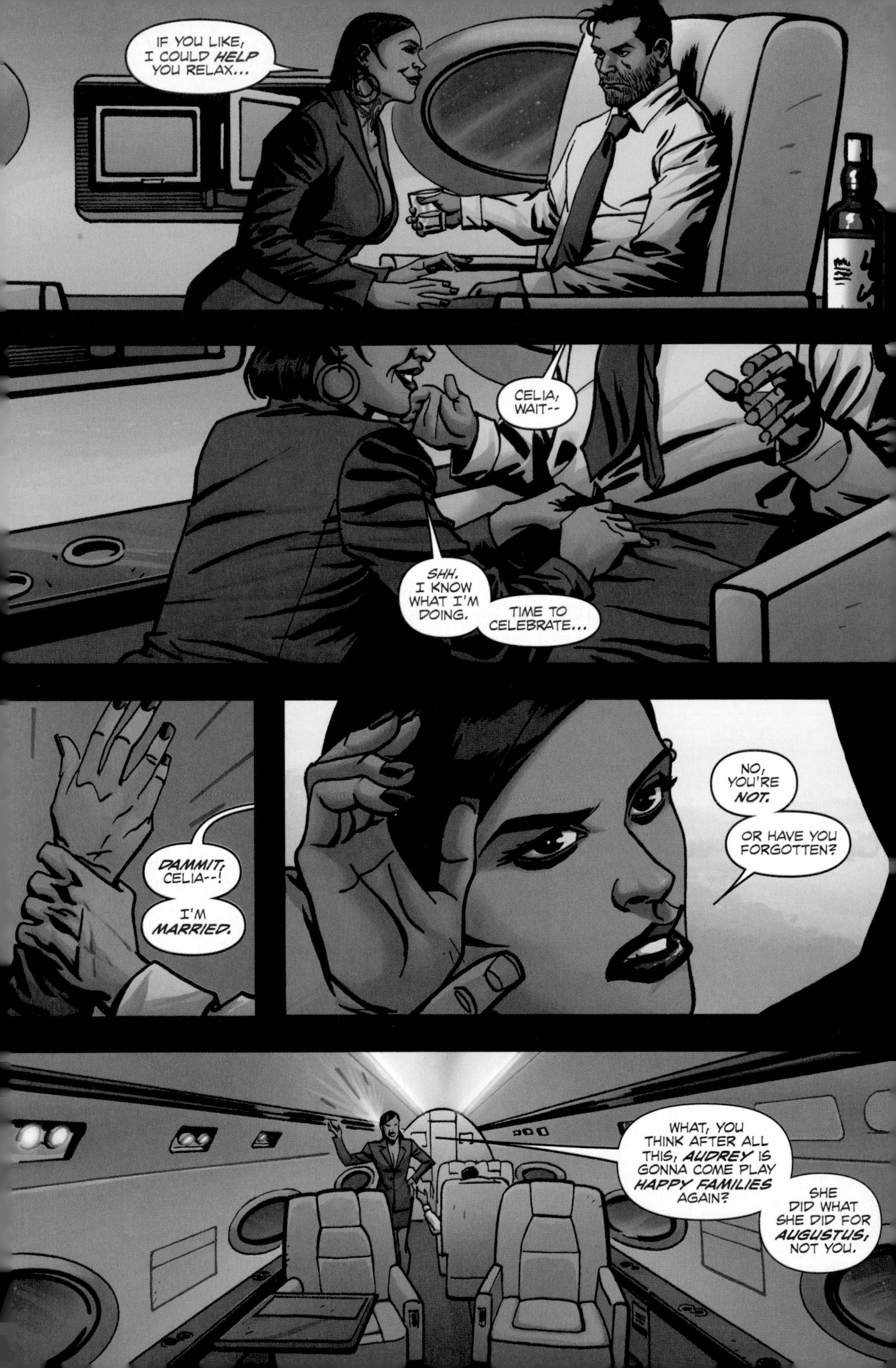
IF YOU LIKE, I COULD *HELP* YOU RELAX...
CELIA, WAIT--
SHH. I KNOW WHAT I'M DOING.
TIME TO CELEBRATE...
DAMMIT, CELIA--!
I'M *MARRIED.*
NO, YOU'RE *NOT.*
OR HAVE YOU FORGOTTEN?
WHAT, YOU THINK AFTER ALL THIS, *AUDREY* IS GONNA COME PLAY *HAPPY FAMILIES* AGAIN?
SHE DID WHAT SHE DID FOR *AUGUSTUS,* NOT YOU.

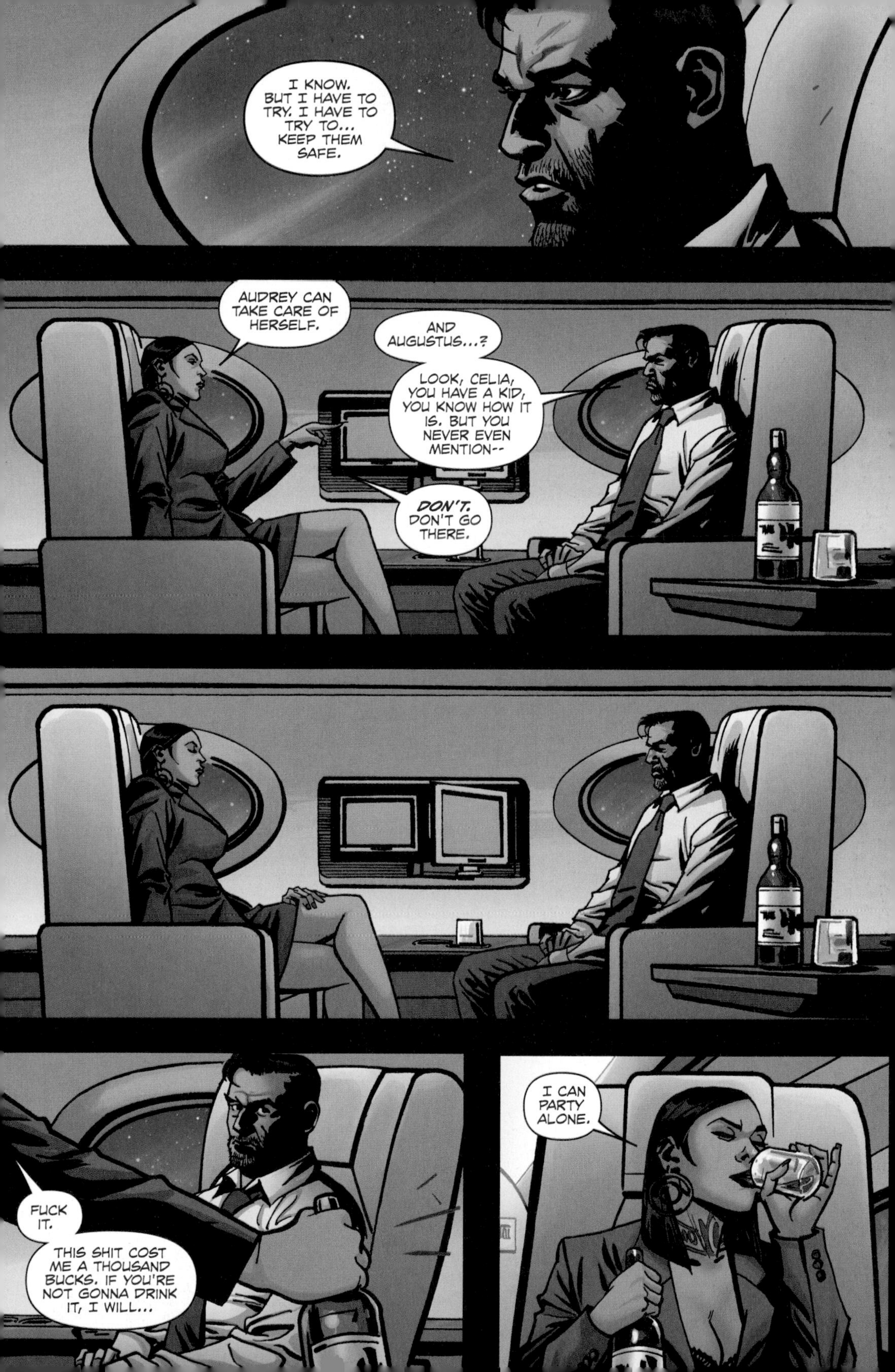
I KNOW. BUT I HAVE TO TRY. I HAVE TO TRY TO... KEEP THEM SAFE.
AUDREY CAN TAKE CARE OF HERSELF.
AND AUGUSTUS...?
LOOK, CELIA, YOU HAVE A KID, YOU KNOW HOW IT IS. BUT YOU NEVER EVEN MENTION--
DON'T. DON'T GO THERE.
FUCK IT.
THIS SHIT COST ME A THOUSAND BUCKS. IF YOU'RE NOT GONNA DRINK IT, I WILL...
I CAN PARTY ALONE.

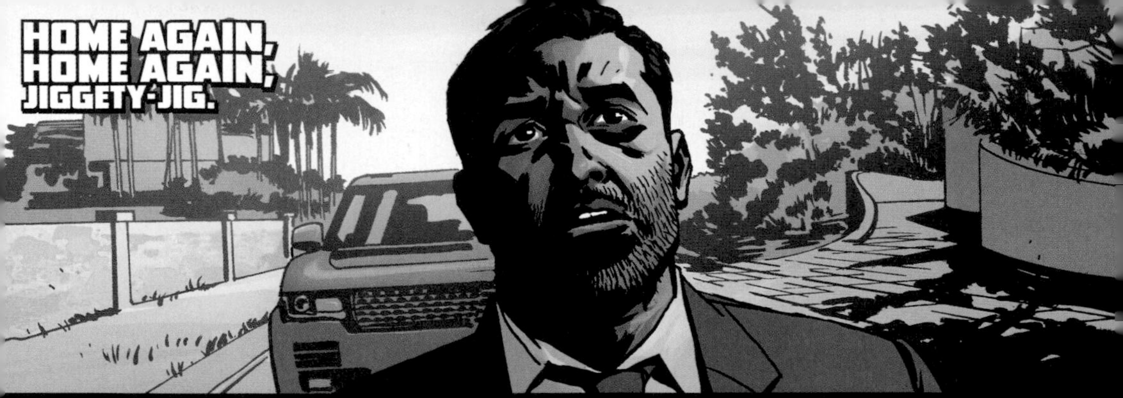
HOME AGAIN, HOME AGAIN, JIGGETY-JIG.

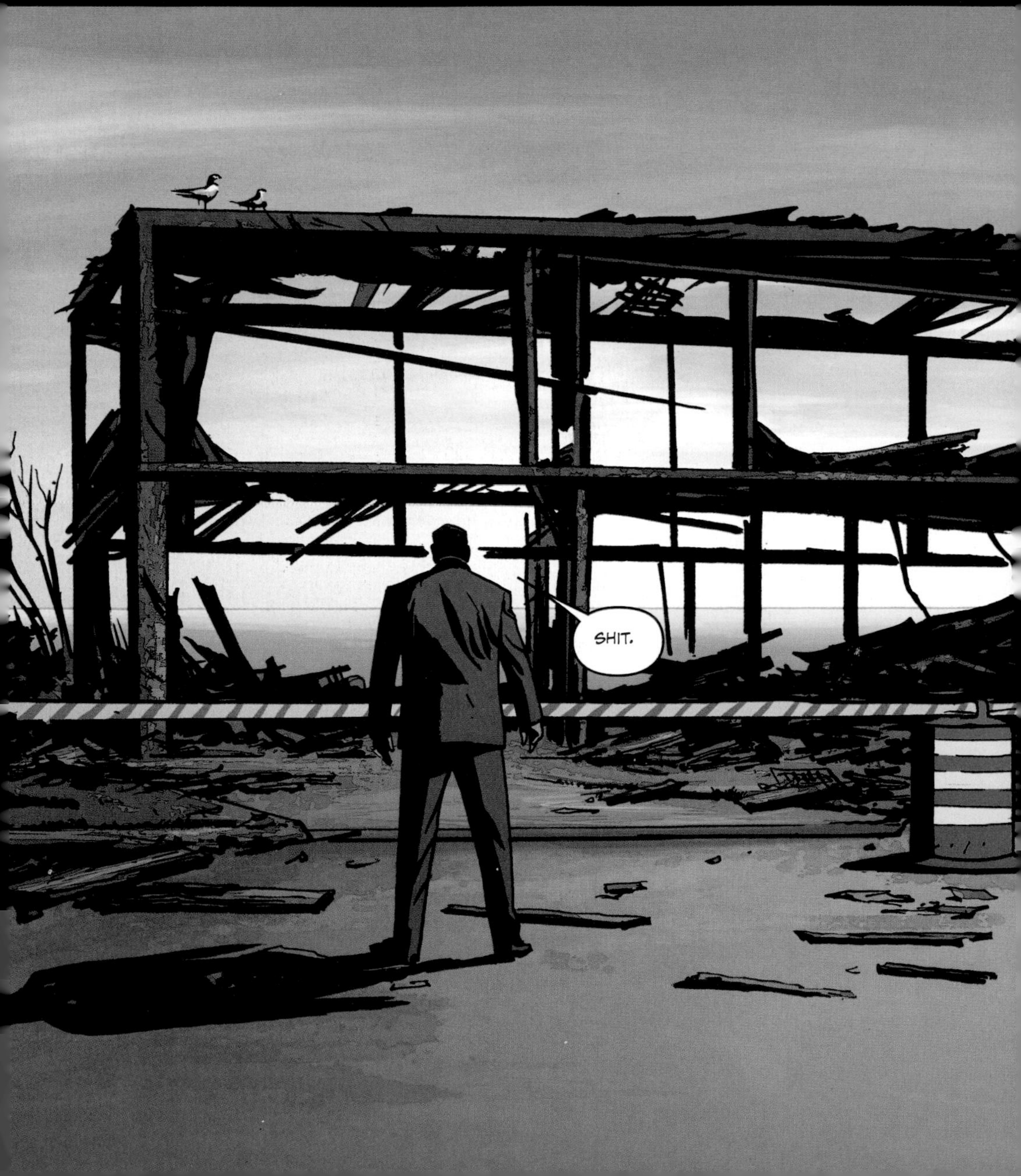
SHIT.

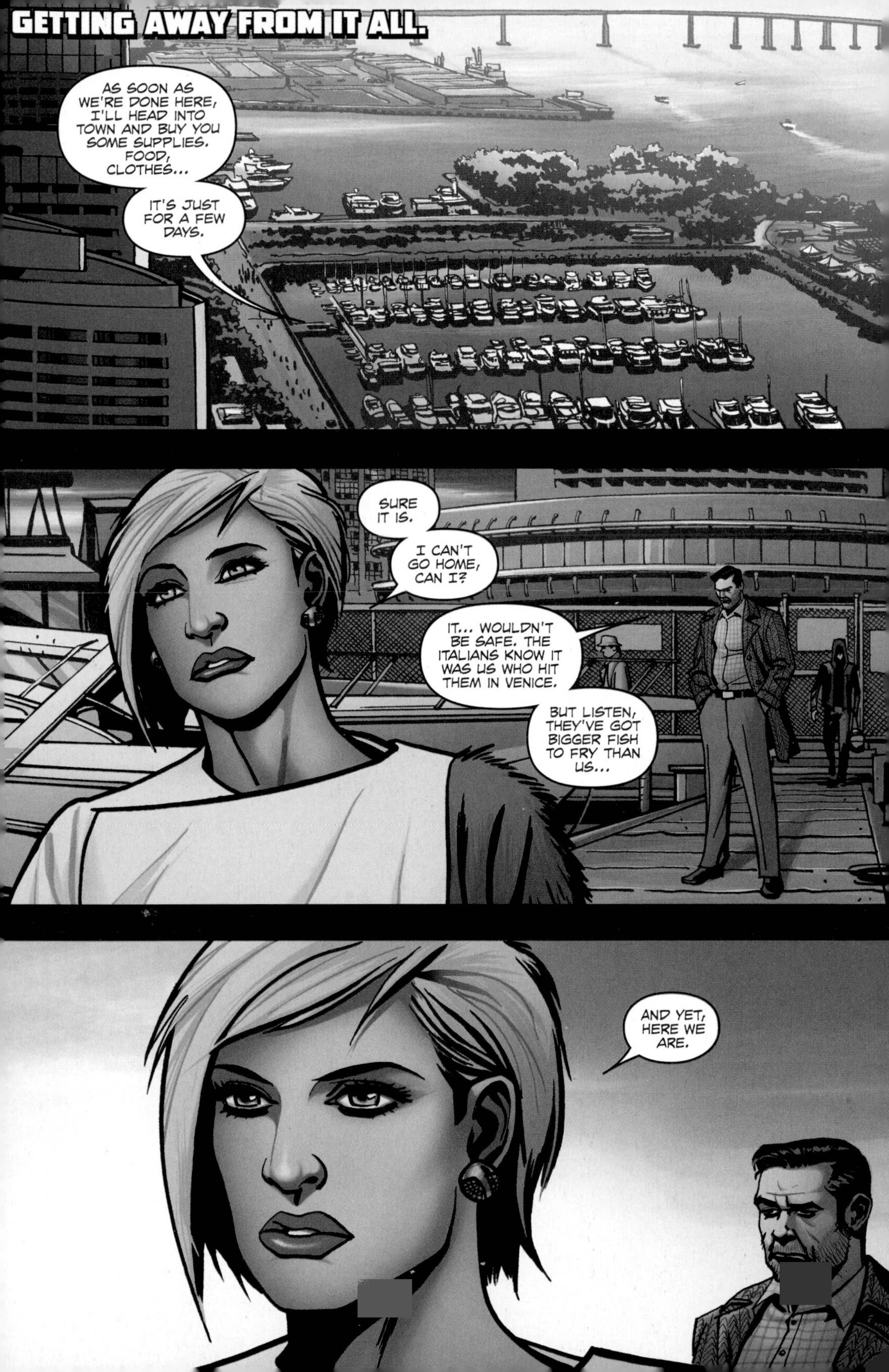
GETTING AWAY FROM IT ALL.
AS SOON AS WE'RE DONE HERE, I'LL HEAD INTO TOWN AND BUY YOU SOME SUPPLIES. FOOD, CLOTHES...
IT'S JUST FOR A FEW DAYS.
SURE IT IS.
I CAN'T GO HOME, CAN I?
IT... WOULDN'T BE SAFE. THE ITALIANS KNOW IT WAS US WHO HIT THEM IN VENICE.
BUT LISTEN, THEY'VE GOT BIGGER FISH TO FRY THAN US...
AND YET, HERE WE ARE.

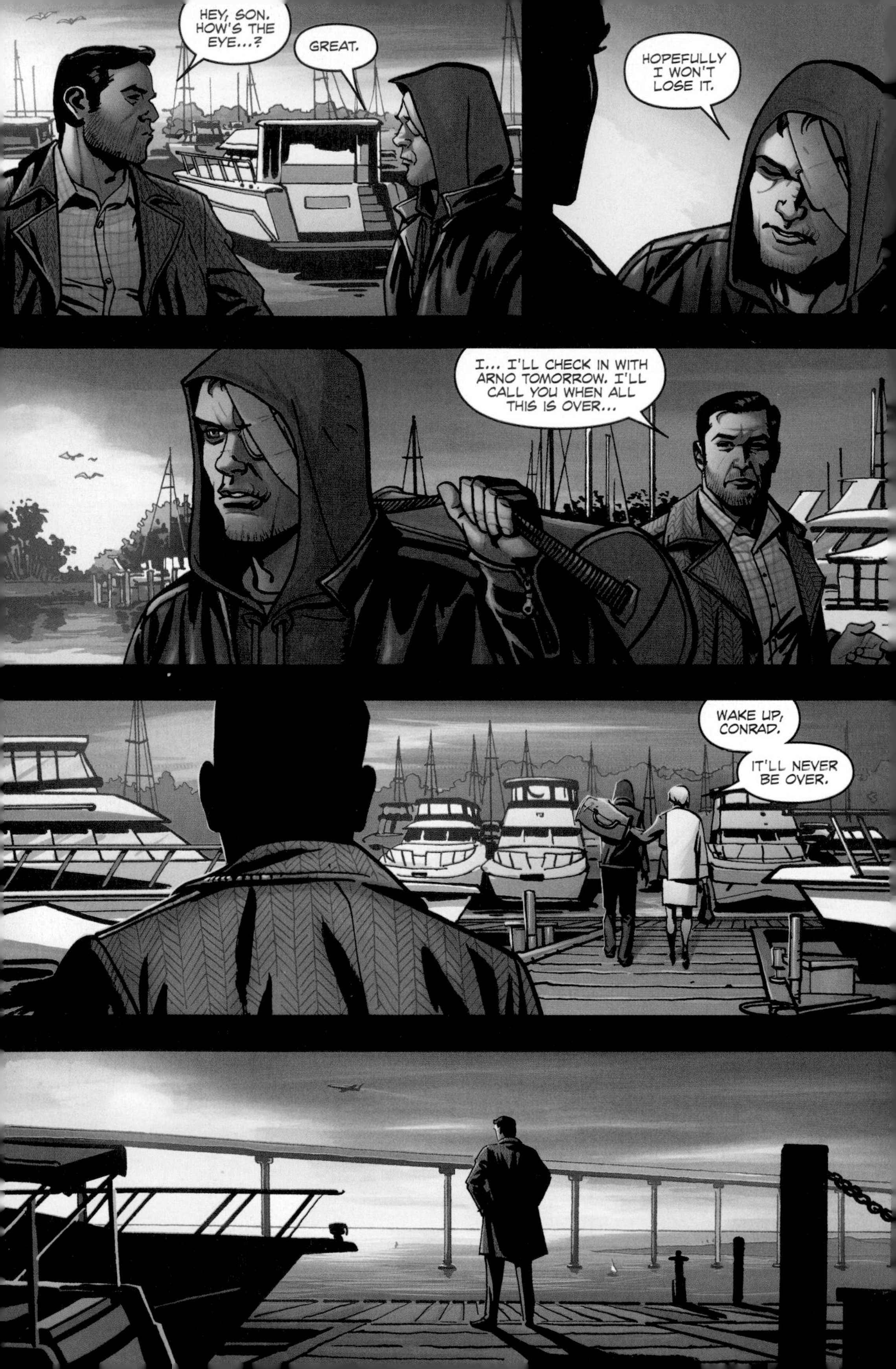
HEY, SON. HOW'S THE EYE...?
GREAT.
HOPEFULLY I WON'T LOSE IT.
I... I'LL CHECK IN WITH ARNO TOMORROW. I'LL CALL YOU WHEN ALL THIS IS OVER...
WAKE UP, CONRAD.
IT'LL NEVER BE OVER.

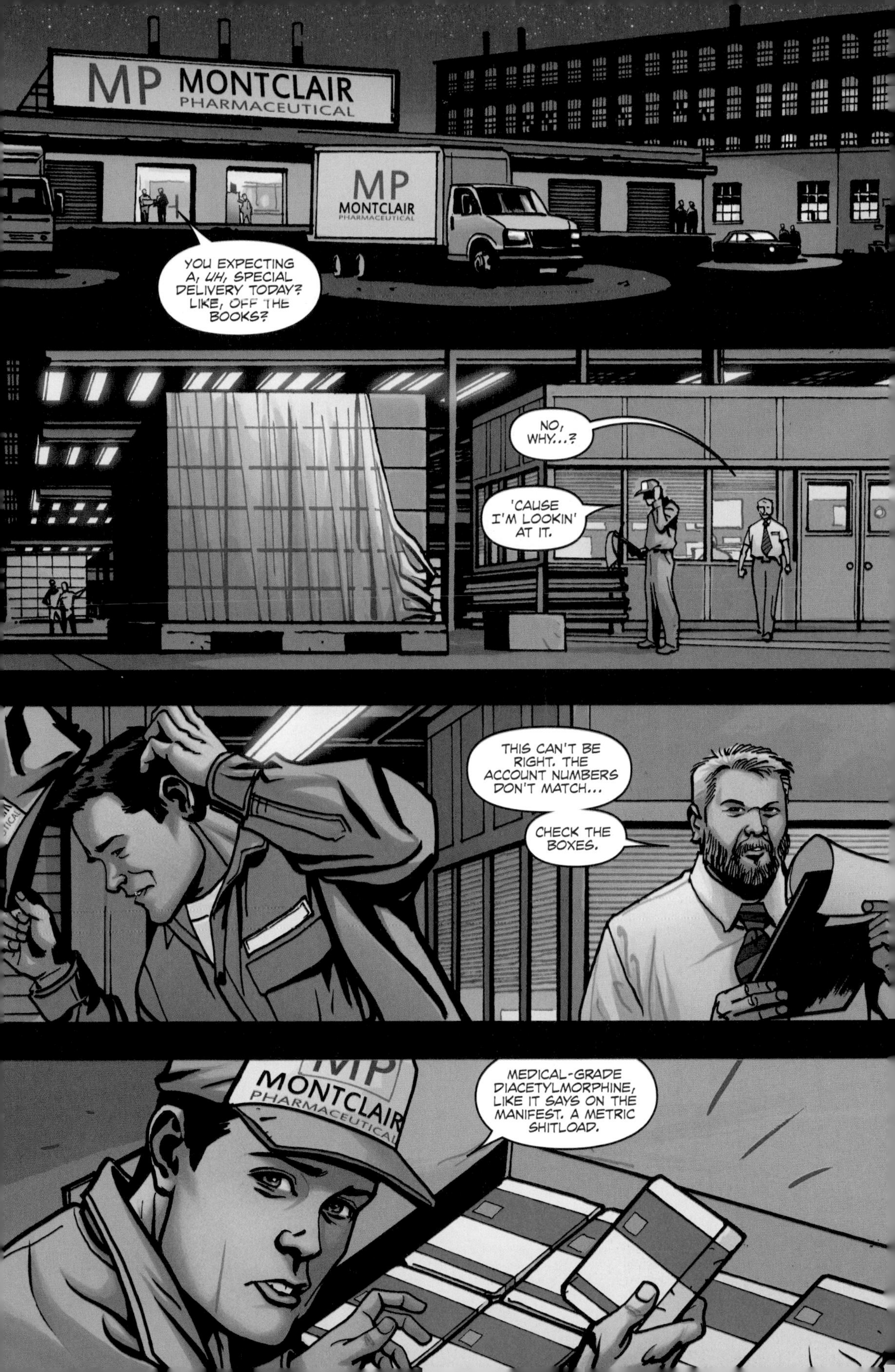
MP MONTCLAIR PHARMACEUTICAL
MP MONTCLAIR PHARMACEUTICAL
YOU EXPECTING A, *UH*, SPECIAL DELIVERY TODAY? LIKE, OFF THE BOOKS?
NO, WHY...?
'CAUSE I'M LOOKIN' AT IT.
THIS CAN'T BE RIGHT. THE ACCOUNT NUMBERS DON'T MATCH...
CHECK THE BOXES.
MP MONTCLAIR PHARMACEUTICAL
MEDICAL-GRADE DIACETYLMORPHINE, LIKE IT SAYS ON THE MANIFEST. A METRIC SHITLOAD.

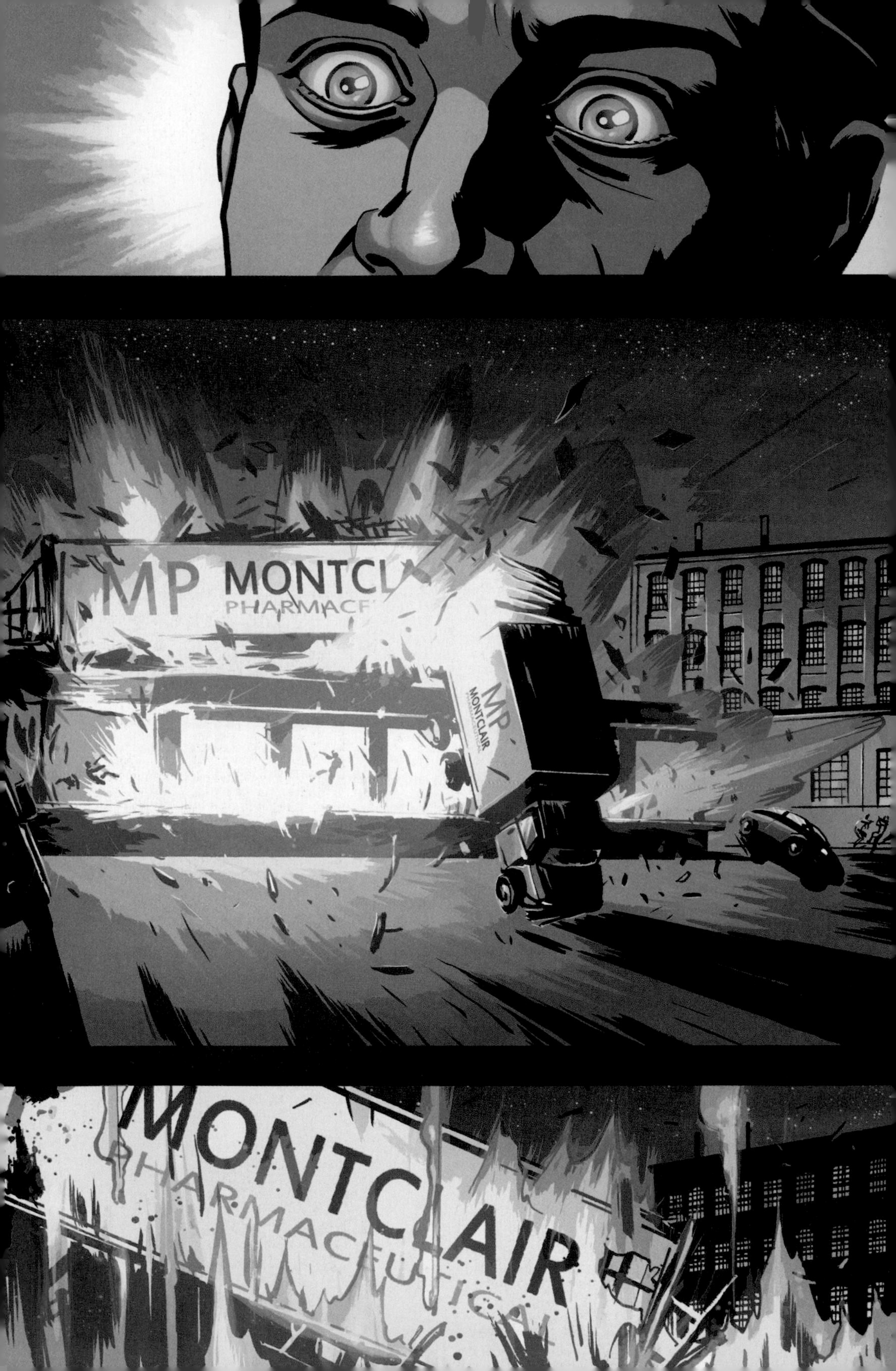
MP MONTCL
PHARMACE
MP
MONTCLAIR
MONTCLAIR

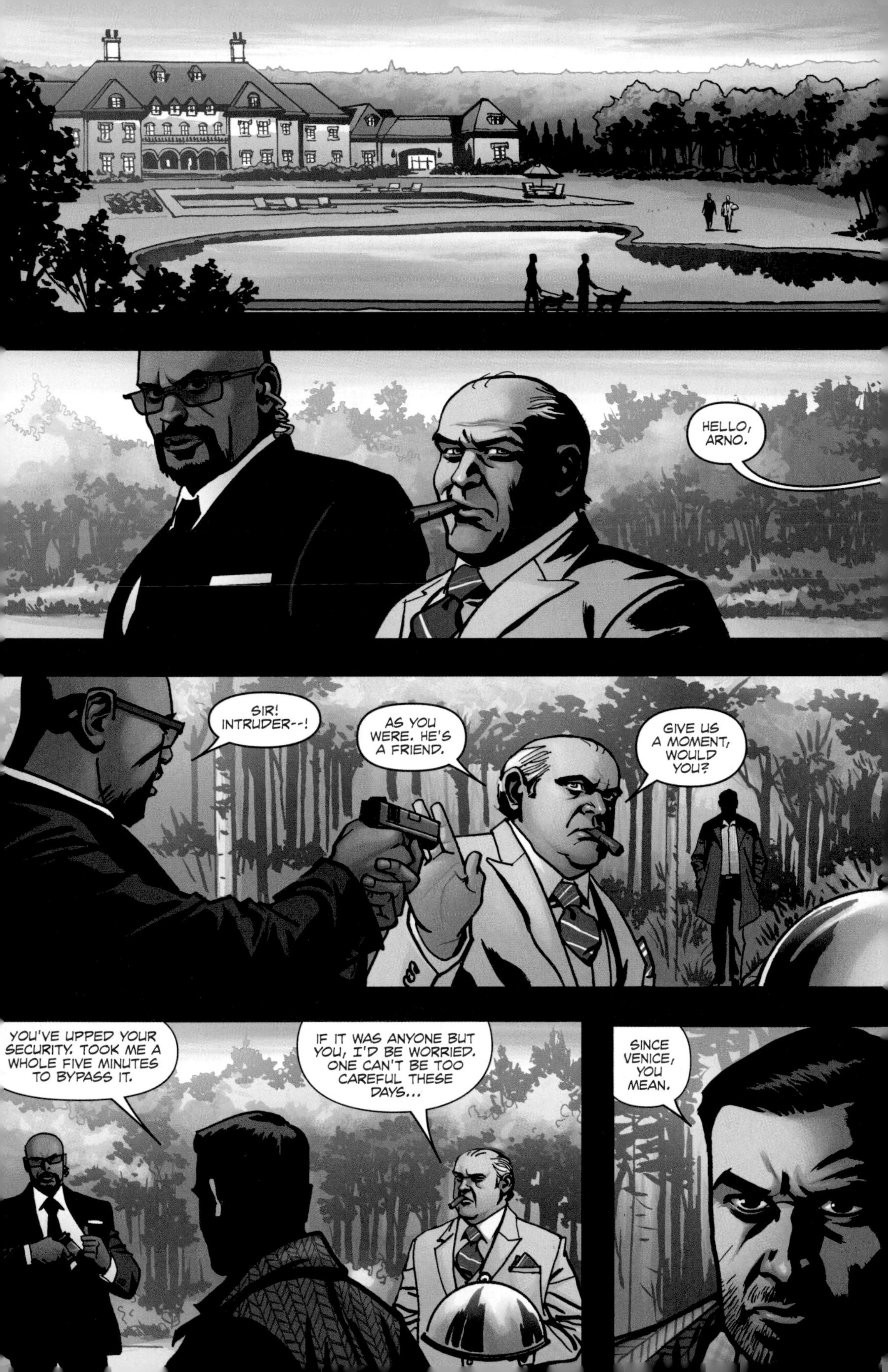
HELLO, ARNO.
SIR! INTRUDER--!
AS YOU WERE. HE'S A FRIEND.
GIVE US A MOMENT, WOULD YOU?
YOU'VE UPPED YOUR SECURITY. TOOK ME A WHOLE FIVE MINUTES TO BYPASS IT.
IF IT WAS ANYONE BUT YOU, I'D BE WORRIED. ONE CAN'T BE TOO CAREFUL THESE DAYS...
SINCE VENICE, YOU MEAN.

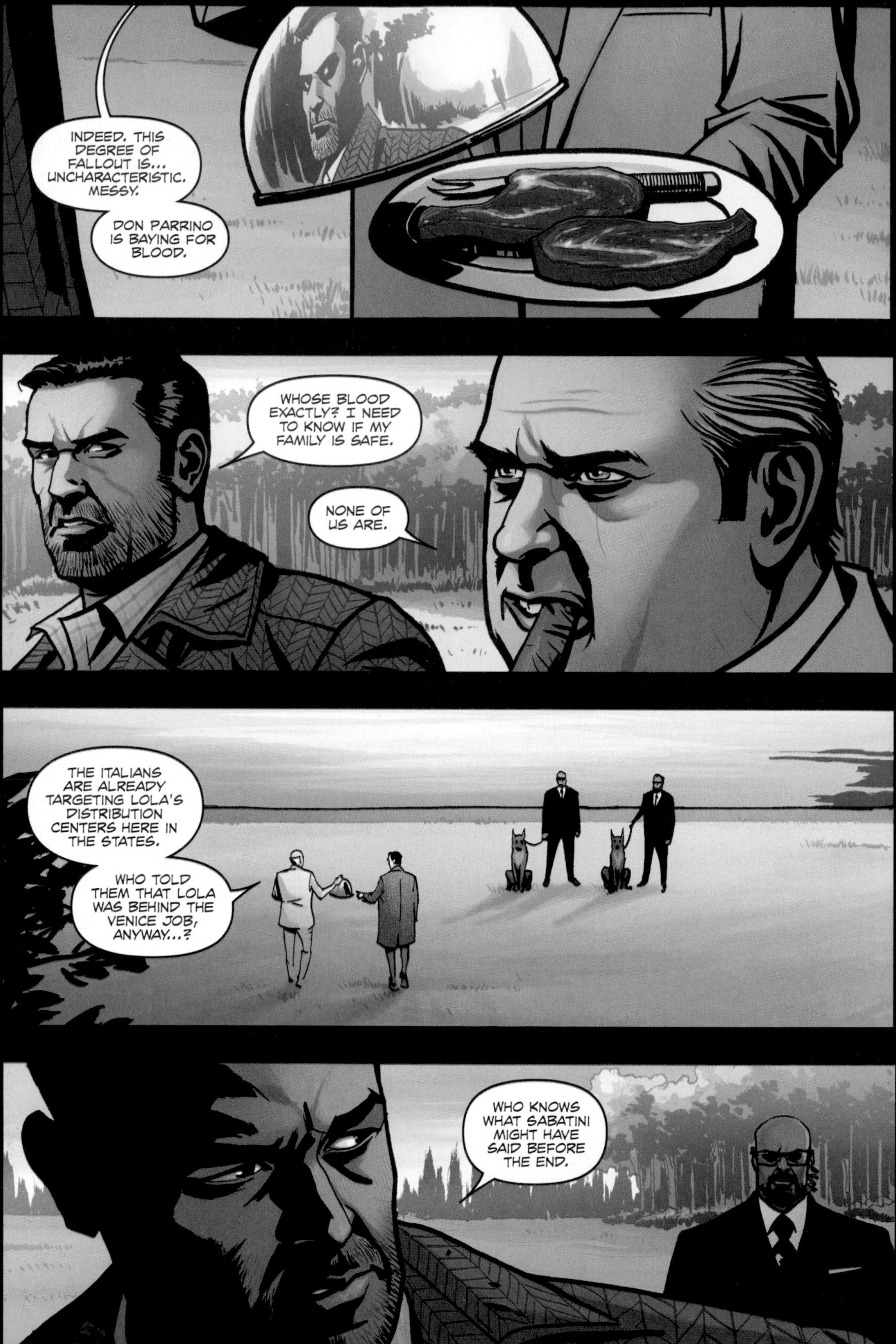
INDEED. THIS DEGREE OF FALLOUT IS... UNCHARACTERISTIC. MESSY.
DON PARRINO IS BAYING FOR BLOOD.
WHOSE BLOOD EXACTLY?? I NEED TO KNOW IF MY FAMILY IS SAFE.
NONE OF US ARE.
THE ITALIANS ARE ALREADY TARGETING LOLA'S DISTRIBUTION CENTERS HERE IN THE STATES.
WHO TOLD THEM THAT LOLA WAS BEHIND THE VENICE JOB, ANYWAY...?
WHO KNOWS WHAT SABATINI MIGHT HAVE SAID BEFORE THE END.

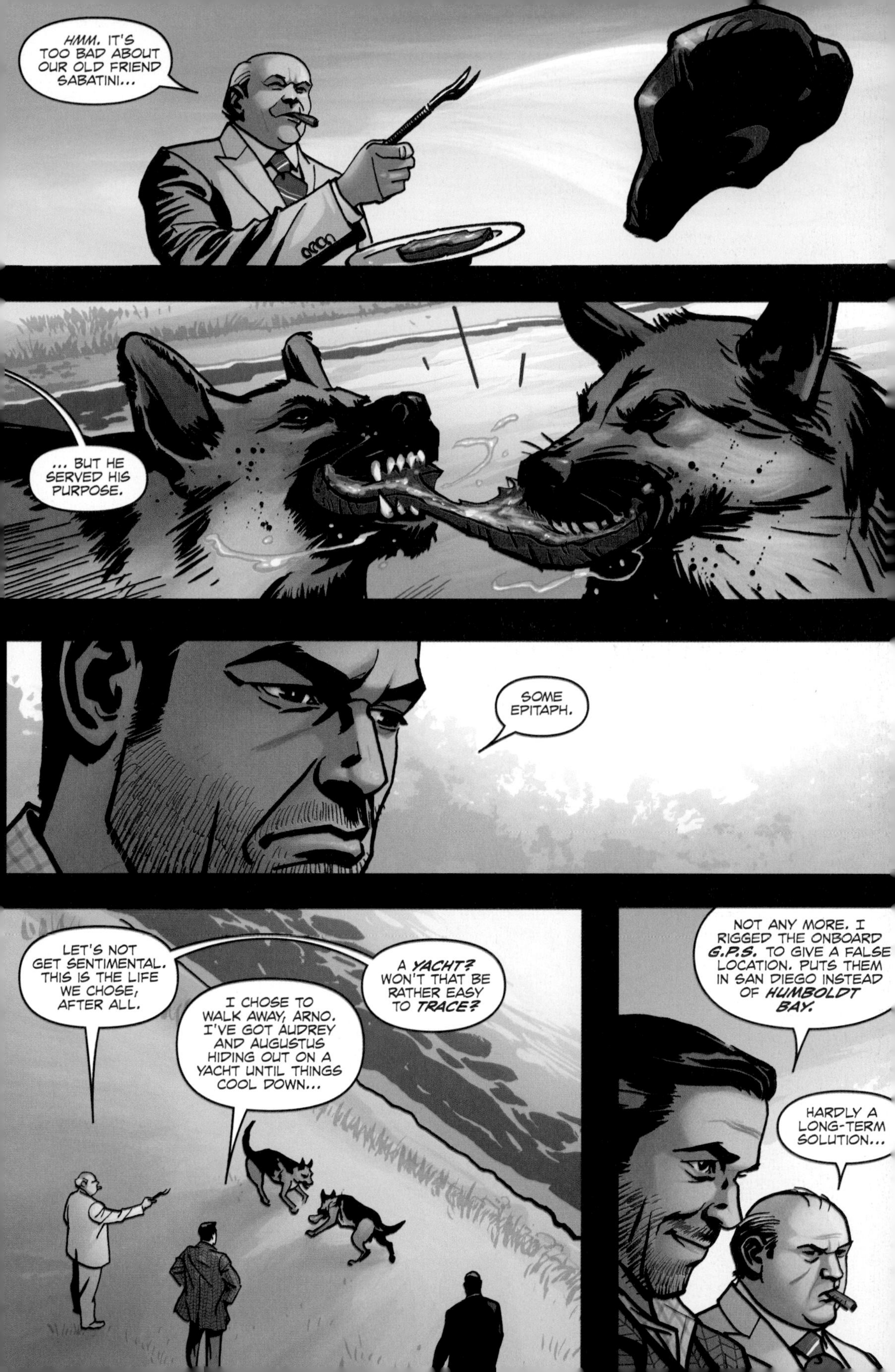
HMM. IT'S TOO BAD ABOUT OUR OLD FRIEND SABATINI...
... BUT HE SERVED HIS PURPOSE.
SOME EPITAPH.
LET'S NOT GET SENTIMENTAL. THIS IS THE LIFE WE CHOSE, AFTER ALL.
I CHOSE TO WALK AWAY, ARNO. I'VE GOT AUDREY AND AUGUSTUS HIDING OUT ON A YACHT UNTIL THINGS COOL DOWN...
A YACHT? WON'T THAT BE RATHER EASY TO TRACE?
NOT ANY MORE. I RIGGED THE ONBOARD G.P.S. TO GIVE A FALSE LOCATION. PUTS THEM IN SAN DIEGO INSTEAD OF HUMBOLDT BAY.
HARDLY A LONG-TERM SOLUTION...

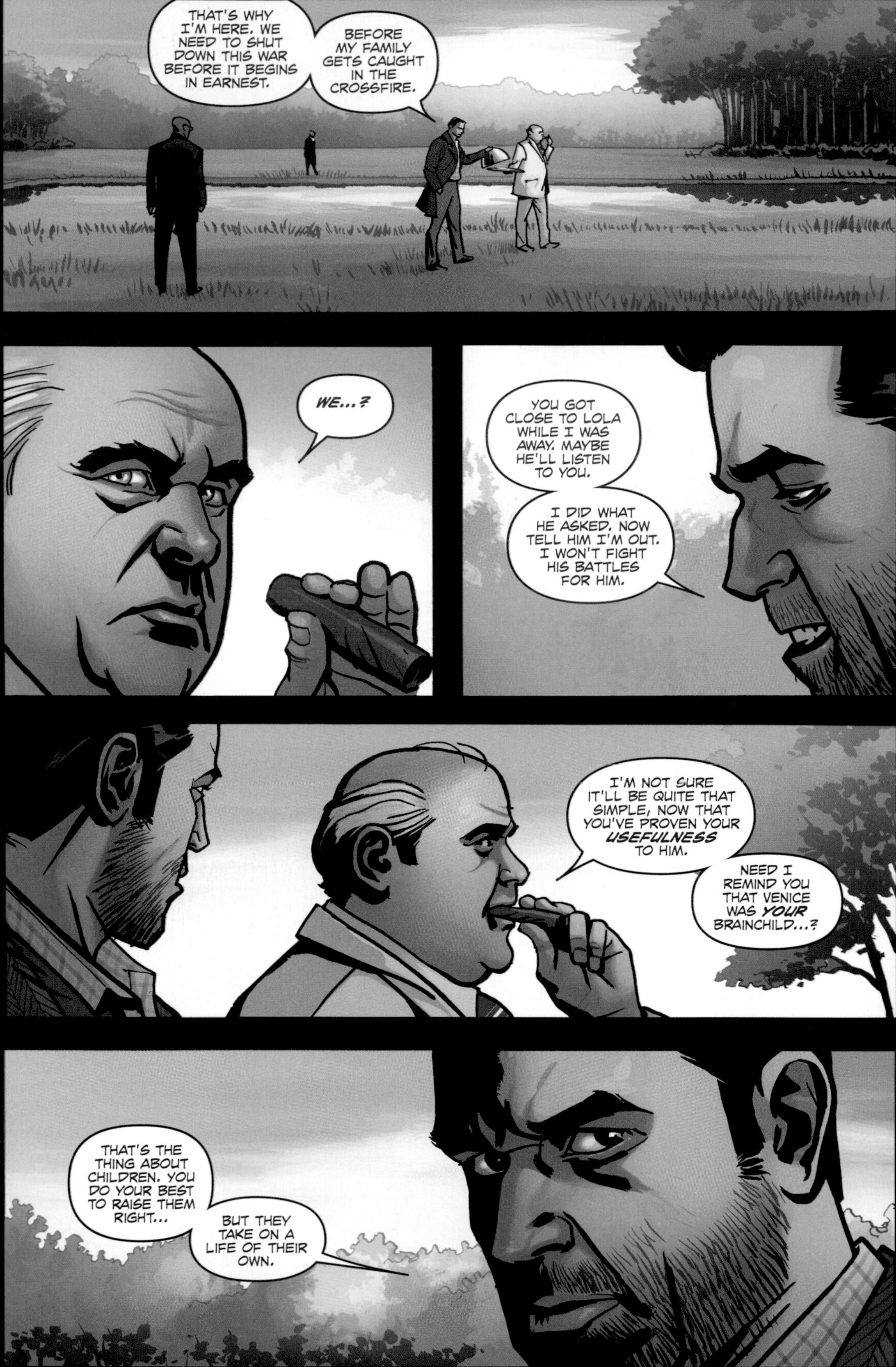
THAT'S WHY I'M HERE. WE NEED TO SHUT DOWN THIS WAR BEFORE IT BEGINS IN EARNEST.
BEFORE MY FAMILY GETS CAUGHT IN THE CROSSFIRE.
WE...?
YOU GOT CLOSE TO LOLA WHILE I WAS AWAY. MAYBE HE'LL LISTEN TO YOU.
I DID WHAT HE ASKED. NOW TELL HIM I'M OUT. I WON'T FIGHT HIS BATTLES FOR HIM.
I'M NOT SURE IT'LL BE QUITE THAT SIMPLE, NOW THAT YOU'VE PROVEN YOUR *USEFULNESS* TO HIM.
NEED I REMIND YOU THAT VENICE WAS *YOUR* BRAINCHILD...?
THAT'S THE THING ABOUT CHILDREN. YOU DO YOUR BEST TO RAISE THEM RIGHT...
BUT THEY TAKE ON A LIFE OF THEIR OWN.

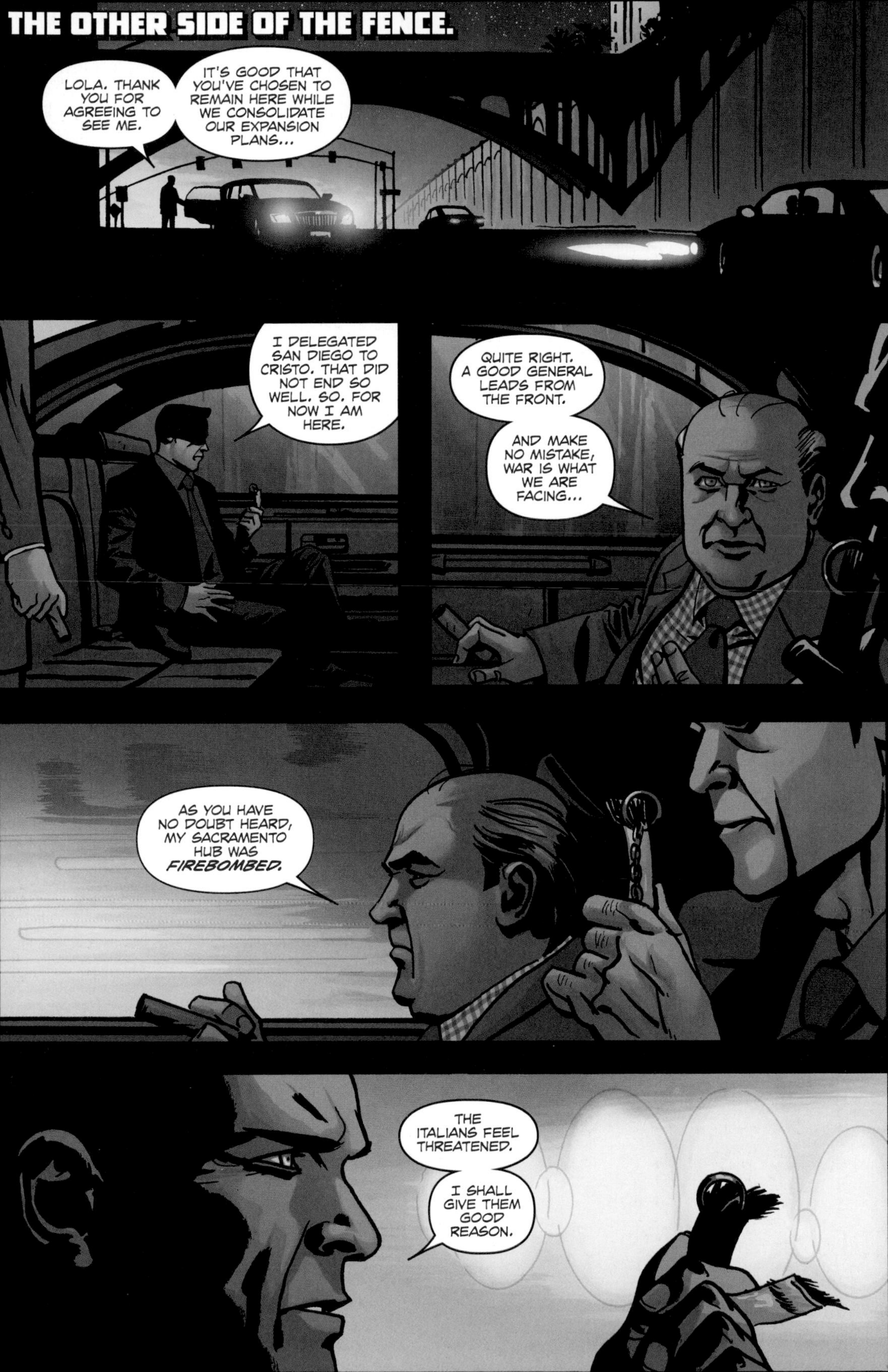
THE OTHER SIDE OF THE FENCE.
LOLA. THANK YOU FOR AGREEING TO SEE ME.
IT'S GOOD THAT YOU'VE CHOSEN TO REMAIN HERE WHILE WE CONSOLIDATE OUR EXPANSION PLANS...
I DELEGATED SAN DIEGO TO CRISTO. THAT DID NOT END SO WELL. SO. FOR NOW I AM HERE.
QUITE RIGHT. A GOOD GENERAL LEADS FROM THE FRONT.
AND MAKE NO MISTAKE, WAR IS WHAT WE ARE FACING...
AS YOU HAVE NO DOUBT HEARD, MY SACRAMENTO HUB WAS FIREBOMBED.
THE ITALIANS FEEL THREATENED.
I SHALL GIVE THEM GOOD REASON.

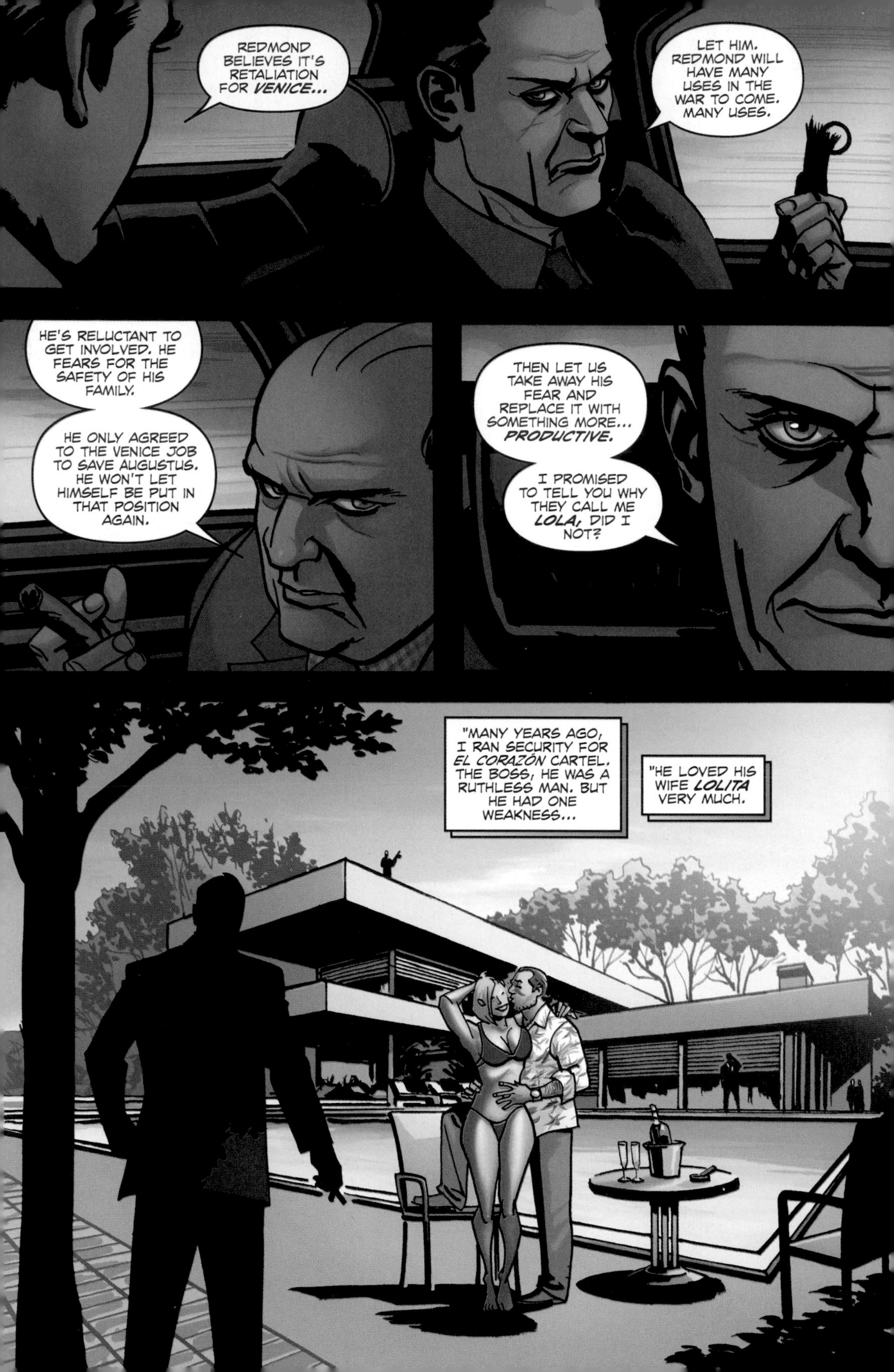
REDMOND BELIEVES IT'S RETALIATION FOR VENICE...
LET HIM. REDMOND WILL HAVE MANY USES IN THE WAR TO COME. MANY USES.
HE'S RELUCTANT TO GET INVOLVED. HE FEARS FOR THE SAFETY OF HIS FAMILY.
HE ONLY AGREED TO THE VENICE JOB TO SAVE AUGUSTUS. HE WON'T LET HIMSELF BE PUT IN THAT POSITION AGAIN.
THEN LET US TAKE AWAY HIS FEAR AND REPLACE IT WITH SOMETHING MORE... PRODUCTIVE.
I PROMISED TO TELL YOU WHY THEY CALL ME LOLA, DID I NOT?
"MANY YEARS AGO, I RAN SECURITY FOR EL CORAZÓN CARTEL. THE BOSS, HE WAS A RUTHLESS MAN. BUT HE HAD ONE WEAKNESS...
"HE LOVED HIS WIFE LOLITA VERY MUCH.

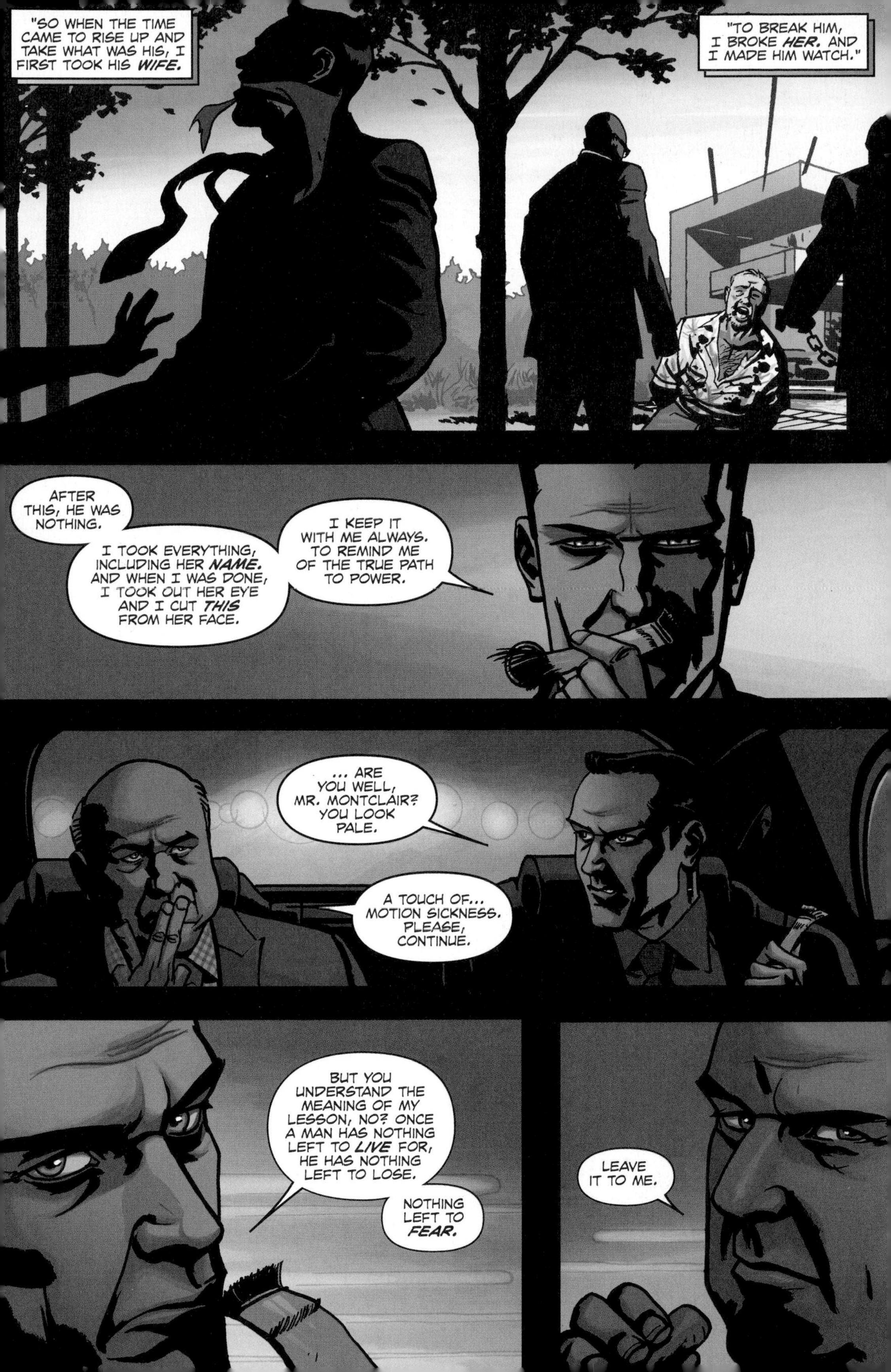
"SO WHEN THE TIME CAME TO RISE UP AND TAKE WHAT WAS HIS, I FIRST TOOK HIS *WIFE.*
"TO BREAK HIM, I BROKE *HER.* AND I MADE HIM WATCH."
AFTER THIS, HE WAS NOTHING.
I TOOK EVERYTHING, INCLUDING HER *NAME.* AND WHEN I WAS DONE, I TOOK OUT HER EYE AND I CUT *THIS* FROM HER FACE.
I KEEP IT WITH ME ALWAYS. TO REMIND ME OF THE TRUE PATH TO POWER.
... ARE YOU WELL, MR. MONTCLAIR? YOU LOOK PALE.
A TOUCH OF... MOTION SICKNESS. PLEASE, CONTINUE.
BUT YOU UNDERSTAND THE MEANING OF MY LESSON, NO? ONCE A MAN HAS NOTHING LEFT TO *LIVE* FOR, HE HAS NOTHING LEFT TO LOSE.
NOTHING LEFT TO *FEAR.*
LEAVE IT TO ME.

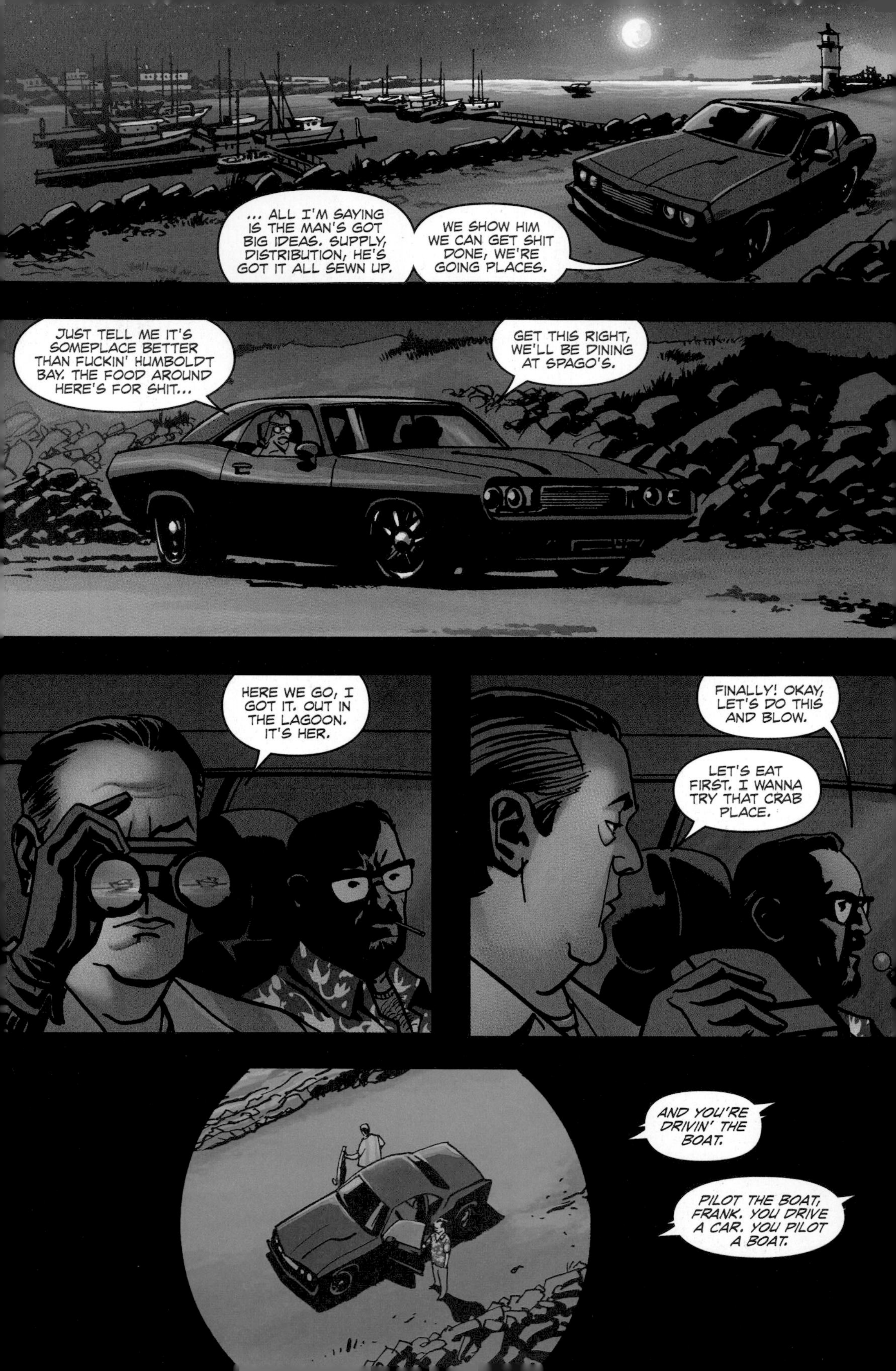
... ALL I'M SAYING IS THE MAN'S GOT BIG IDEAS. SUPPLY, DISTRIBUTION, HE'S GOT IT ALL SEWN UP.
WE SHOW HIM WE CAN GET SHIT DONE, WE'RE GOING PLACES.
JUST TELL ME IT'S SOMEPLACE BETTER THAN FUCKIN' HUMBOLDT BAY. THE FOOD AROUND HERE'S FOR SHIT...
GET THIS RIGHT, WE'LL BE DINING AT SPAGO'S.
HERE WE GO, I GOT IT. OUT IN THE LAGOON. IT'S HER.
FINALLY! OKAY, LET'S DO THIS AND BLOW.
LET'S EAT FIRST. I WANNA TRY THAT CRAB PLACE.
AND YOU'RE DRIVIN' THE BOAT.
PILOT THE BOAT, FRANK. YOU DRIVE A CAR. YOU PILOT A BOAT.

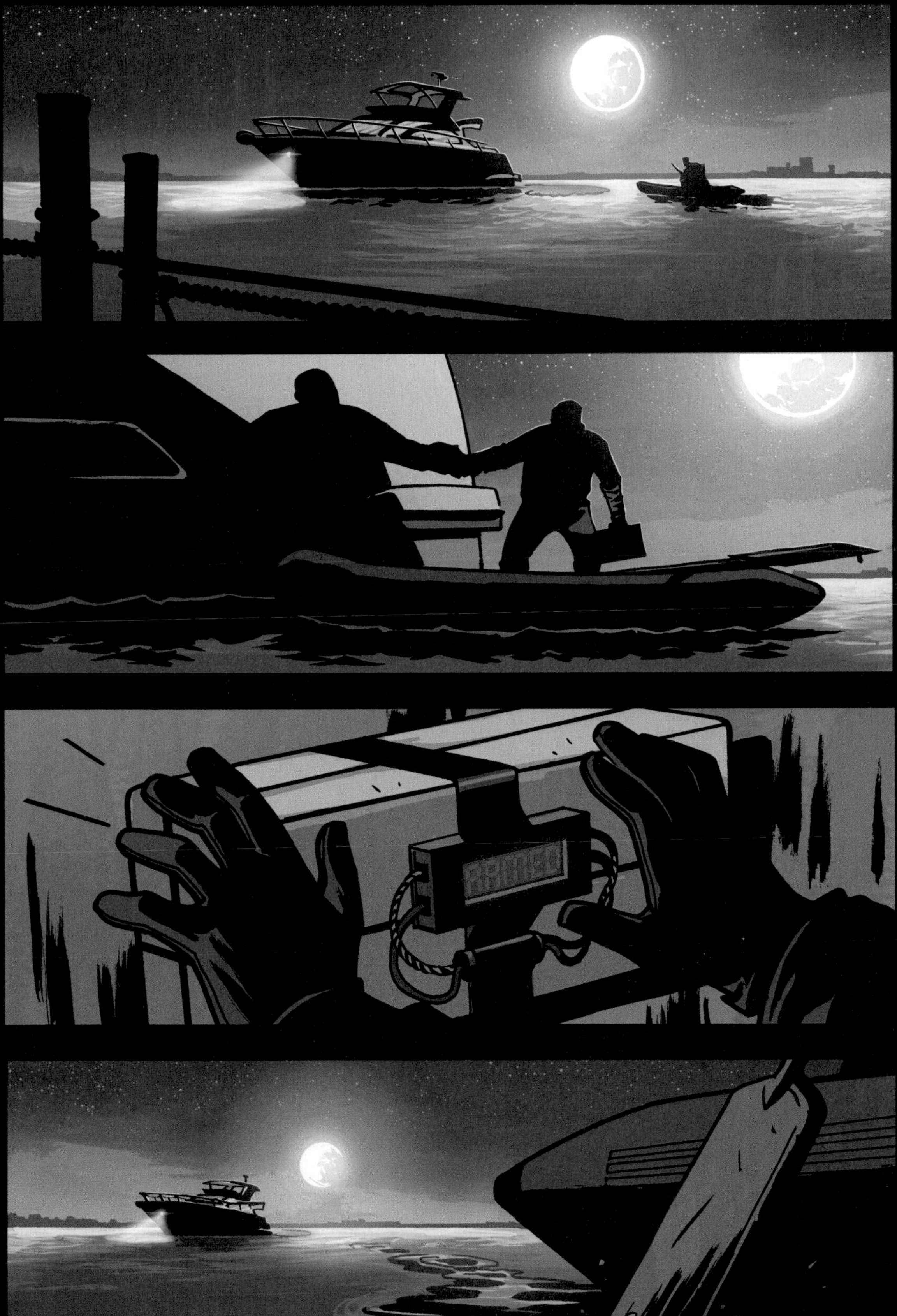
ARMED

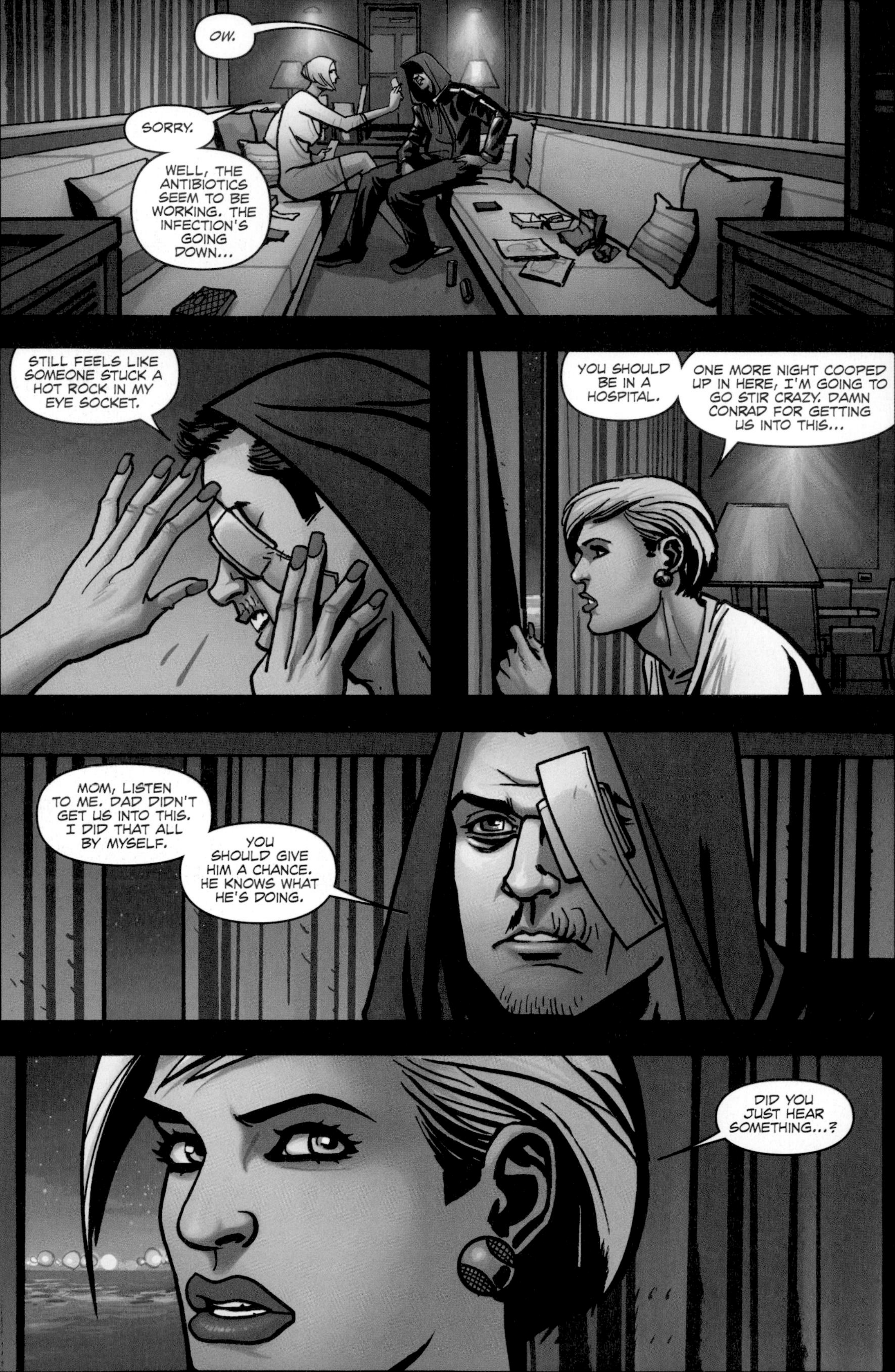
OW.
SORRY.
WELL, THE ANTIBIOTICS SEEM TO BE WORKING. THE INFECTION'S GOING DOWN...
STILL FEELS LIKE SOMEONE STUCK A HOT ROCK IN MY EYE SOCKET.
YOU SHOULD BE IN A HOSPITAL.
ONE MORE NIGHT COOPED UP IN HERE, I'M GOING TO GO STIR CRAZY. DAMN CONRAD FOR GETTING US INTO THIS...
MOM, LISTEN TO ME. DAD DIDN'T GET US INTO THIS. I DID THAT ALL BY MYSELF.
YOU SHOULD GIVE HIM A CHANCE. HE KNOWS WHAT HE'S DOING.
DID YOU JUST HEAR SOMETHING...?

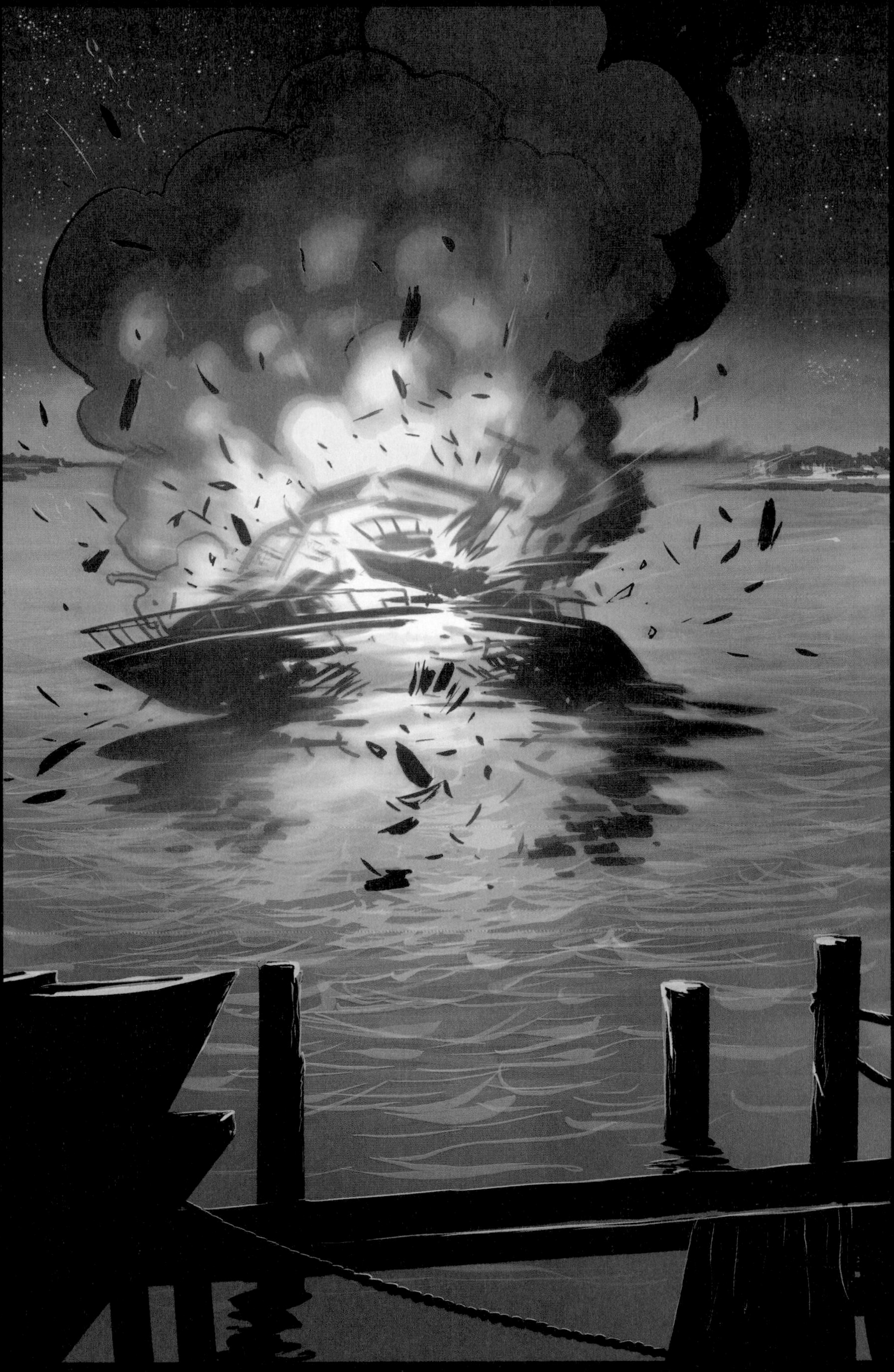

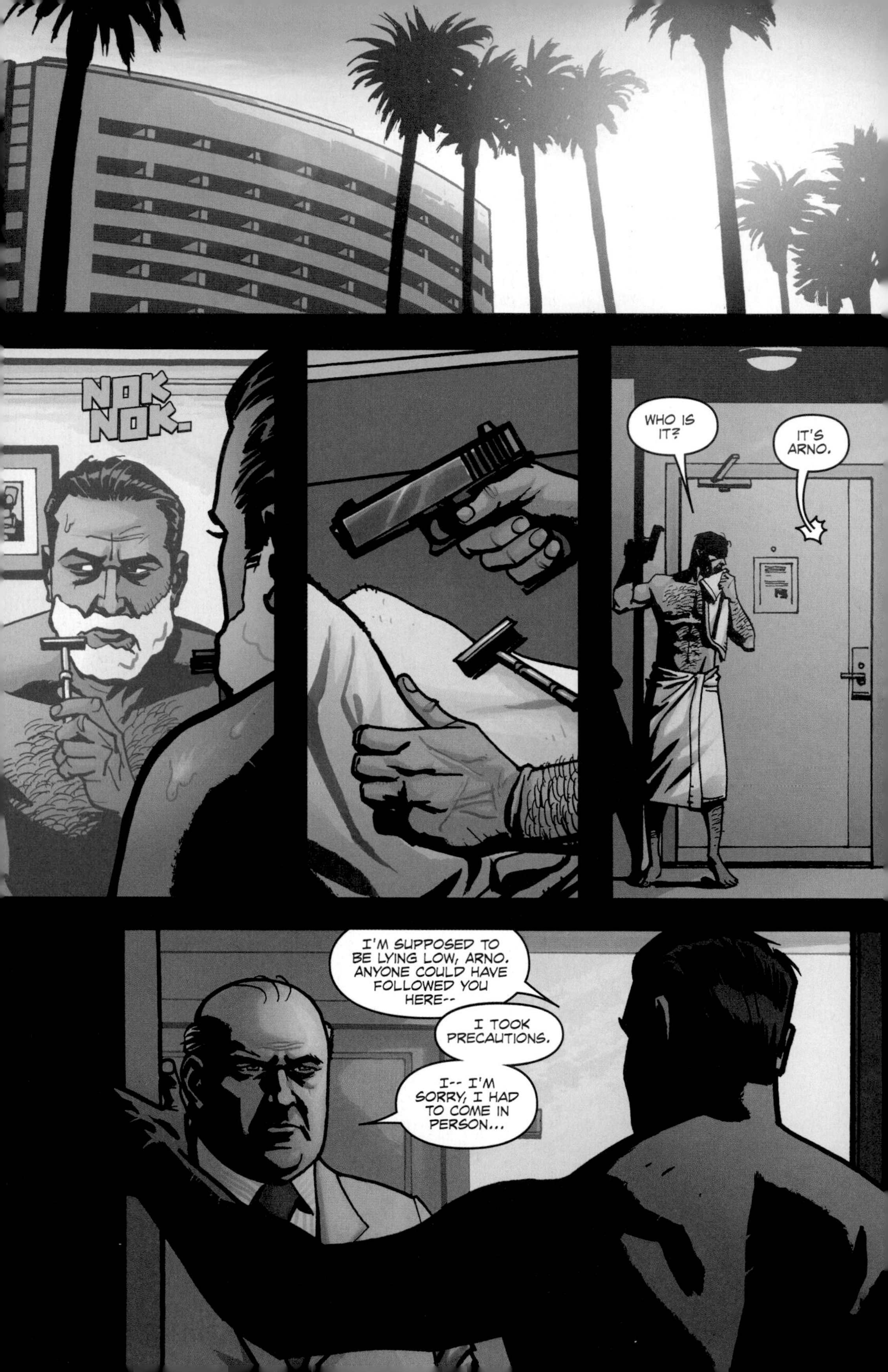
NOK NOK.
WHO IS IT?
IT'S ARNO.
I'M SUPPOSED TO BE LYING LOW, ARNO. ANYONE COULD HAVE FOLLOWED YOU HERE--
I TOOK PRECAUTIONS.
I-- I'M SORRY, I HAD TO COME IN PERSON...

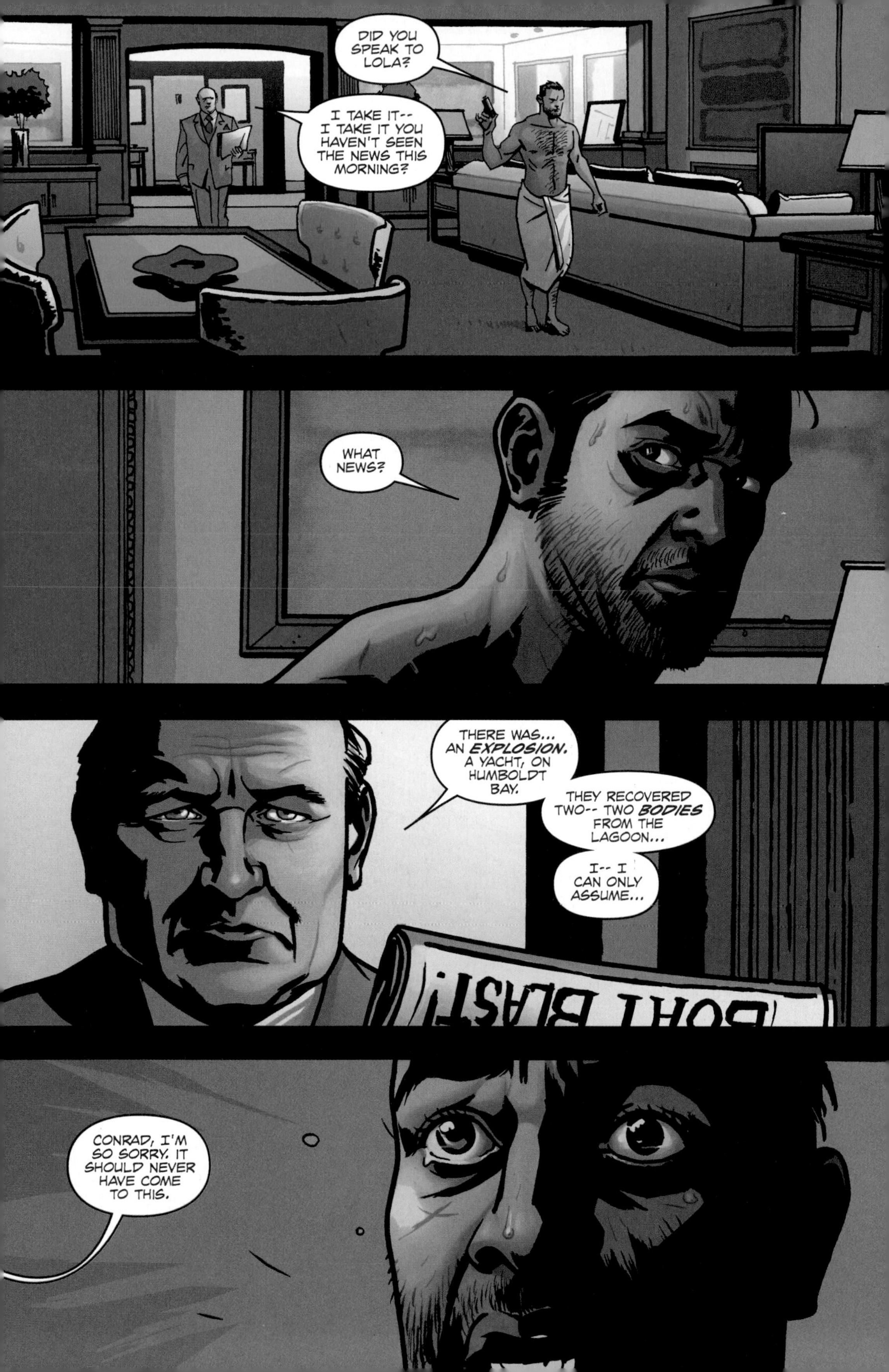
DID YOU SPEAK TO LOLA?
I TAKE IT-- I TAKE IT YOU HAVEN'T SEEN THE NEWS THIS MORNING?
WHAT NEWS?
THERE WAS... AN *EXPLOSION.* A YACHT, ON HUMBOLDT BAY.
THEY RECOVERED TWO-- TWO *BODIES* FROM THE LAGOON...
I-- I CAN ONLY ASSUME...
CONRAD, I'M SO SORRY. IT SHOULD NEVER HAVE COME TO THIS.

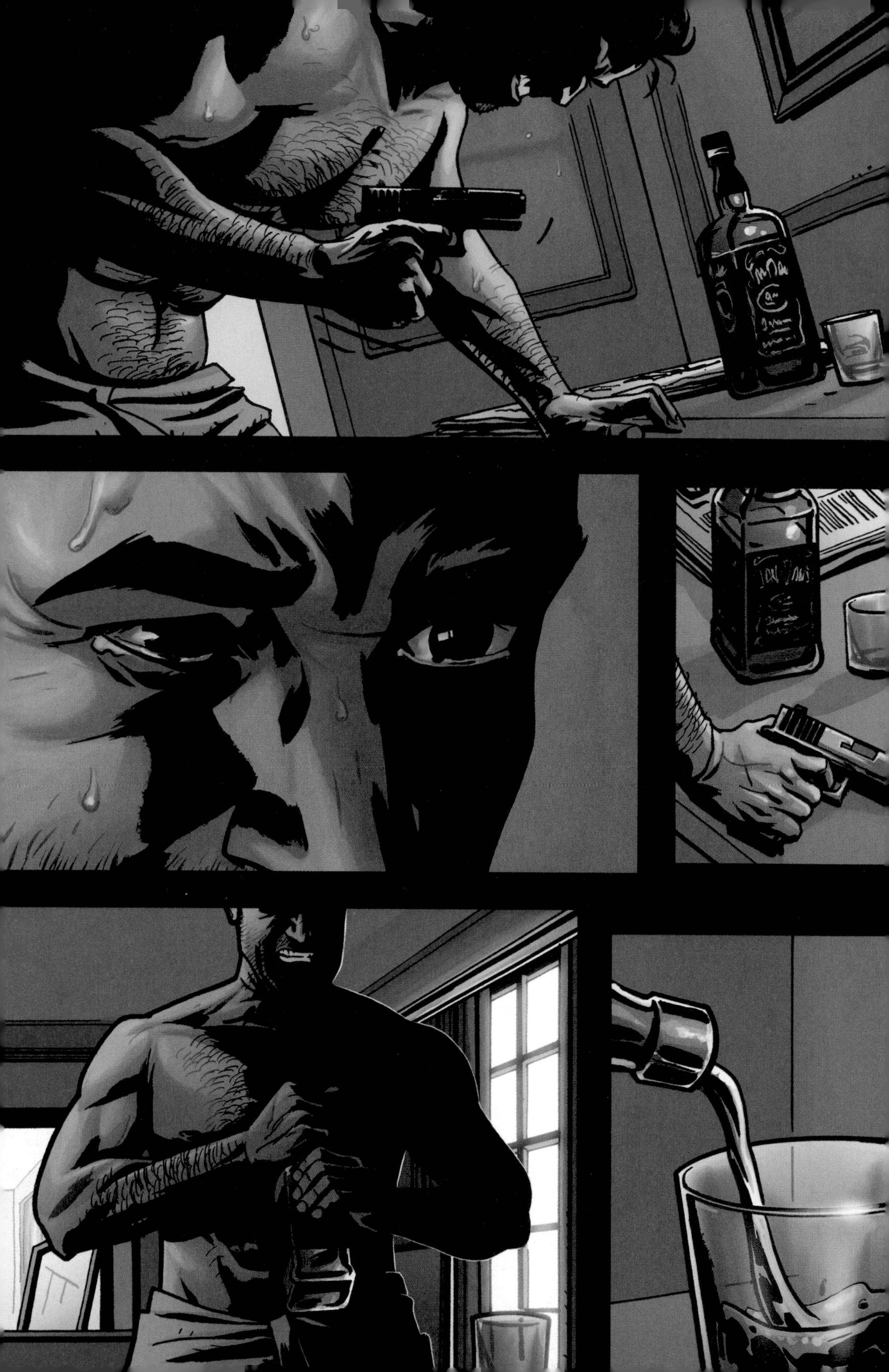

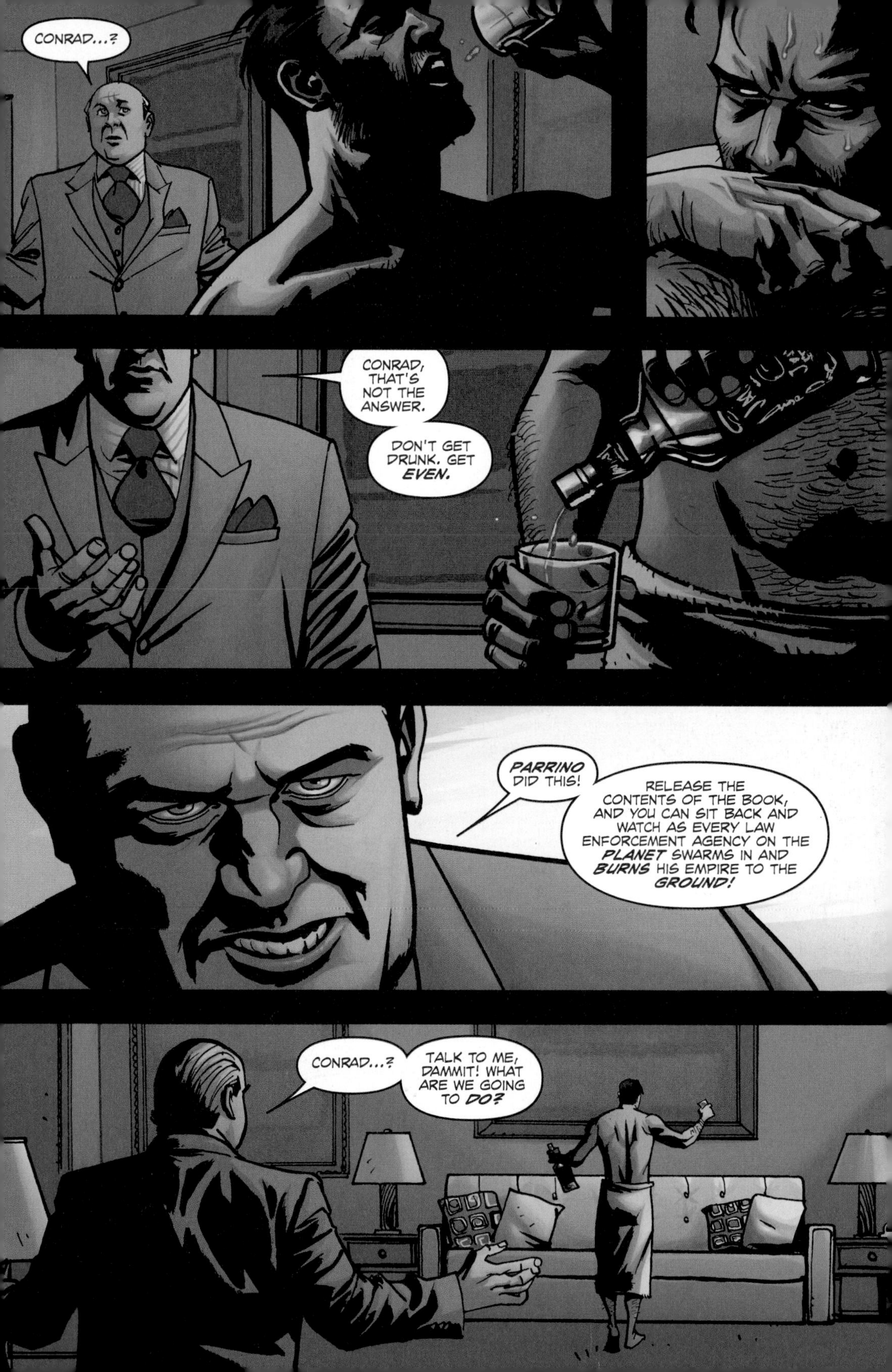
CONRAD...?
CONRAD, THAT'S NOT THE ANSWER.
DON'T GET DRUNK. GET *EVEN.*
PARRINO DID THIS!
RELEASE THE CONTENTS OF THE BOOK, AND YOU CAN SIT BACK AND WATCH AS EVERY LAW ENFORCEMENT AGENCY ON THE *PLANET* SWARMS IN AND *BURNS* HIS EMPIRE TO THE *GROUND!*
CONRAD...?
TALK TO ME, DAMMIT! WHAT ARE WE GOING TO *DO?*

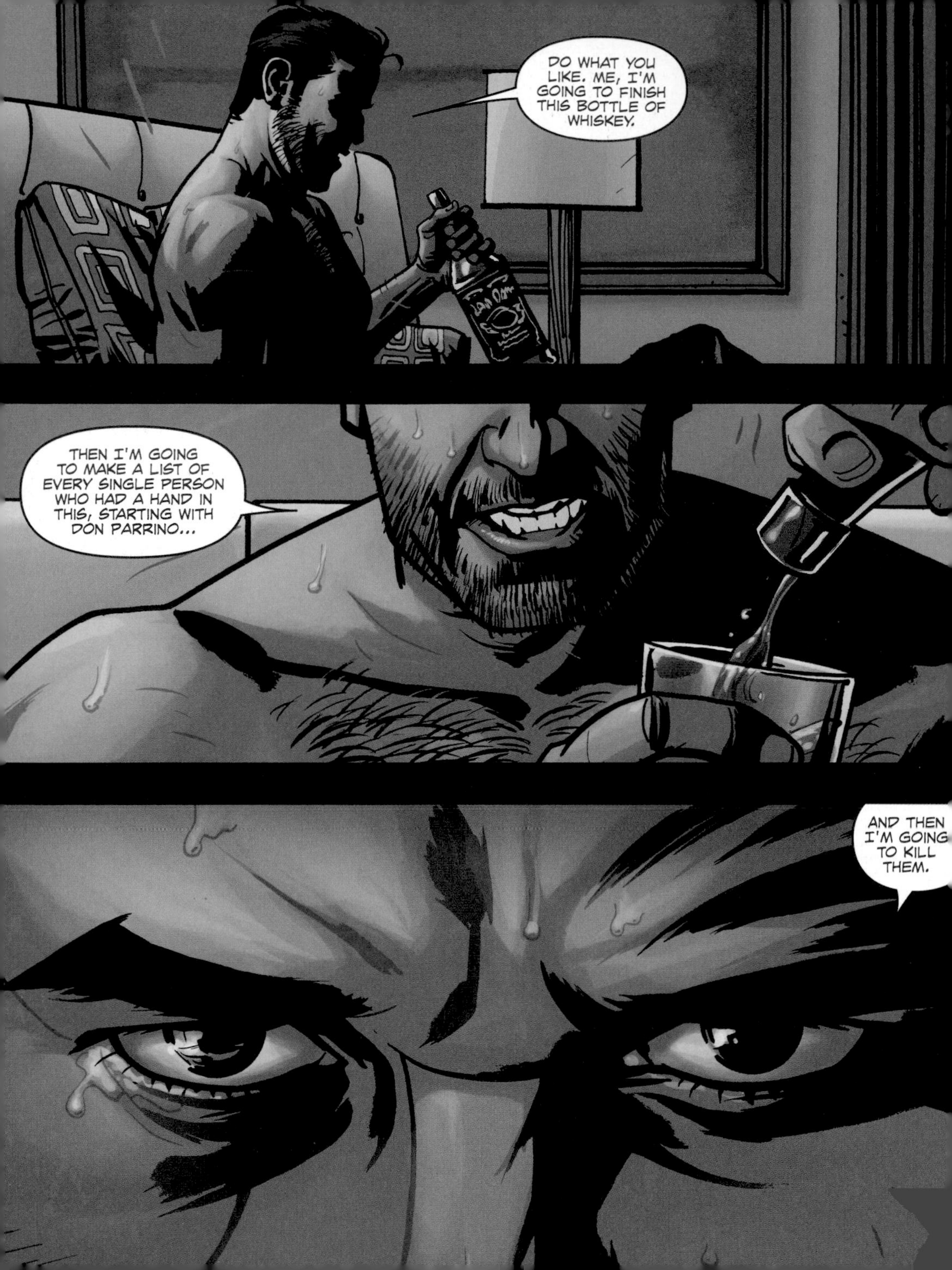
DO WHAT YOU LIKE. ME, I'M GOING TO FINISH THIS BOTTLE OF WHISKEY.
THEN I'M GOING TO MAKE A LIST OF EVERY SINGLE PERSON WHO HAD A HAND IN THIS, STARTING WITH DON PARRINO...
AND THEN I'M GOING TO KILL THEM.

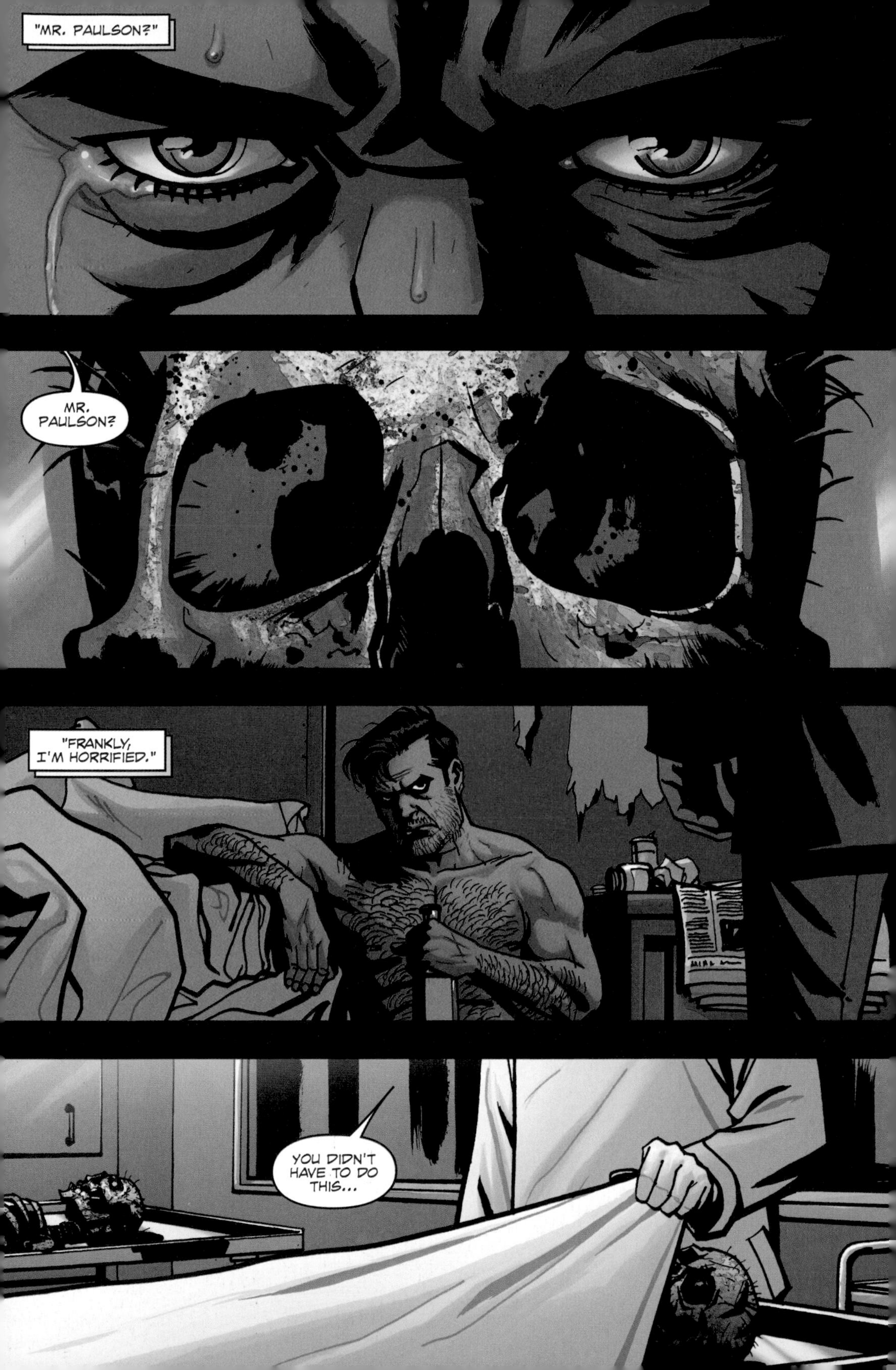
"MR. PAULSON?"
MR. PAULSON?
"FRANKLY, I'M HORRIFIED."
YOU DIDN'T HAVE TO DO THIS...

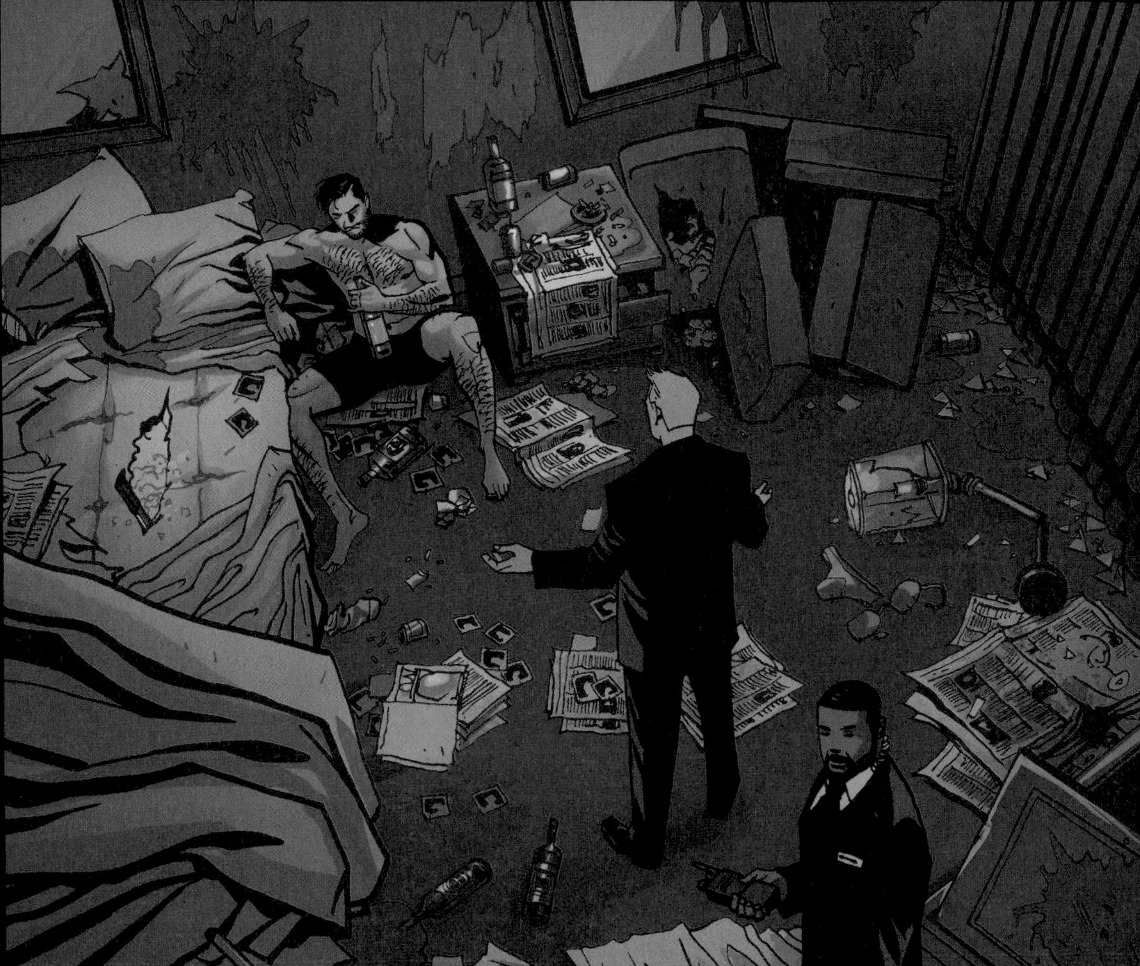
"I'M AFRAID I'M GOING TO HAVE TO ASK YOU TO LEAVE THE HOTEL."

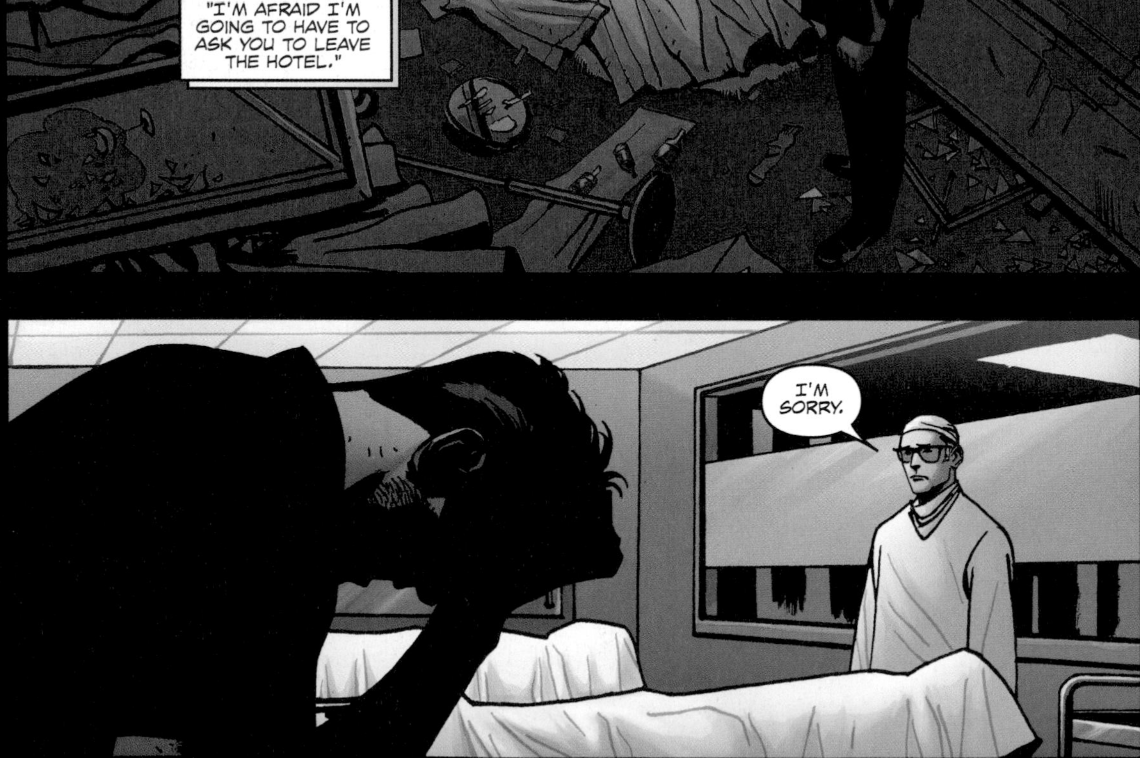
I'M SORRY.

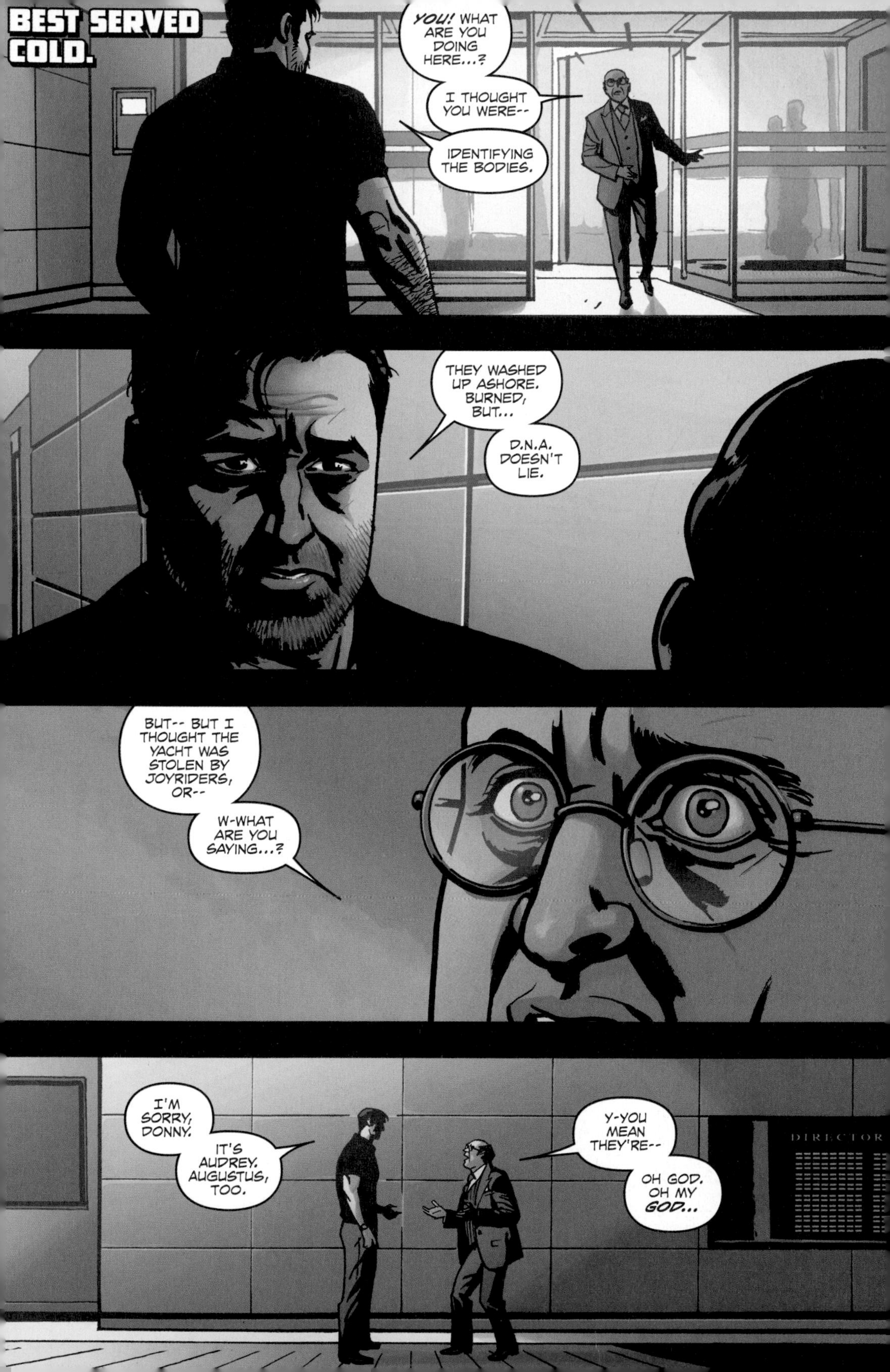
BEST SERVED COLD.
YOU! WHAT ARE YOU DOING HERE...?
I THOUGHT YOU WERE--
IDENTIFYING THE BODIES.
THEY WASHED UP ASHORE. BURNED, BUT...
D.N.A. DOESN'T LIE.
BUT-- BUT I THOUGHT THE YACHT WAS STOLEN BY JOYRIDERS, OR--
W-WHAT ARE YOU SAYING...?
I'M SORRY, DONNY.
IT'S AUDREY. AUGUSTUS, TOO.
Y-YOU MEAN THEY'RE--
OH GOD. OH MY GOD...
DIRECTOR

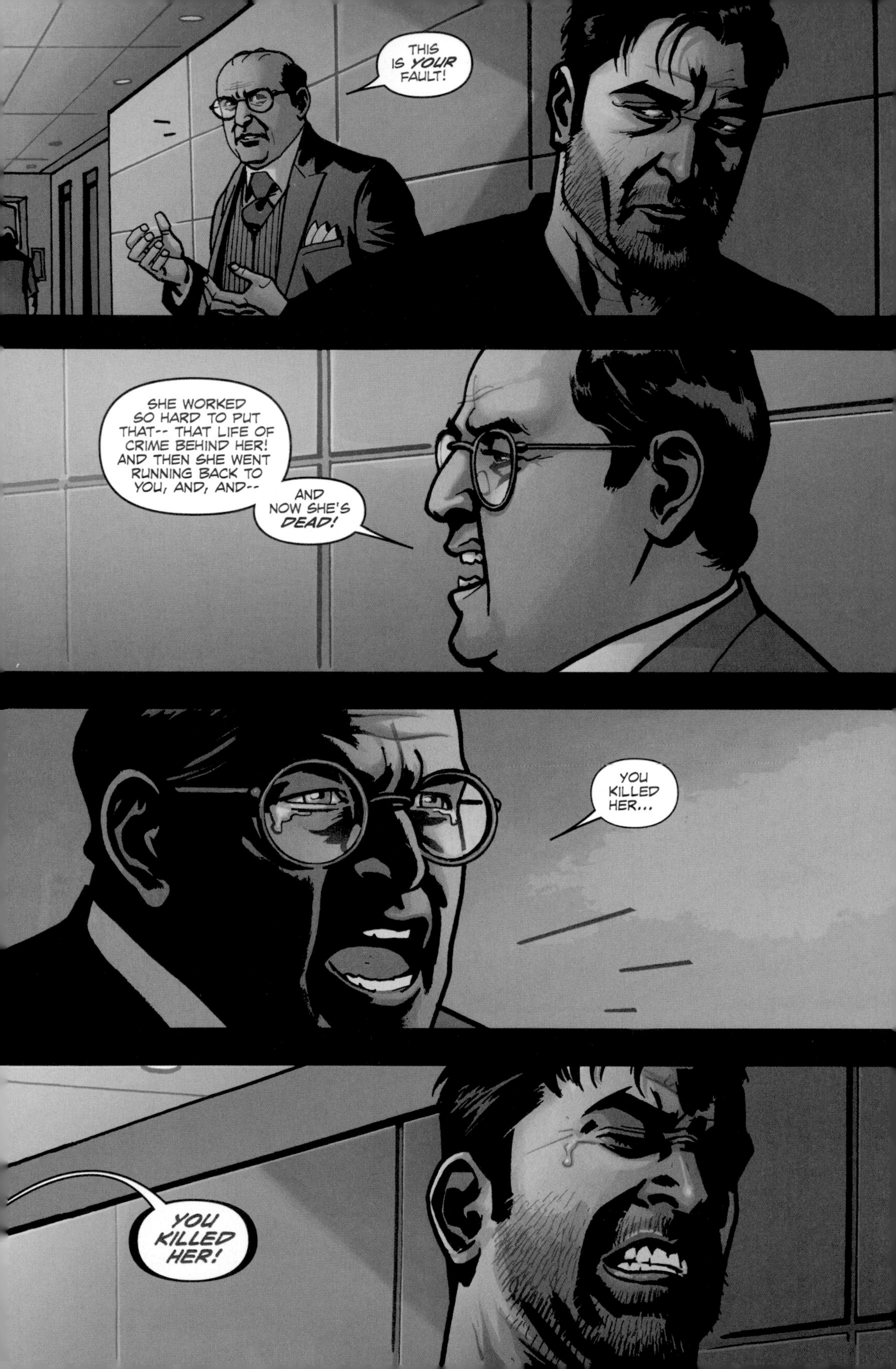
THIS IS *YOUR* FAULT!
SHE WORKED SO HARD TO PUT THAT-- THAT LIFE OF CRIME BEHIND HER! AND THEN SHE WENT RUNNING BACK TO YOU, AND, AND--
AND NOW SHE'S *DEAD!*
YOU KILLED HER...
YOU KILLED HER!

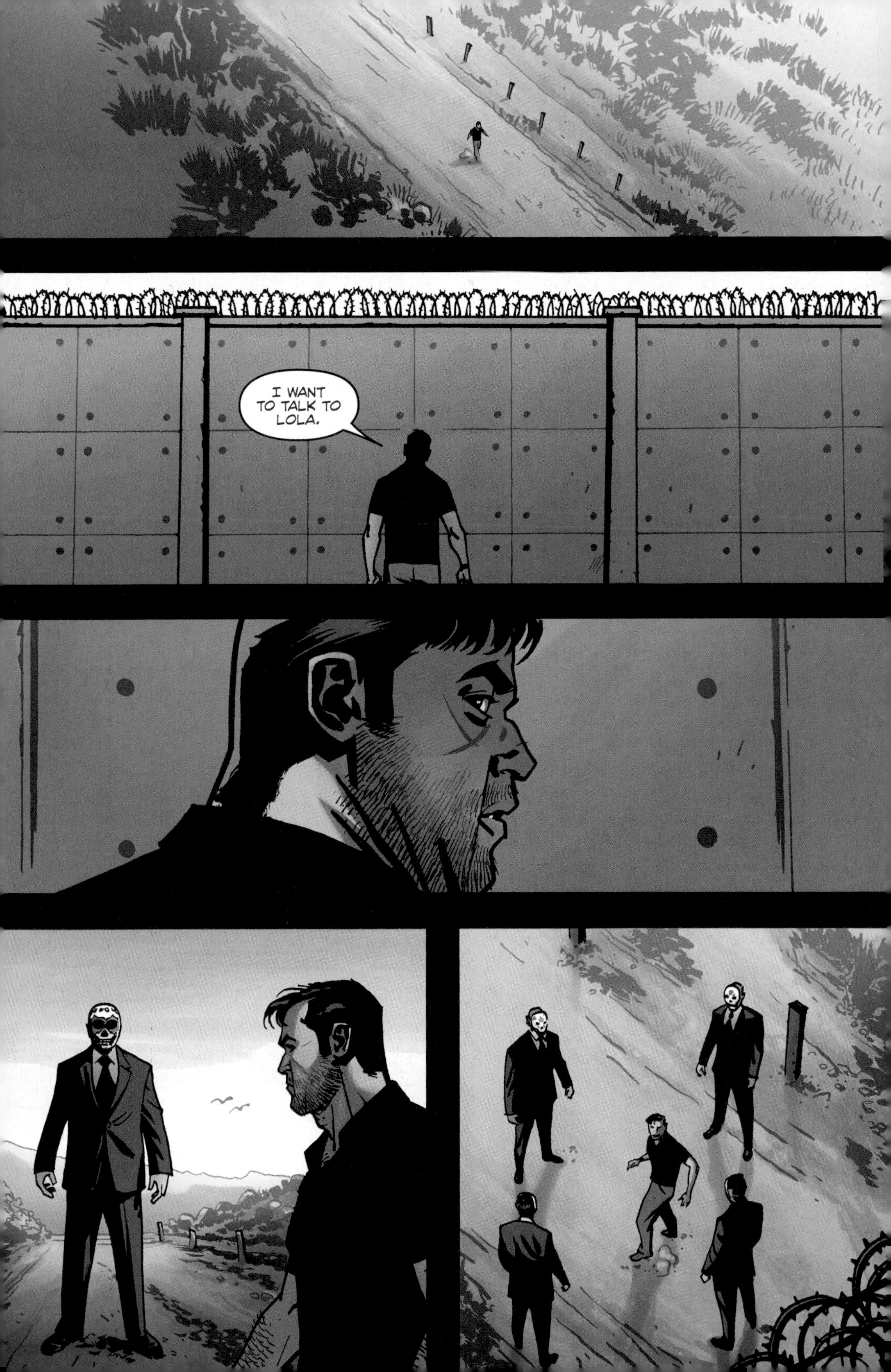
I WANT TO TALK TO LOLA.

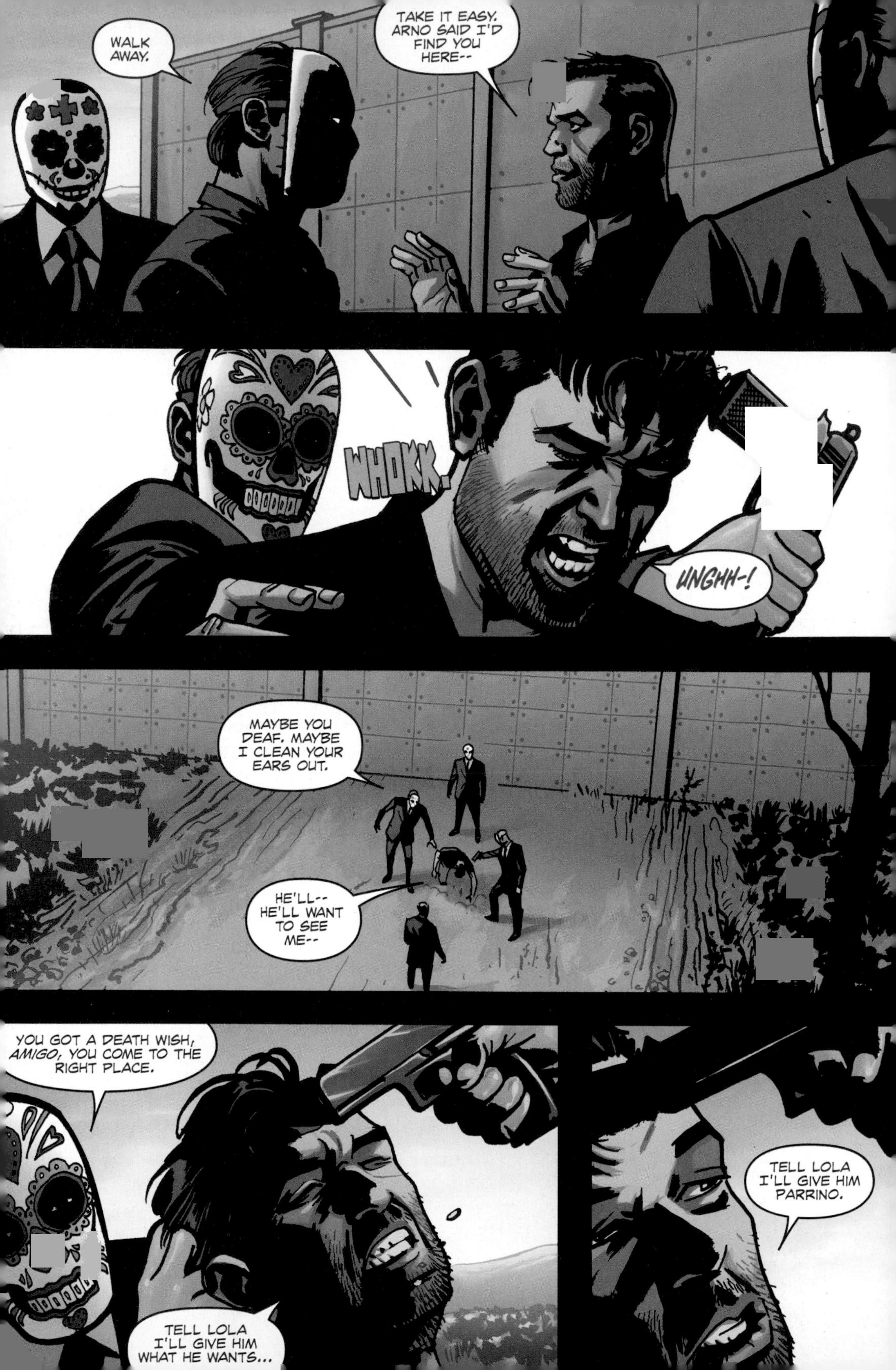
WALK AWAY.
TAKE IT EASY. ARNO SAID I'D FIND YOU HERE--
WHOKK.
UNGHH-!
MAYBE YOU DEAF. MAYBE I CLEAN YOUR EARS OUT.
HE'LL-- HE'LL WANT TO SEE ME--
YOU GOT A DEATH WISH, *AMIGO*, YOU COME TO THE RIGHT PLACE.
TELL LOLA I'LL GIVE HIM WHAT HE WANTS...
TELL LOLA I'LL GIVE HIM PARRINO.

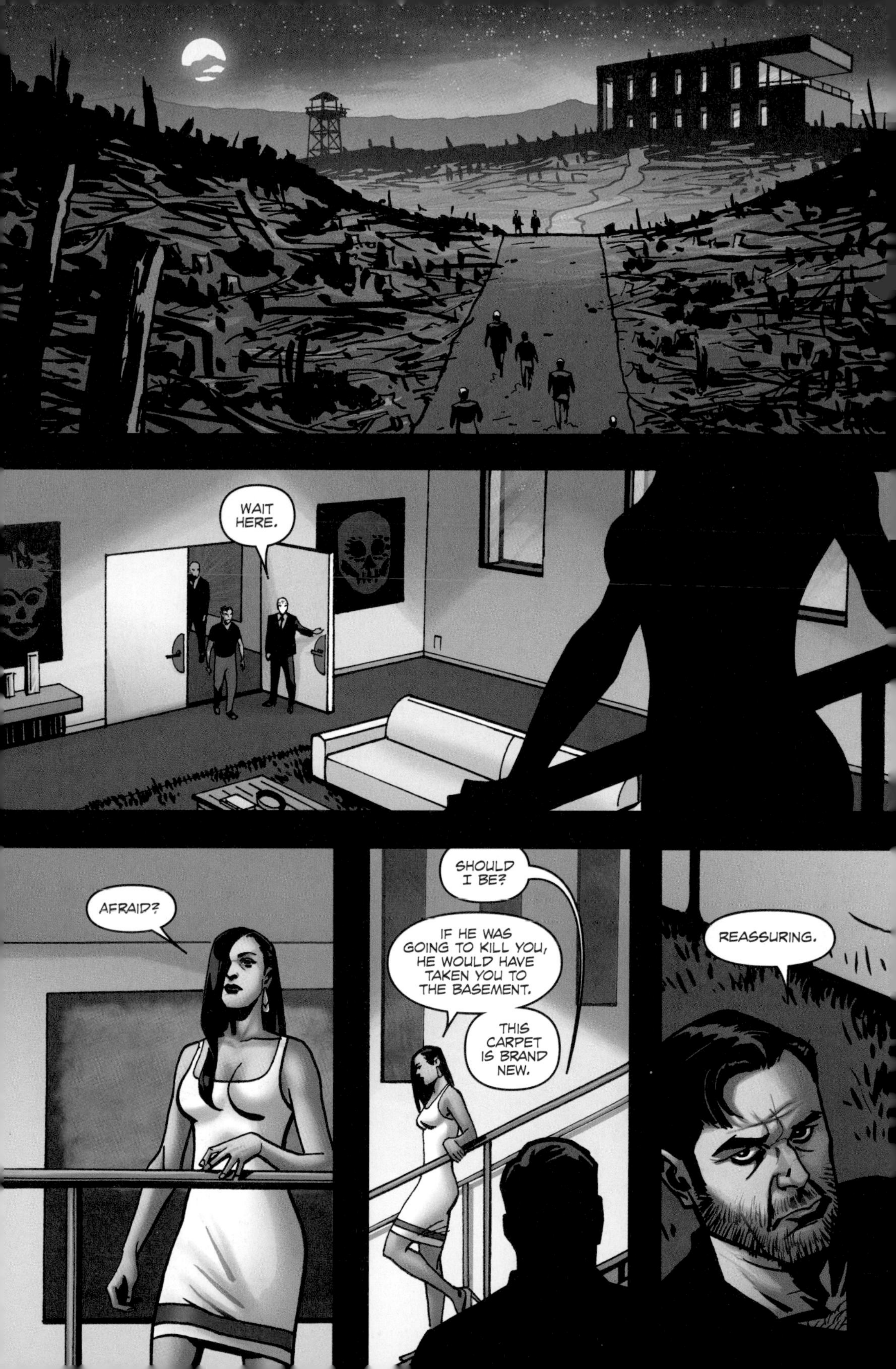
WAIT HERE.
AFRAID?
SHOULD I BE?
IF HE WAS GOING TO KILL YOU, HE WOULD HAVE TAKEN YOU TO THE BASEMENT.
THIS CARPET IS BRAND NEW.
REASSURING.

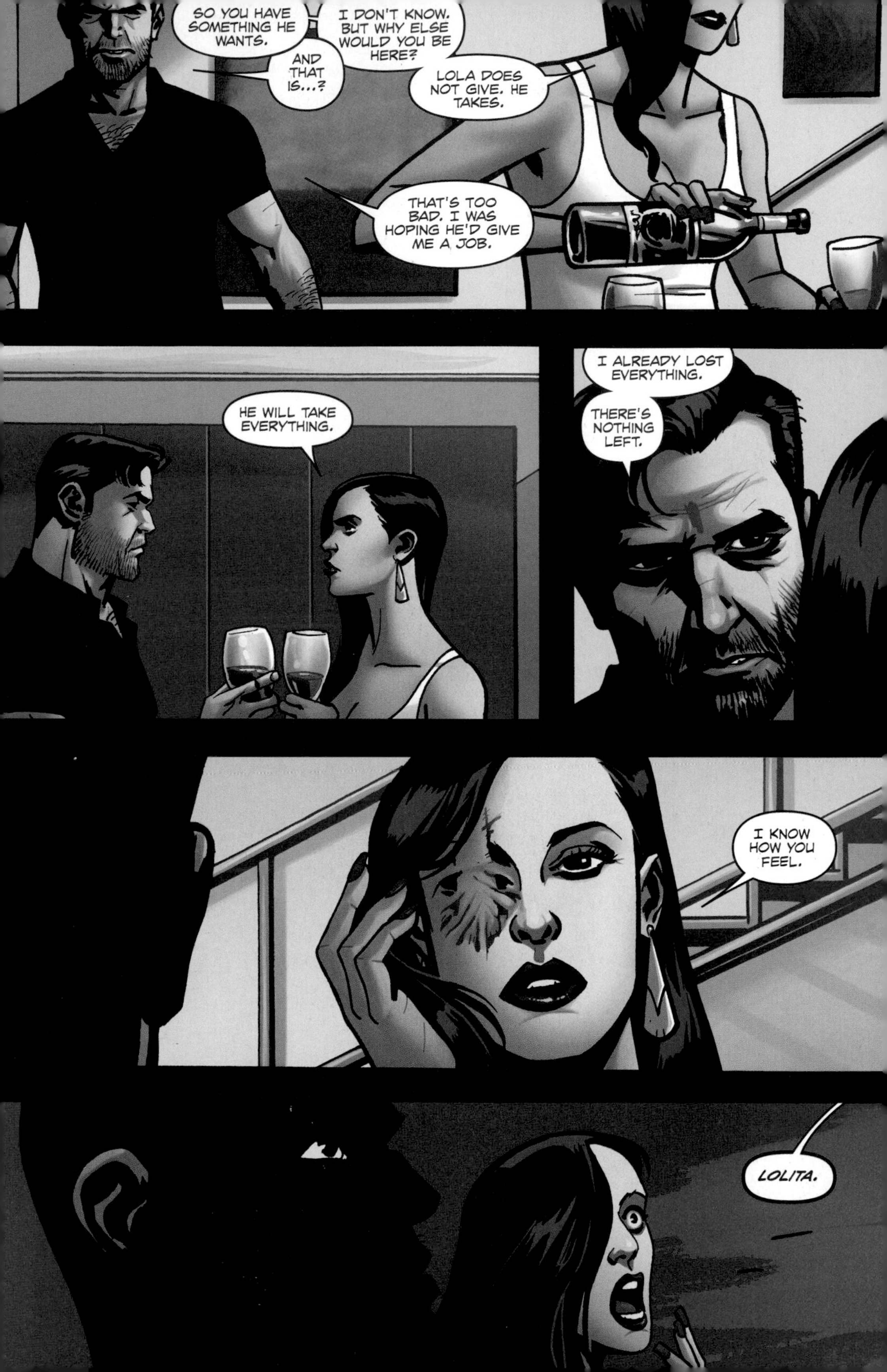
SO YOU HAVE SOMETHING HE WANTS.
I DON'T KNOW. BUT WHY ELSE WOULD YOU BE HERE?
AND THAT IS...?
LOLA DOES NOT GIVE. HE TAKES.
THAT'S TOO BAD. I WAS HOPING HE'D GIVE ME A JOB.
HE WILL TAKE EVERYTHING.
I ALREADY LOST EVERYTHING.
THERE'S NOTHING LEFT.
I KNOW HOW YOU FEEL.
LOLITA.

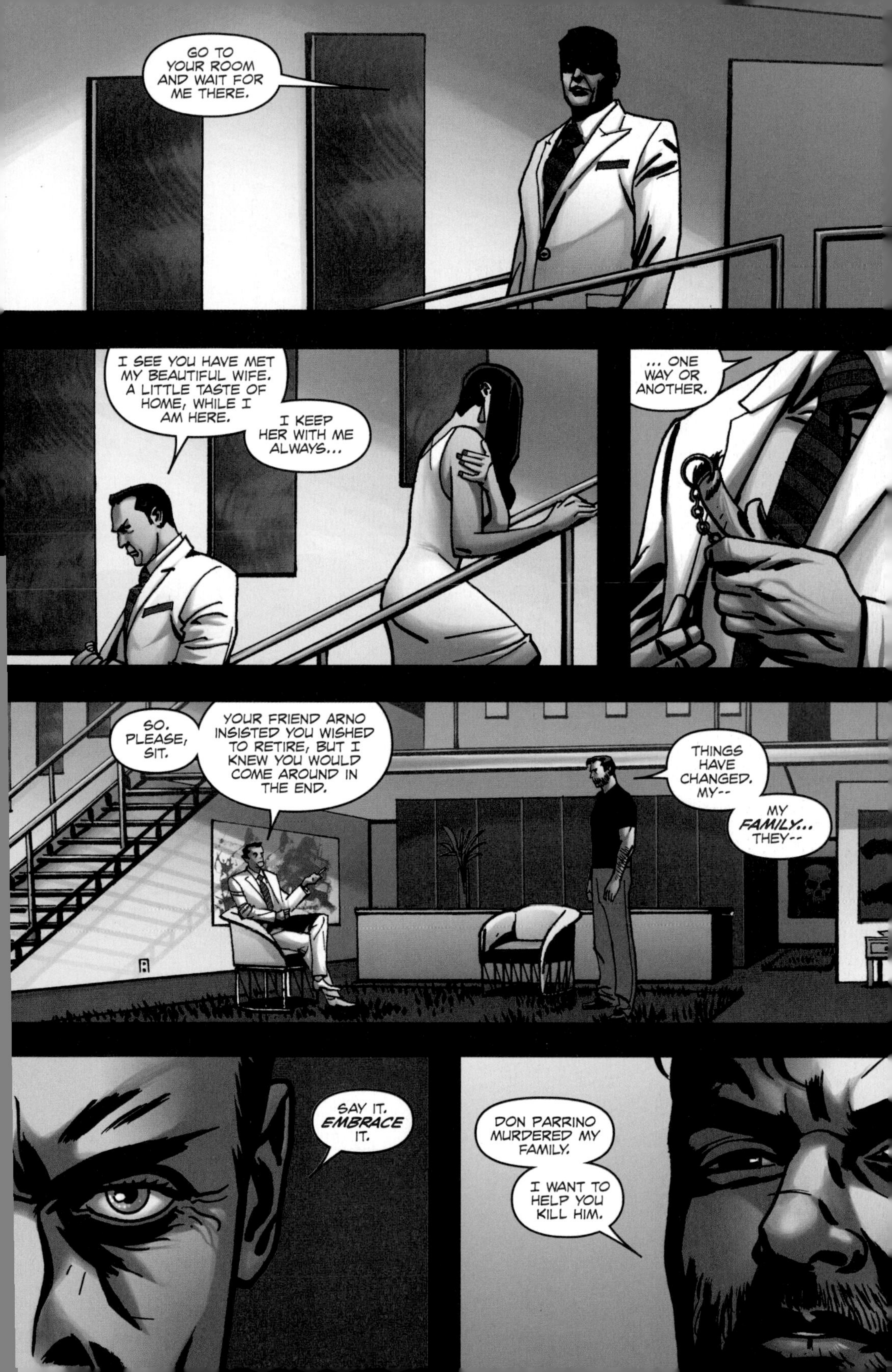
GO TO YOUR ROOM AND WAIT FOR ME THERE.
I SEE YOU HAVE MET MY BEAUTIFUL WIFE. A LITTLE TASTE OF HOME, WHILE I AM HERE.
I KEEP HER WITH ME ALWAYS...
... ONE WAY OR ANOTHER.
SO. PLEASE, SIT.
YOUR FRIEND ARNO INSISTED YOU WISHED TO RETIRE, BUT I KNEW YOU WOULD COME AROUND IN THE END.
THINGS HAVE CHANGED. MY--
MY *FAMILY...* THEY--
SAY IT. ***EMBRACE*** IT.
DON PARRINO MURDERED MY FAMILY.
I WANT TO HELP YOU KILL HIM.

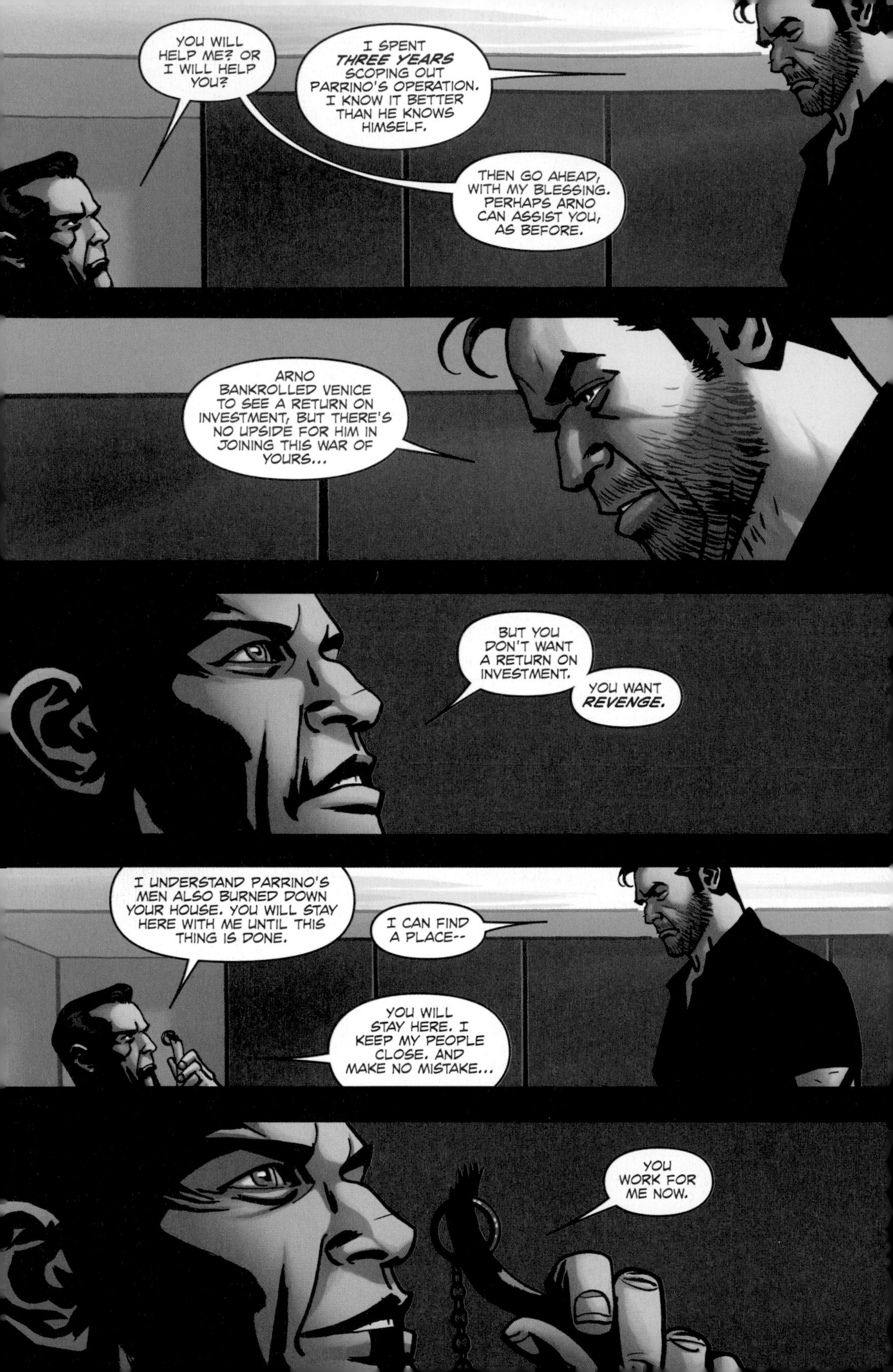

YOU WILL HELP ME? OR I WILL HELP YOU?
I SPENT THREE YEARS SCOPING OUT PARRINO'S OPERATION. I KNOW IT BETTER THAN HE KNOWS HIMSELF.
THEN GO AHEAD, WITH MY BLESSING. PERHAPS ARNO CAN ASSIST YOU, AS BEFORE.
ARNO BANKROLLED VENICE TO SEE A RETURN ON INVESTMENT, BUT THERE'S NO UPSIDE FOR HIM IN JOINING THIS WAR OF YOURS...
BUT YOU DON'T WANT A RETURN ON INVESTMENT.
YOU WANT REVENGE.
I UNDERSTAND PARRINO'S MEN ALSO BURNED DOWN YOUR HOUSE. YOU WILL STAY HERE WITH ME UNTIL THIS THING IS DONE.
I CAN FIND A PLACE--
YOU WILL STAY HERE. I KEEP MY PEOPLE CLOSE. AND MAKE NO MISTAKE...
YOU WORK FOR ME NOW.

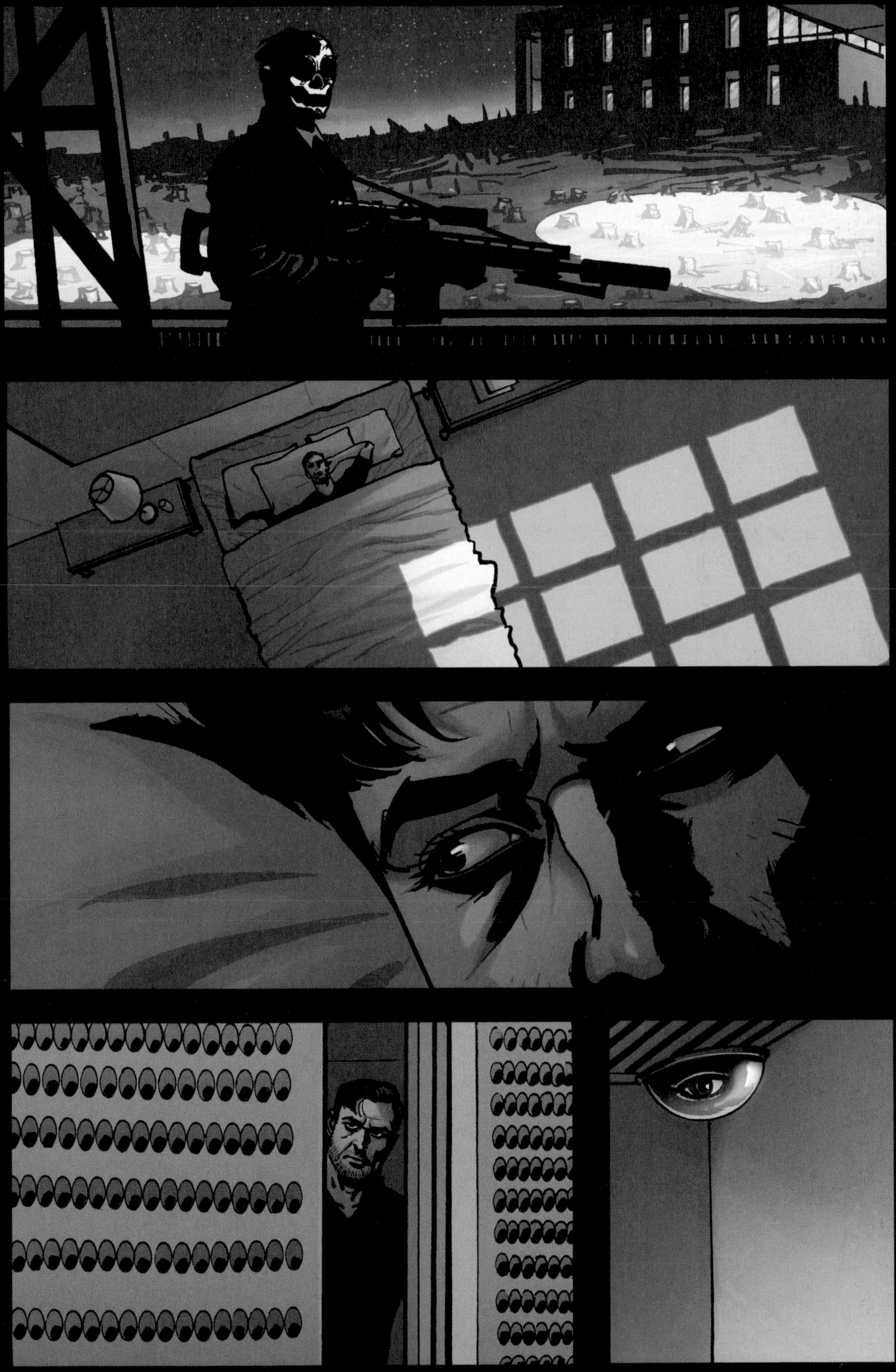

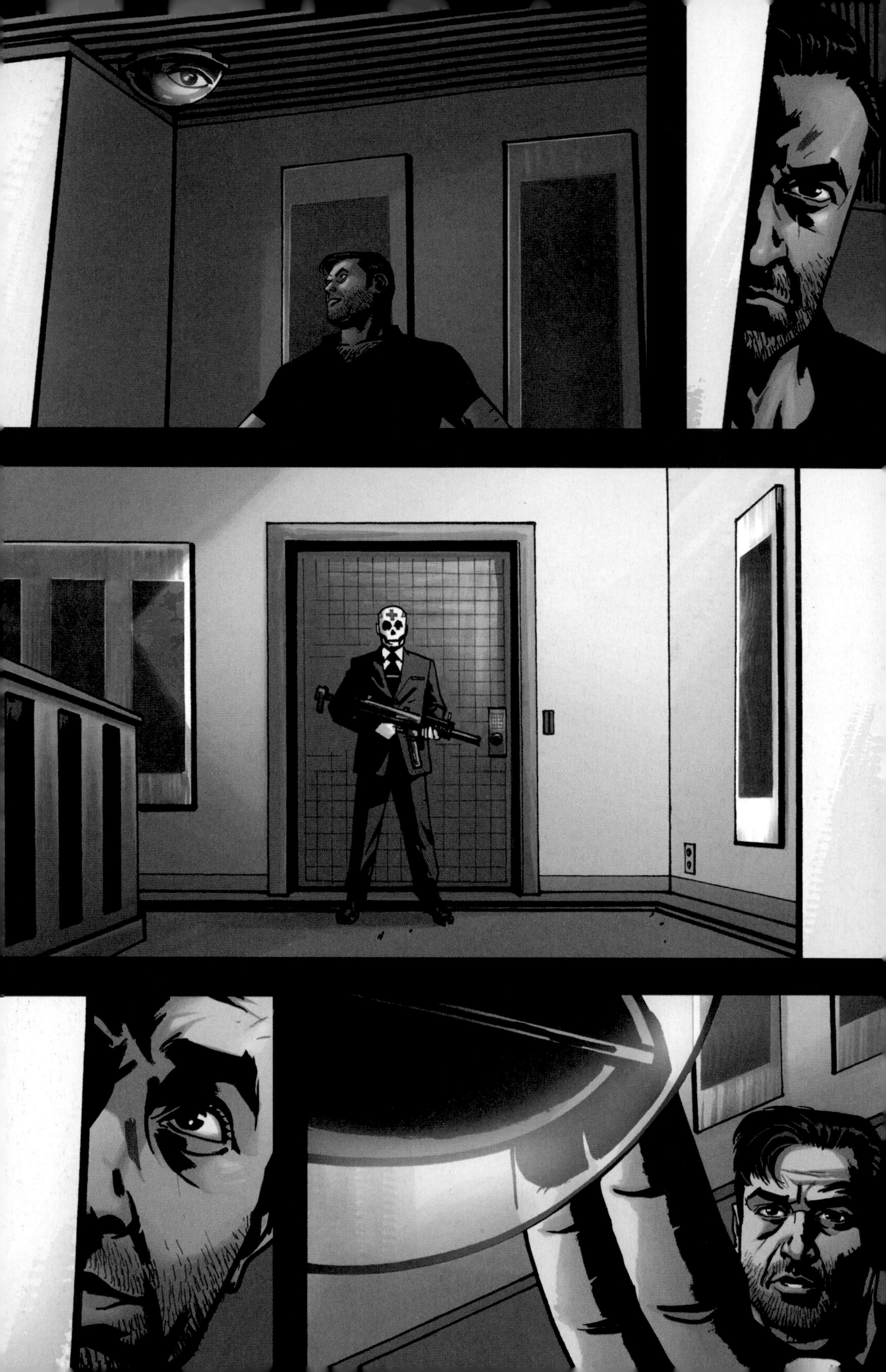

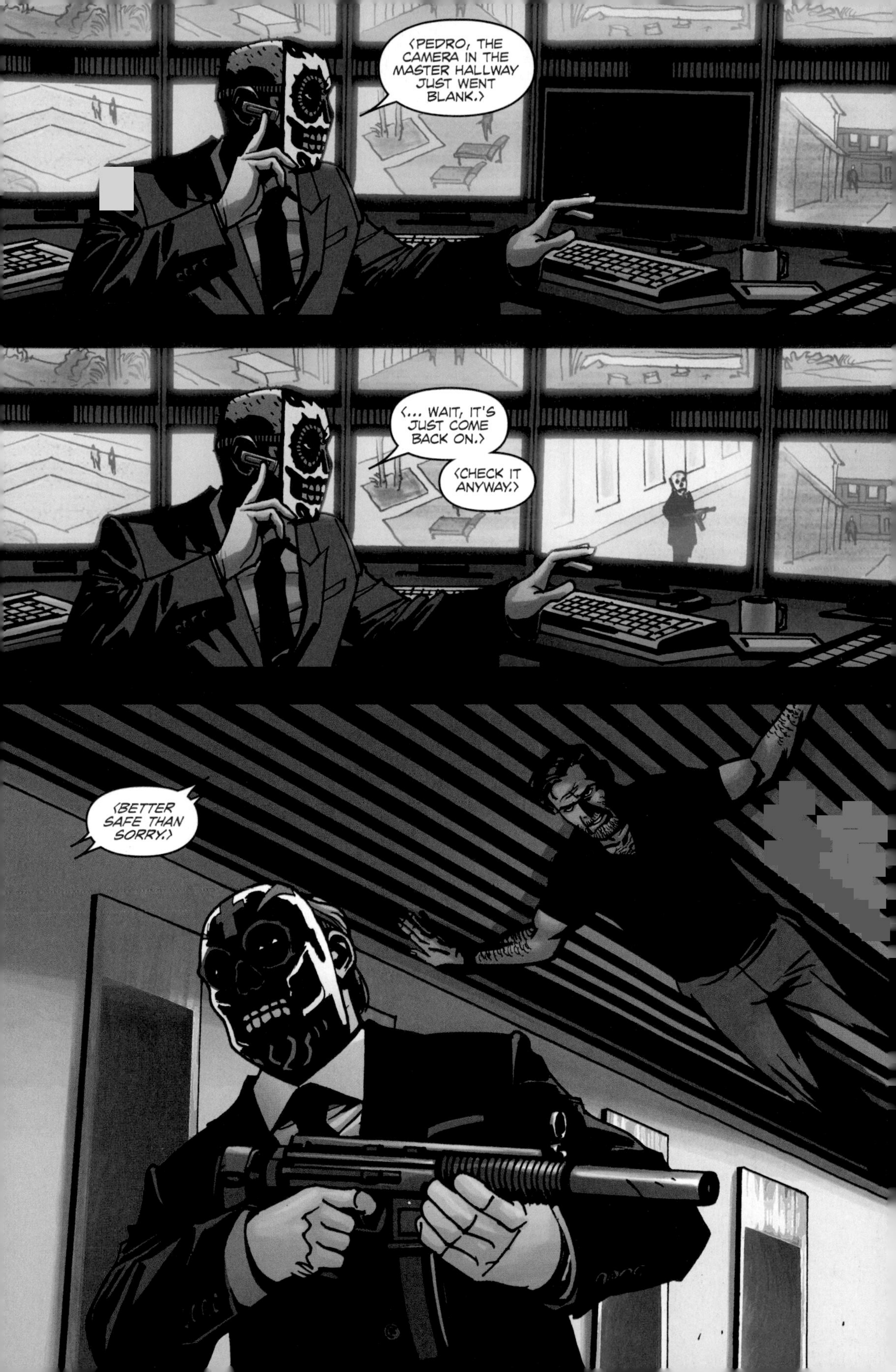
‹PEDRO, THE CAMERA IN THE MASTER HALLWAY JUST WENT BLANK.›
‹... WAIT, IT'S JUST COME BACK ON.›
‹CHECK IT ANYWAY.›
‹BETTER SAFE THAN SORRY.›

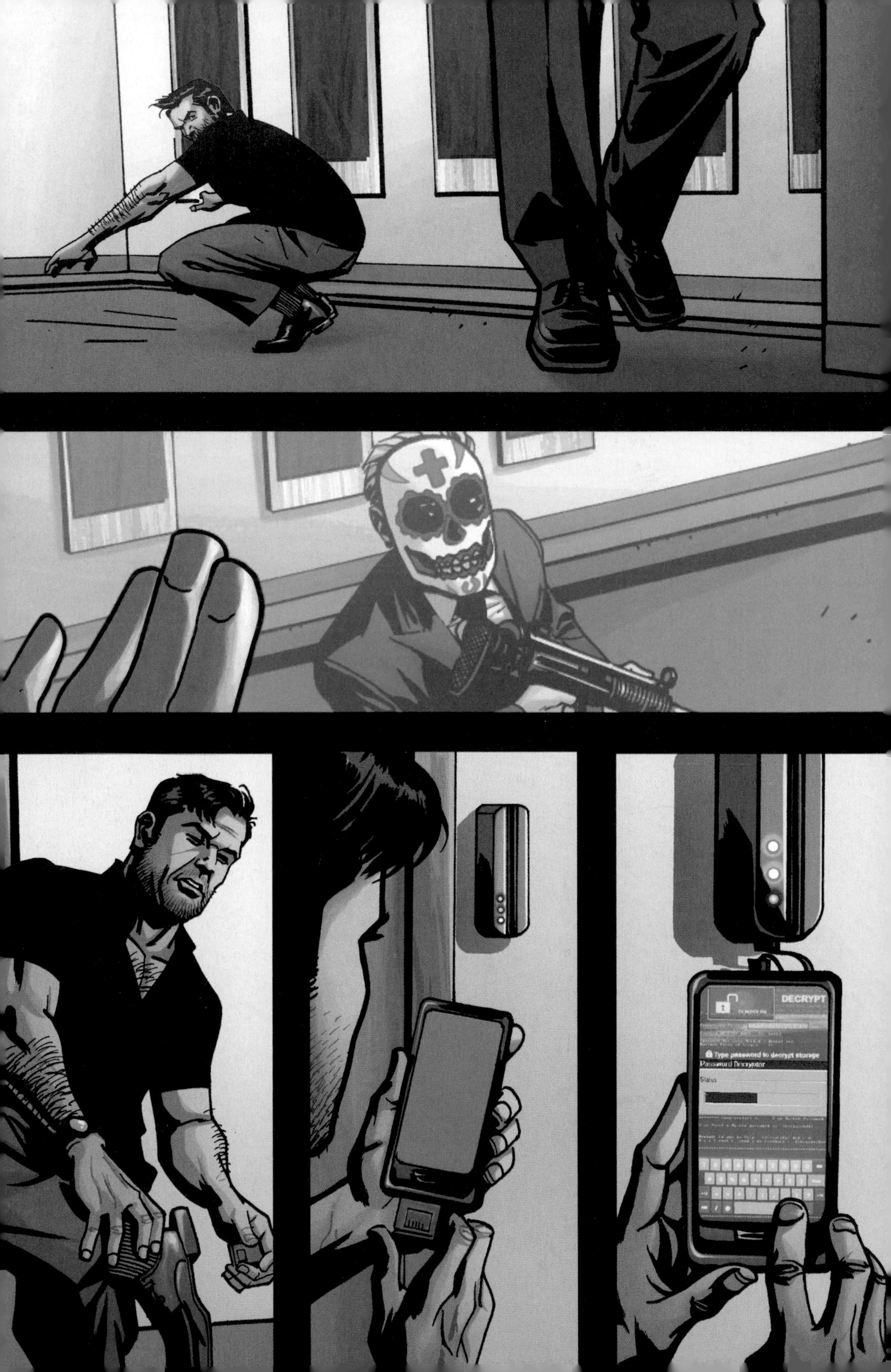
DECRYPT
TX BLOCK ON
Type password to decrypt storage
Password Decryptor
Status

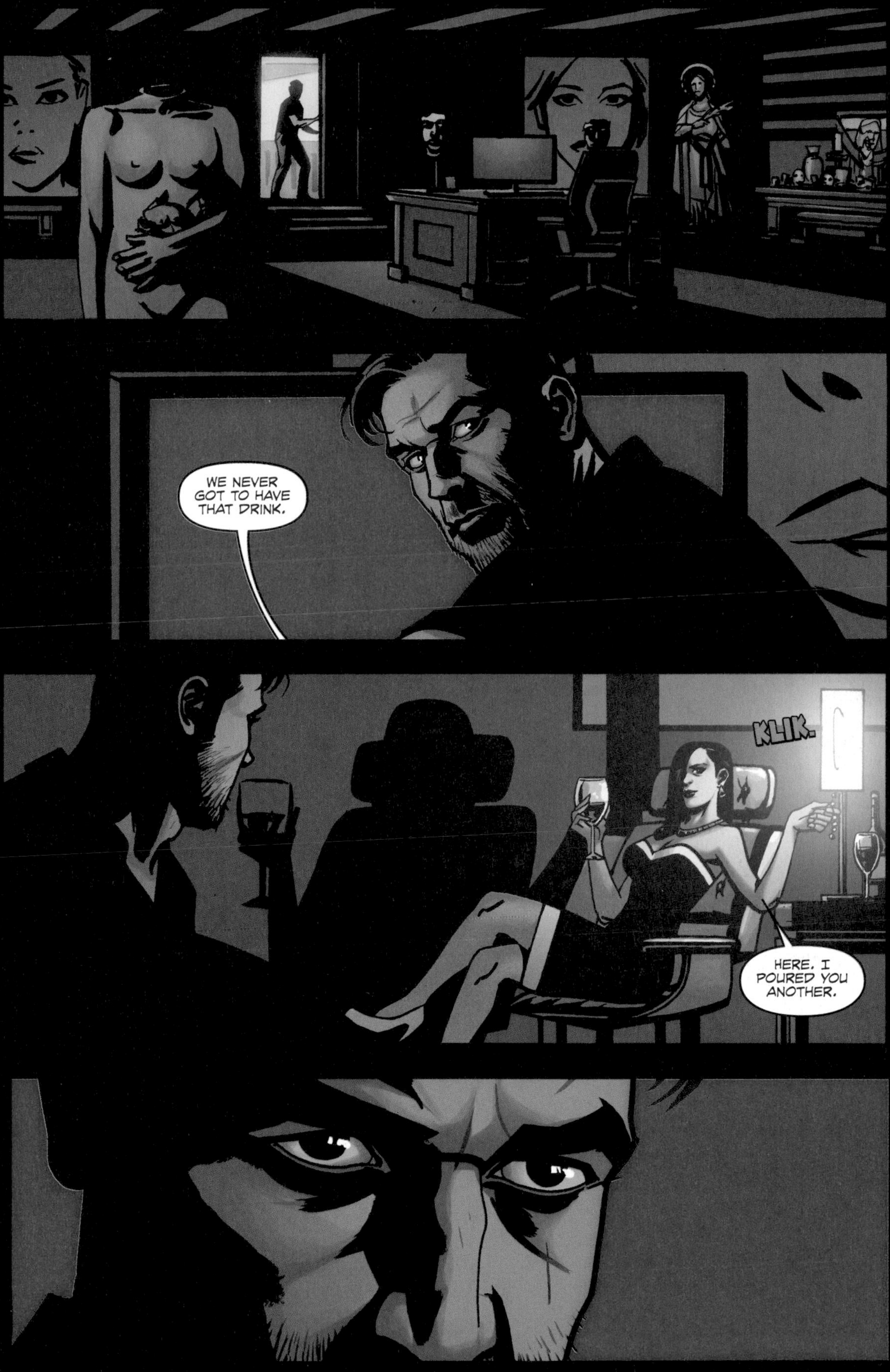
WE NEVER GOT TO HAVE THAT DRINK.
KLIK.
HERE. I POURED YOU ANOTHER.

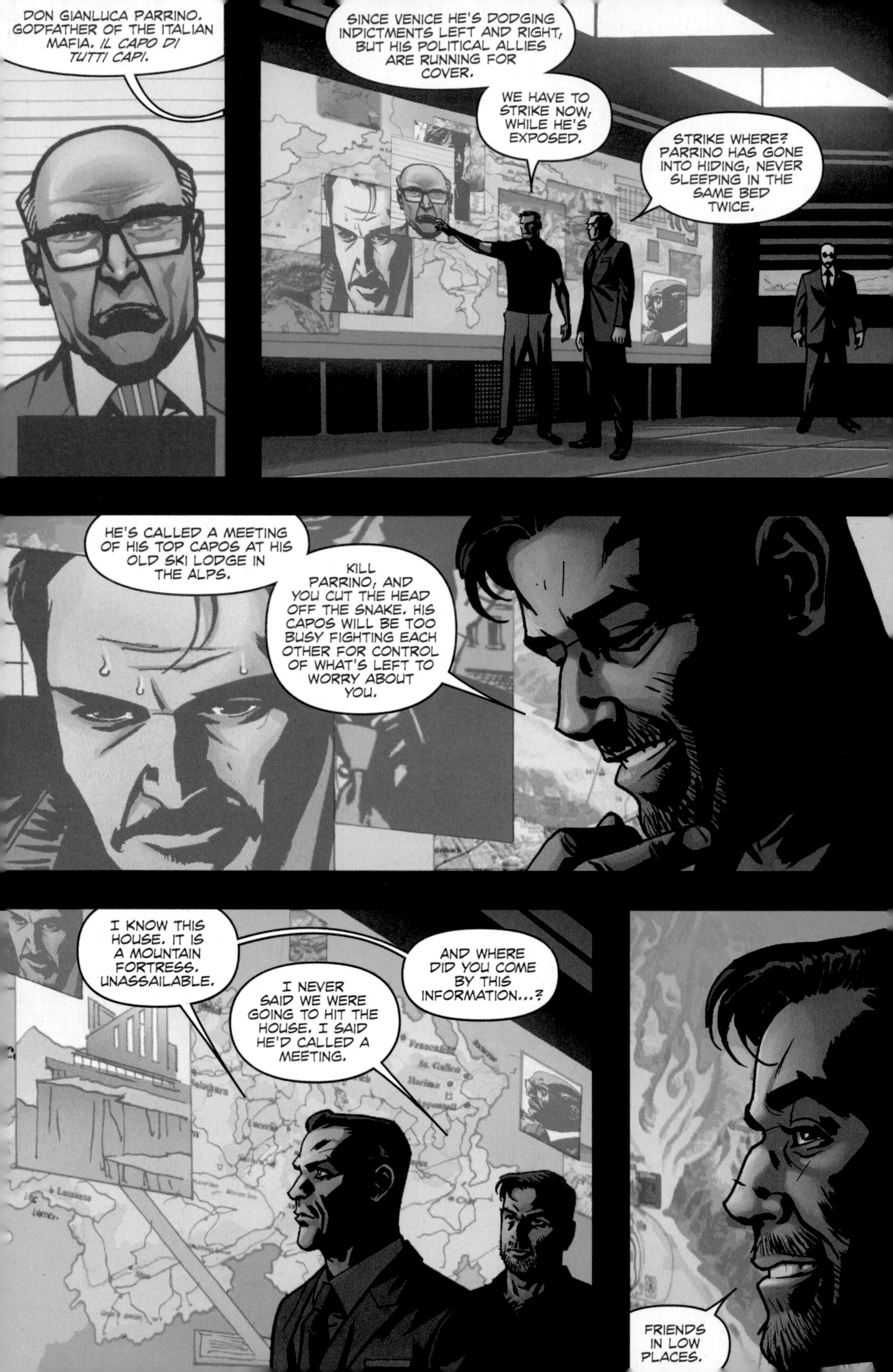
DON GIANLUCA PARRINO. GODFATHER OF THE ITALIAN MAFIA. *IL CAPO DI TUTTI CAPI.*
SINCE VENICE HE'S DODGING INDICTMENTS LEFT AND RIGHT, BUT HIS POLITICAL ALLIES ARE RUNNING FOR COVER.
WE HAVE TO STRIKE NOW, WHILE HE'S EXPOSED.
STRIKE WHERE? PARRINO HAS GONE INTO HIDING, NEVER SLEEPING IN THE SAME BED TWICE.
HE'S CALLED A MEETING OF HIS TOP CAPOS AT HIS OLD SKI LODGE IN THE ALPS.
KILL PARRINO, AND YOU CUT THE HEAD OFF THE SNAKE. HIS CAPOS WILL BE TOO BUSY FIGHTING EACH OTHER FOR CONTROL OF WHAT'S LEFT TO WORRY ABOUT YOU.
I KNOW THIS HOUSE. IT IS A MOUNTAIN FORTRESS. UNASSAILABLE.
I NEVER SAID WE WERE GOING TO HIT THE HOUSE. I SAID HE'D CALLED A MEETING.
AND WHERE DID YOU COME BY THIS INFORMATION...?
FRIENDS IN LOW PLACES.

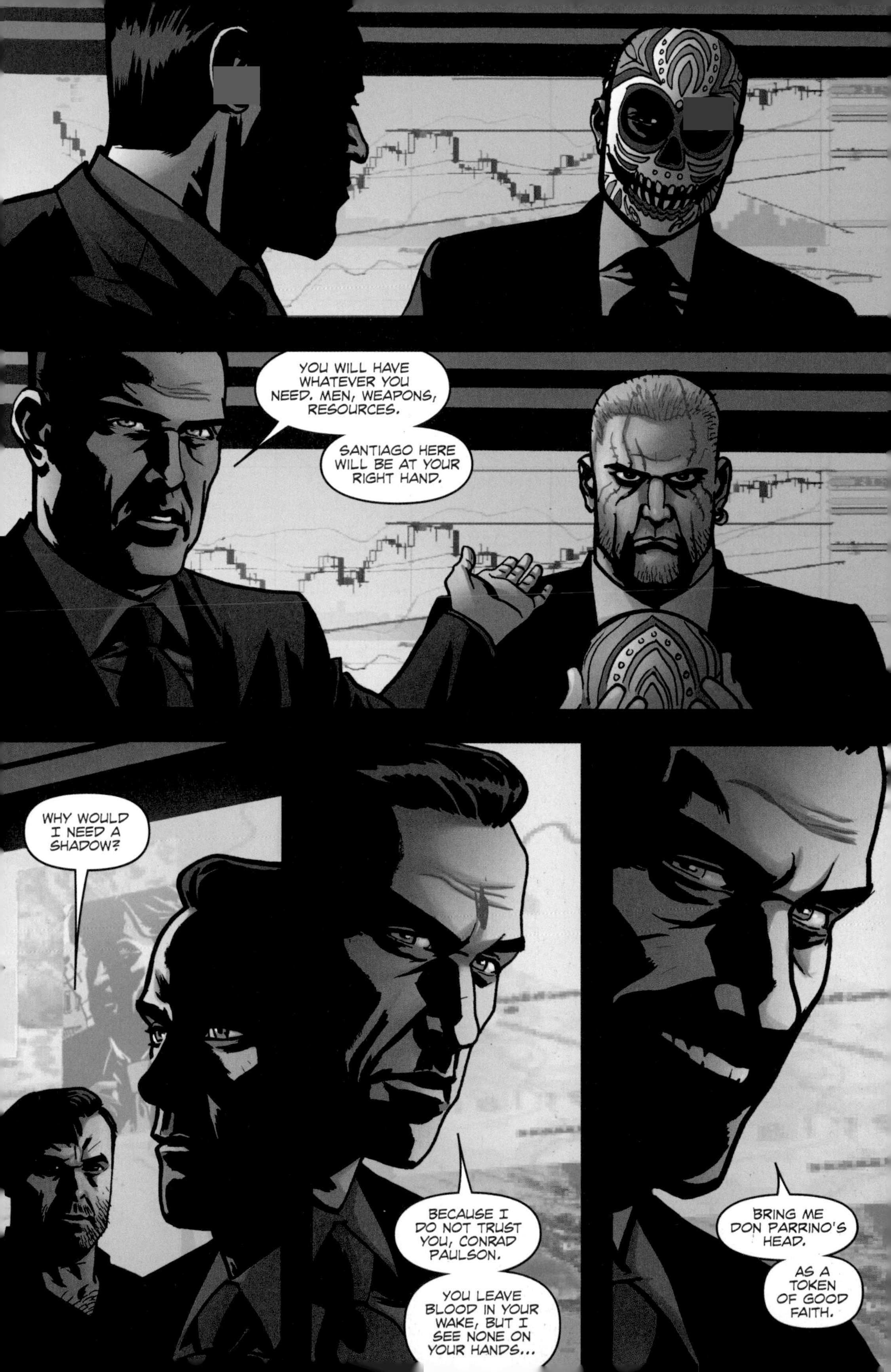
YOU WILL HAVE WHATEVER YOU NEED. MEN, WEAPONS, RESOURCES.
SANTIAGO HERE WILL BE AT YOUR RIGHT HAND.
WHY WOULD I NEED A SHADOW?
BECAUSE I DO NOT TRUST YOU, CONRAD PAULSON.
YOU LEAVE BLOOD IN YOUR WAKE, BUT I SEE NONE ON YOUR HANDS...
BRING ME DON PARRINO'S HEAD.
AS A TOKEN OF GOOD FAITH.

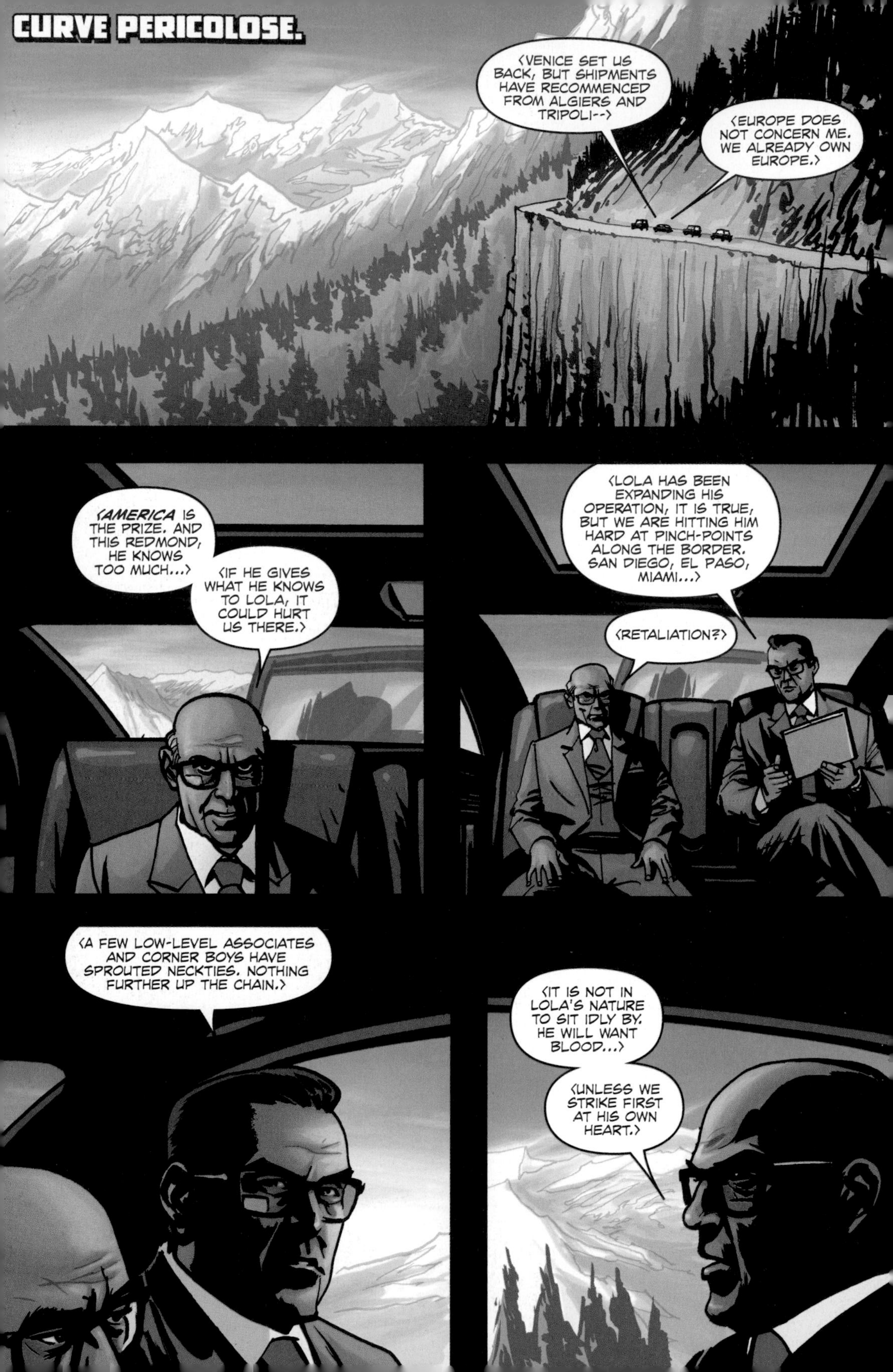
CURVE PERICOLOSE.
<VENICE SET US BACK, BUT SHIPMENTS HAVE RECOMMENCED FROM ALGIERS AND TRIPOLI-->
<EUROPE DOES NOT CONCERN ME. WE ALREADY OWN EUROPE.>
<AMERICA IS THE PRIZE. AND THIS REDMOND, HE KNOWS TOO MUCH...>
<IF HE GIVES WHAT HE KNOWS TO LOLA, IT COULD HURT US THERE.>
<LOLA HAS BEEN EXPANDING HIS OPERATION, IT IS TRUE, BUT WE ARE HITTING HIM HARD AT PINCH-POINTS ALONG THE BORDER. SAN DIEGO, EL PASO, MIAMI...>
<RETALIATION?>
<A FEW LOW-LEVEL ASSOCIATES AND CORNER BOYS HAVE SPROUTED NECKTIES. NOTHING FURTHER UP THE CHAIN.>
<IT IS NOT IN LOLA'S NATURE TO SIT IDLY BY. HE WILL WANT BLOOD...>
<UNLESS WE STRIKE FIRST AT HIS OWN HEART.>

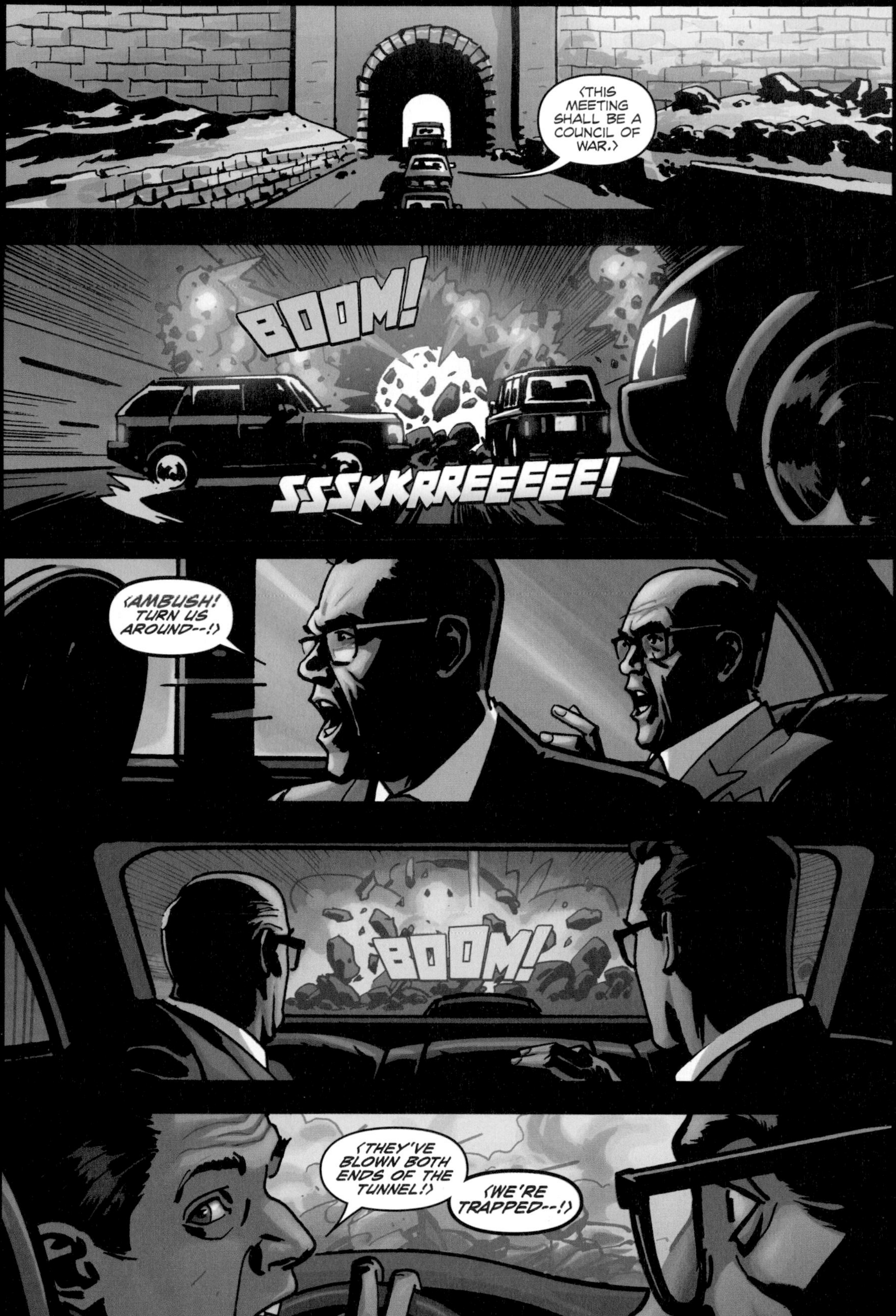

<THIS MEETING SHALL BE A COUNCIL OF WAR.>
BOOM!
SSSKKRREEEEEE!
<AMBUSH! TURN US AROUND--!>
BOOM!
<THEY'VE BLOWN BOTH ENDS OF THE TUNNEL!>
<WE'RE TRAPPED--!>

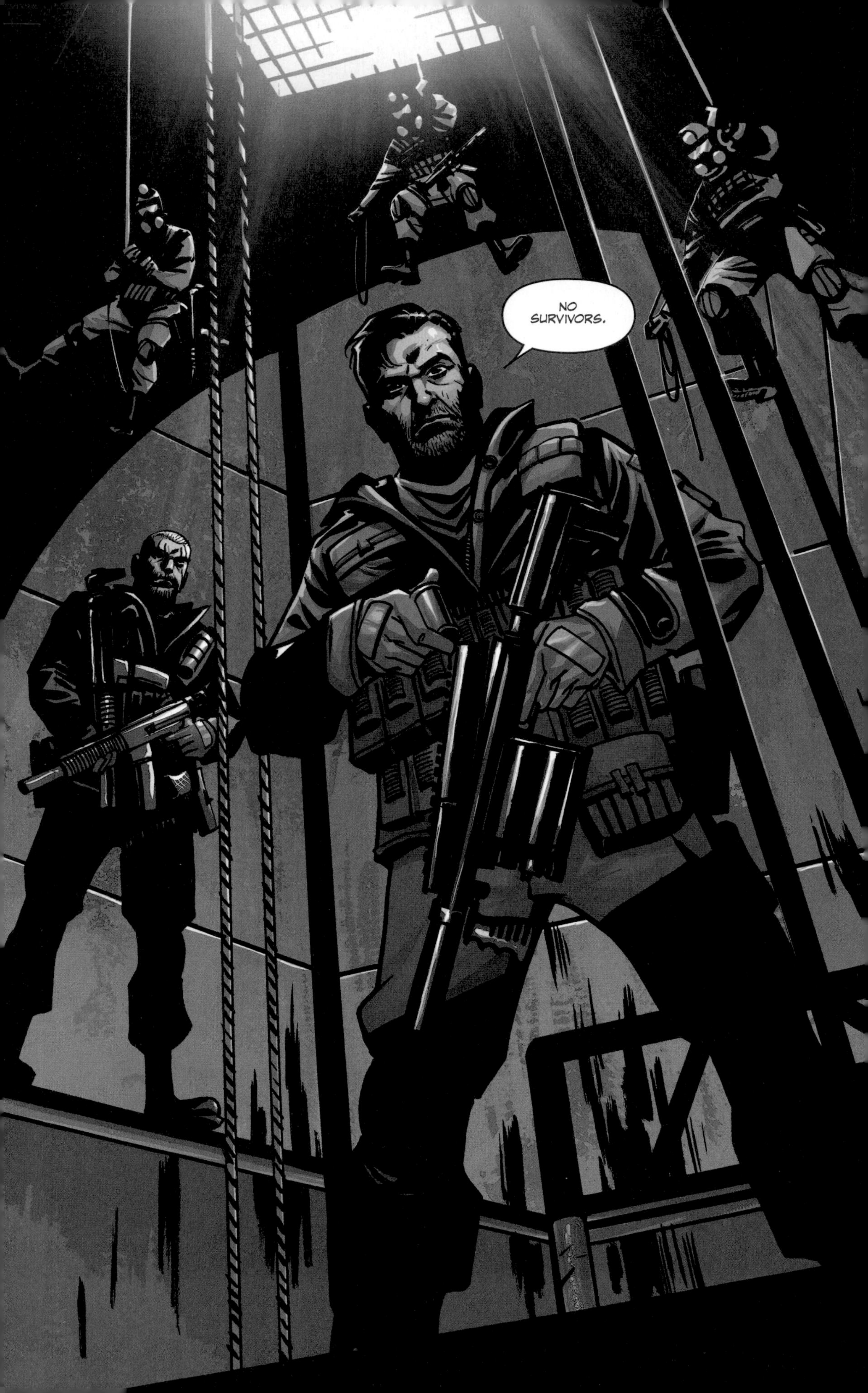
NO SURVIVORS.

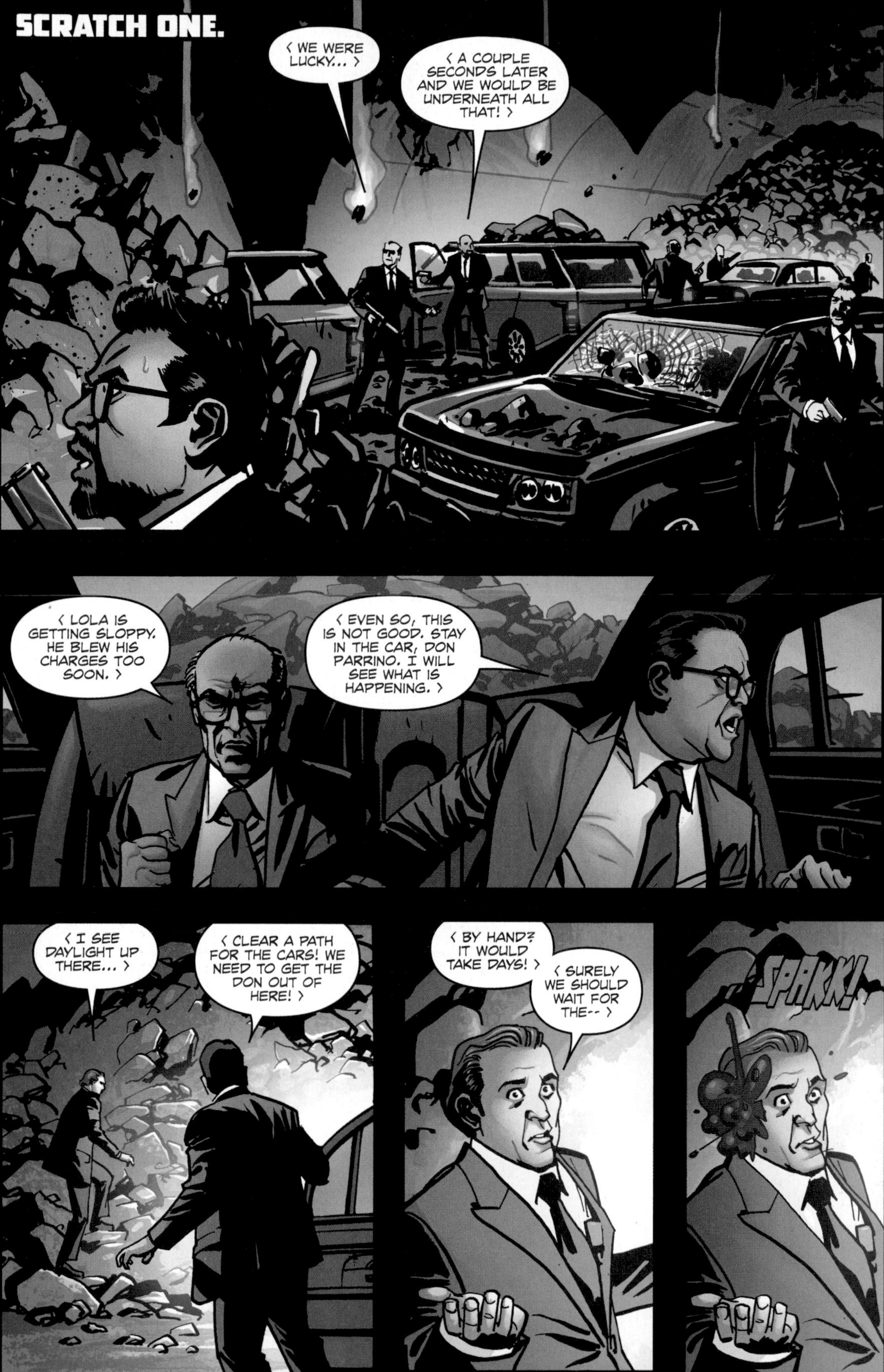
SCRATCH ONE.
< WE WERE LUCKY... >
< A COUPLE SECONDS LATER AND WE WOULD BE UNDERNEATH ALL THAT! >
< LOLA IS GETTING SLOPPY. HE BLEW HIS CHARGES TOO SOON. >
< EVEN SO, THIS IS NOT GOOD. STAY IN THE CAR, DON PARRINO. I WILL SEE WHAT IS HAPPENING. >
< I SEE DAYLIGHT UP THERE... >
< CLEAR A PATH FOR THE CARS! WE NEED TO GET THE DON OUT OF HERE! >
< BY HAND? IT WOULD TAKE DAYS! >
< SURELY WE SHOULD WAIT FOR THE-- >
SPAKK!

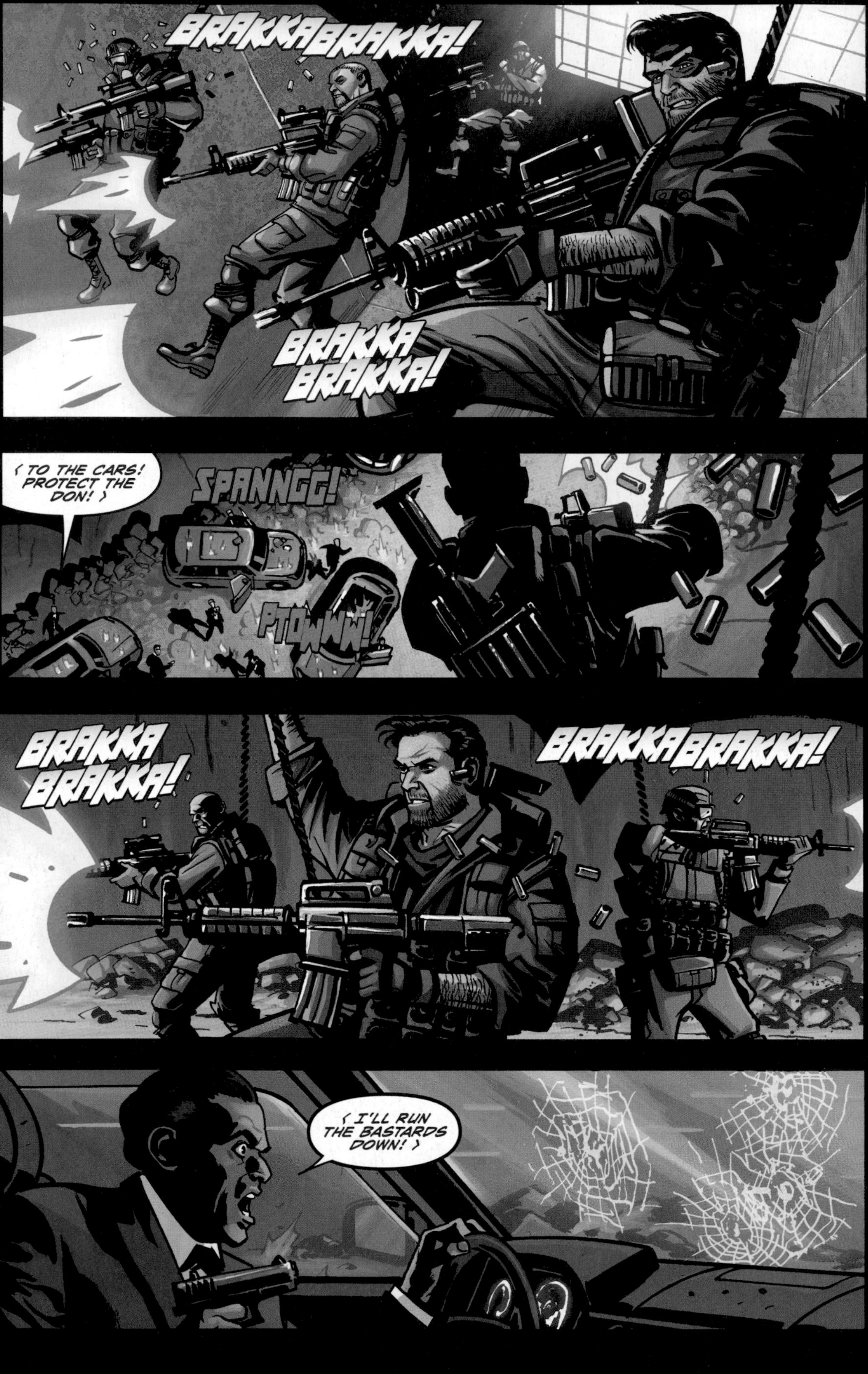
BRAKKABRAKKA!
BRAKKA BRAKKA!
‹ TO THE CARS! PROTECT THE DON! ›
SPANNGG!
PTOWWW!
BRAKKA BRAKKA!
BRAKKABRAKKA!
‹ I'LL RUN THE BASTARDS DOWN! ›

VVVRRRRRMMMMMMM!

FTOOM!

VROOOOOOM!

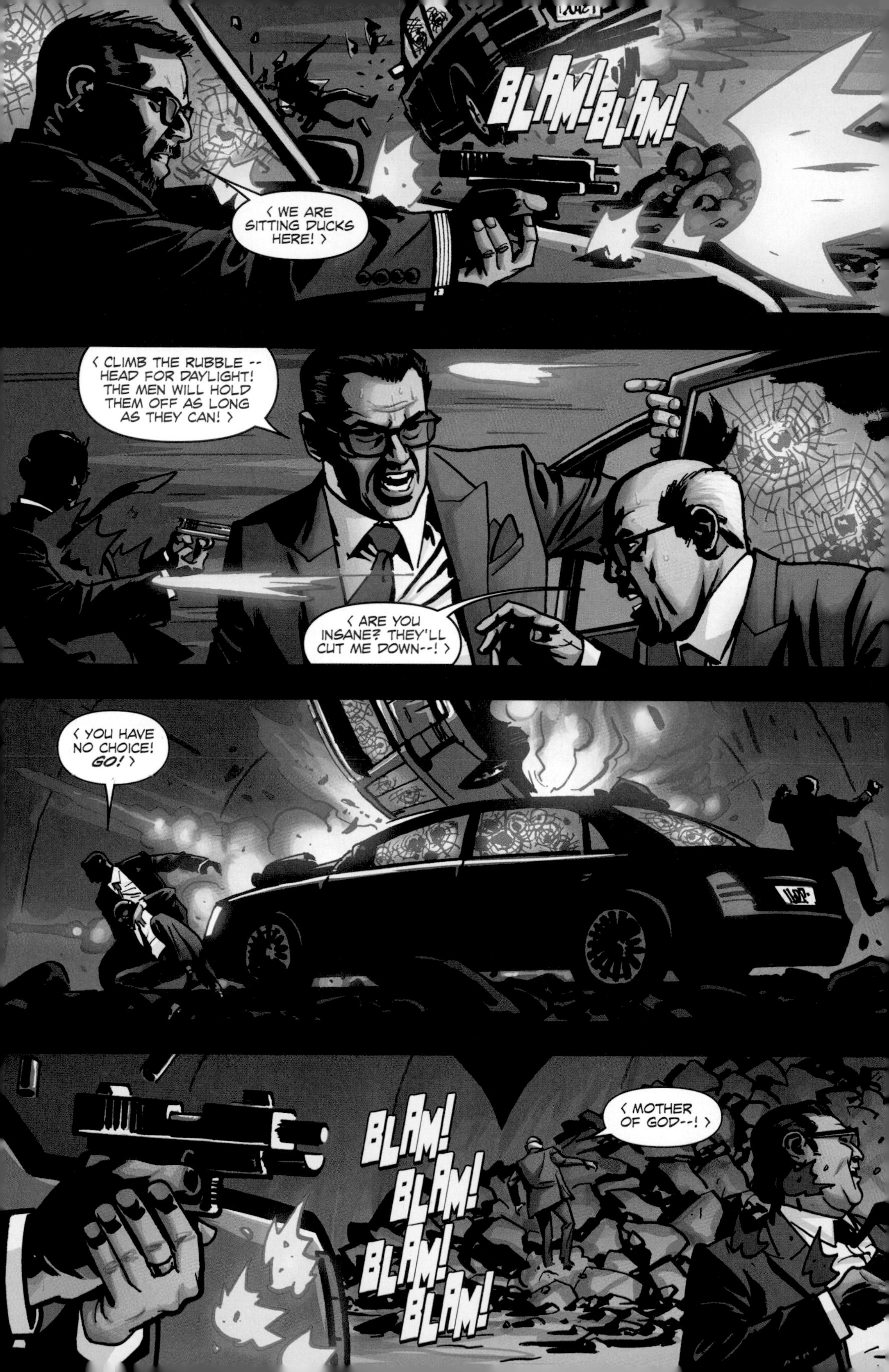
BLAM! BLAM!
< WE ARE SITTING DUCKS HERE! >
< CLIMB THE RUBBLE -- HEAD FOR DAYLIGHT! THE MEN WILL HOLD THEM OFF AS LONG AS THEY CAN! >
< ARE YOU INSANE? THEY'LL CUT ME DOWN--! >
< YOU HAVE NO CHOICE! *GO!* >
BLAM! BLAM! BLAM! BLAM!
< MOTHER OF GOD--! >

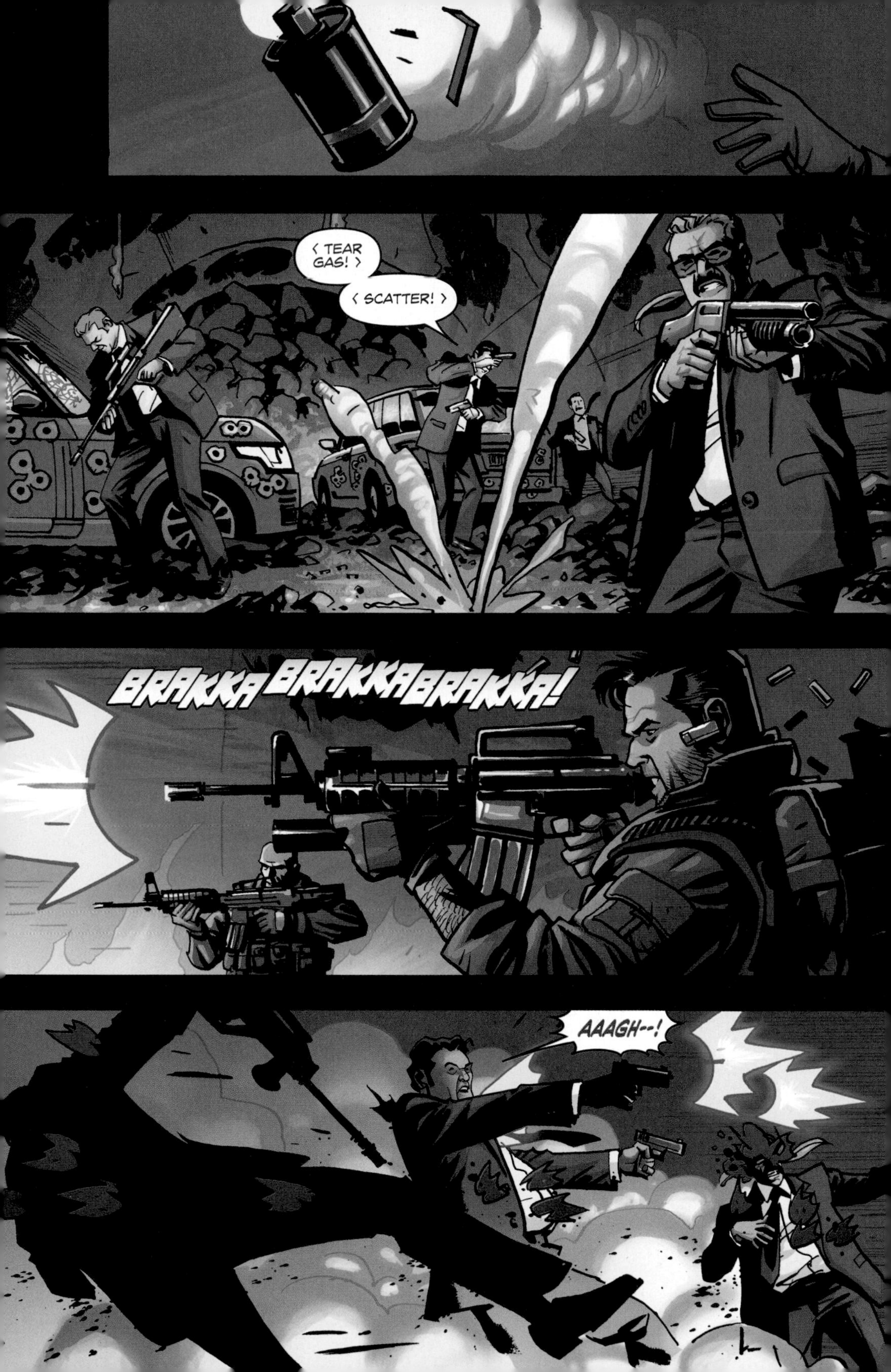
< TEAR GAS! >
< SCATTER! >
BRAKKA BRAKKA BRAKKA!
AAAGH--!

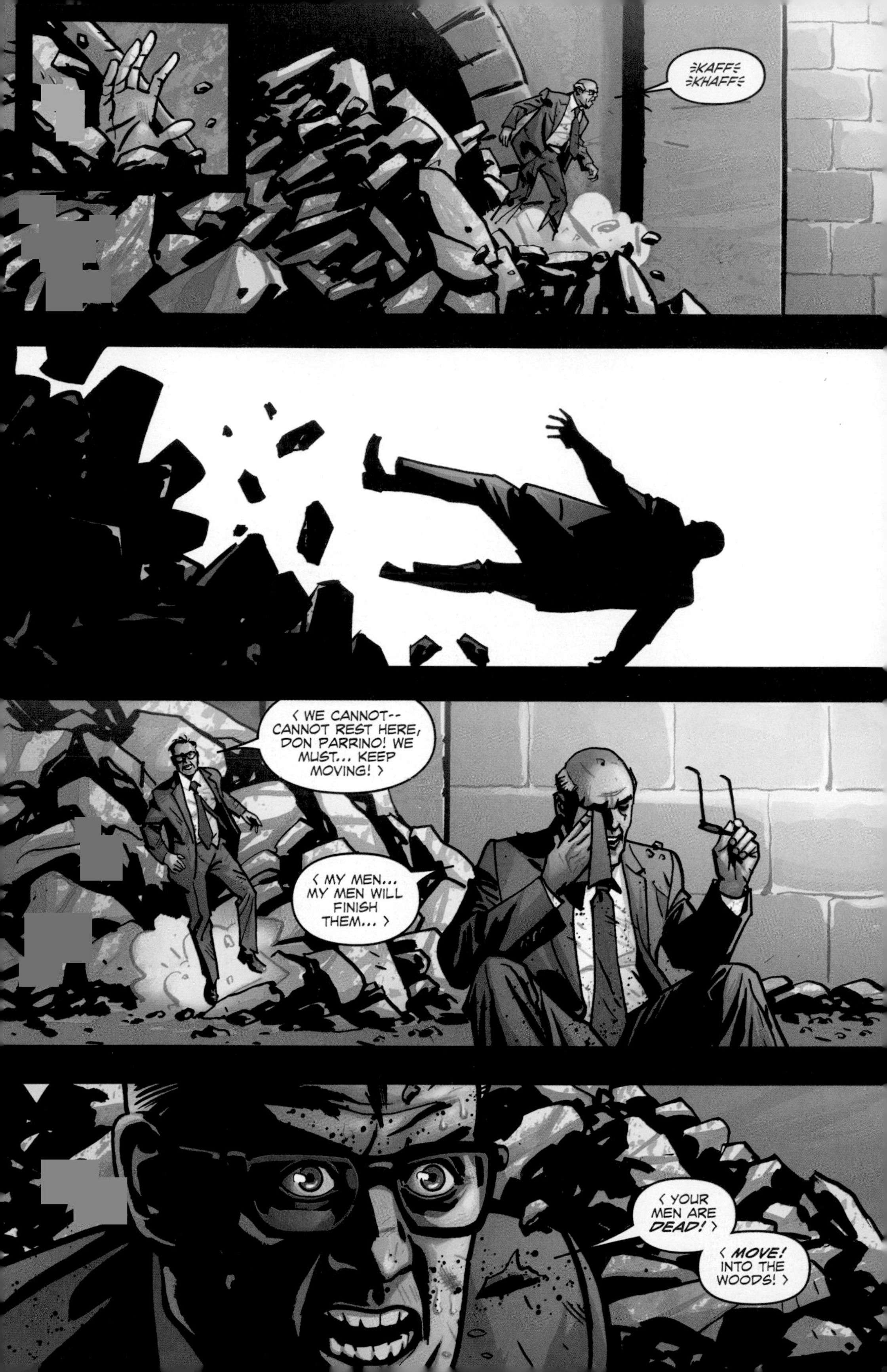
KAFF KHAFF
< WE CANNOT-- CANNOT REST HERE, DON PARRINO! WE MUST... KEEP MOVING! >
< MY MEN... MY MEN WILL FINISH THEM... >
< YOUR MEN ARE DEAD! >
< MOVE! INTO THE WOODS! >

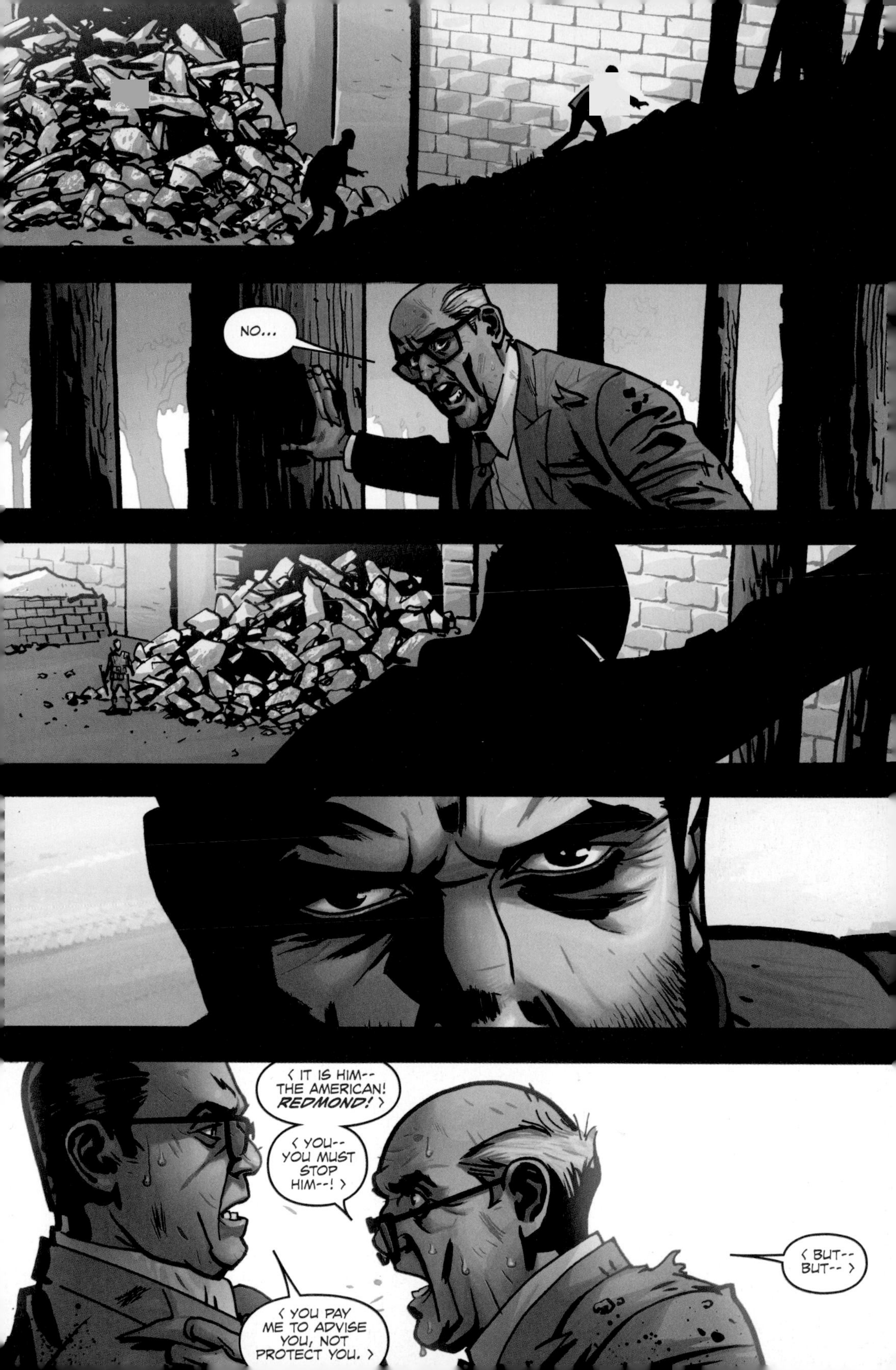
NO...
‹ IT IS HIM-- THE AMERICAN! REDMOND! ›
‹ YOU-- YOU MUST STOP HIM--! ›
‹ YOU PAY ME TO ADVISE YOU, NOT PROTECT YOU. ›
‹ BUT-- BUT-- ›

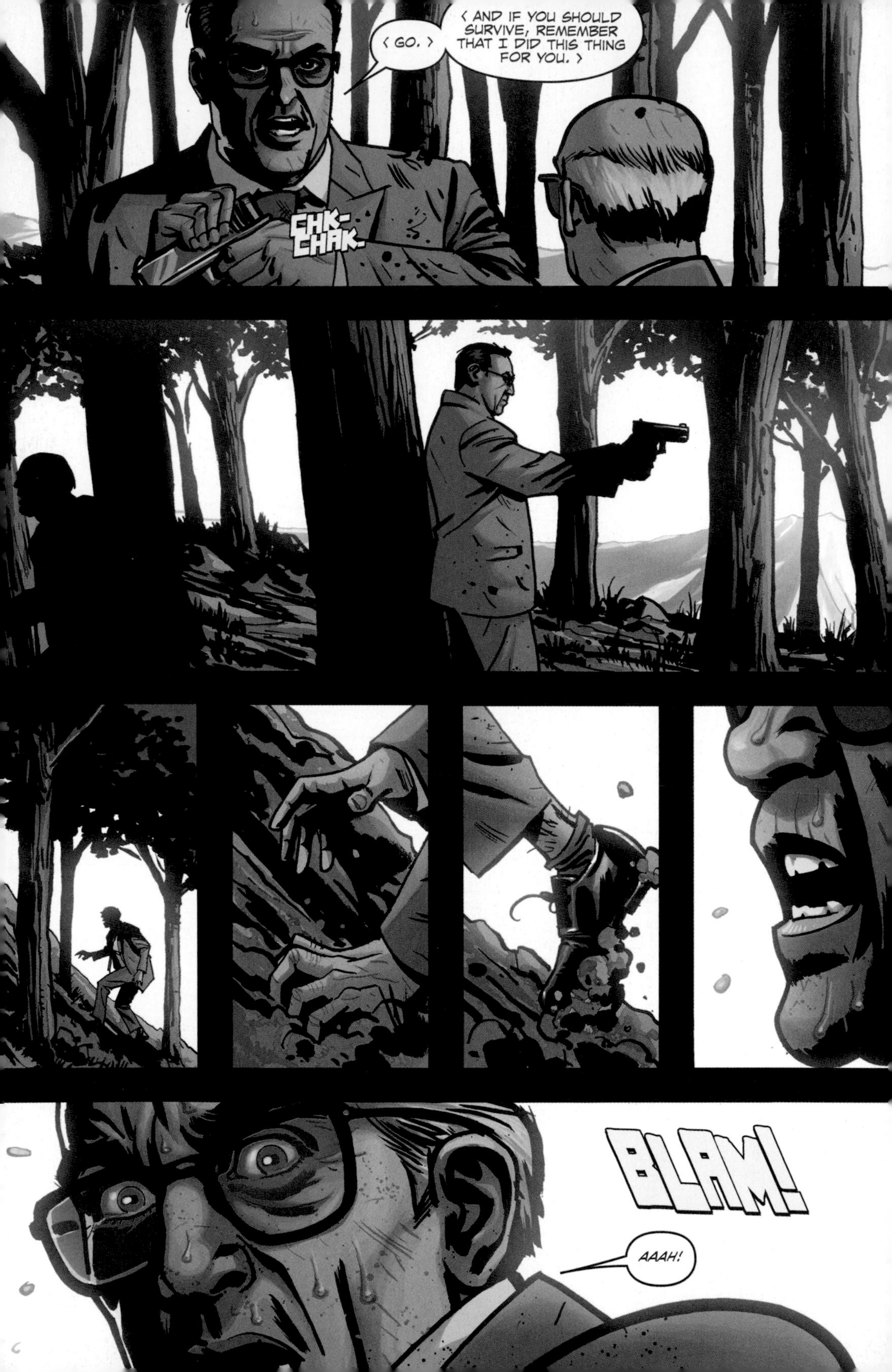
‹ GO. ›
‹ AND IF YOU SHOULD SURVIVE, REMEMBER THAT I DID THIS THING FOR YOU. ›
CHK-CHAK.
BLAM!
AAAH!

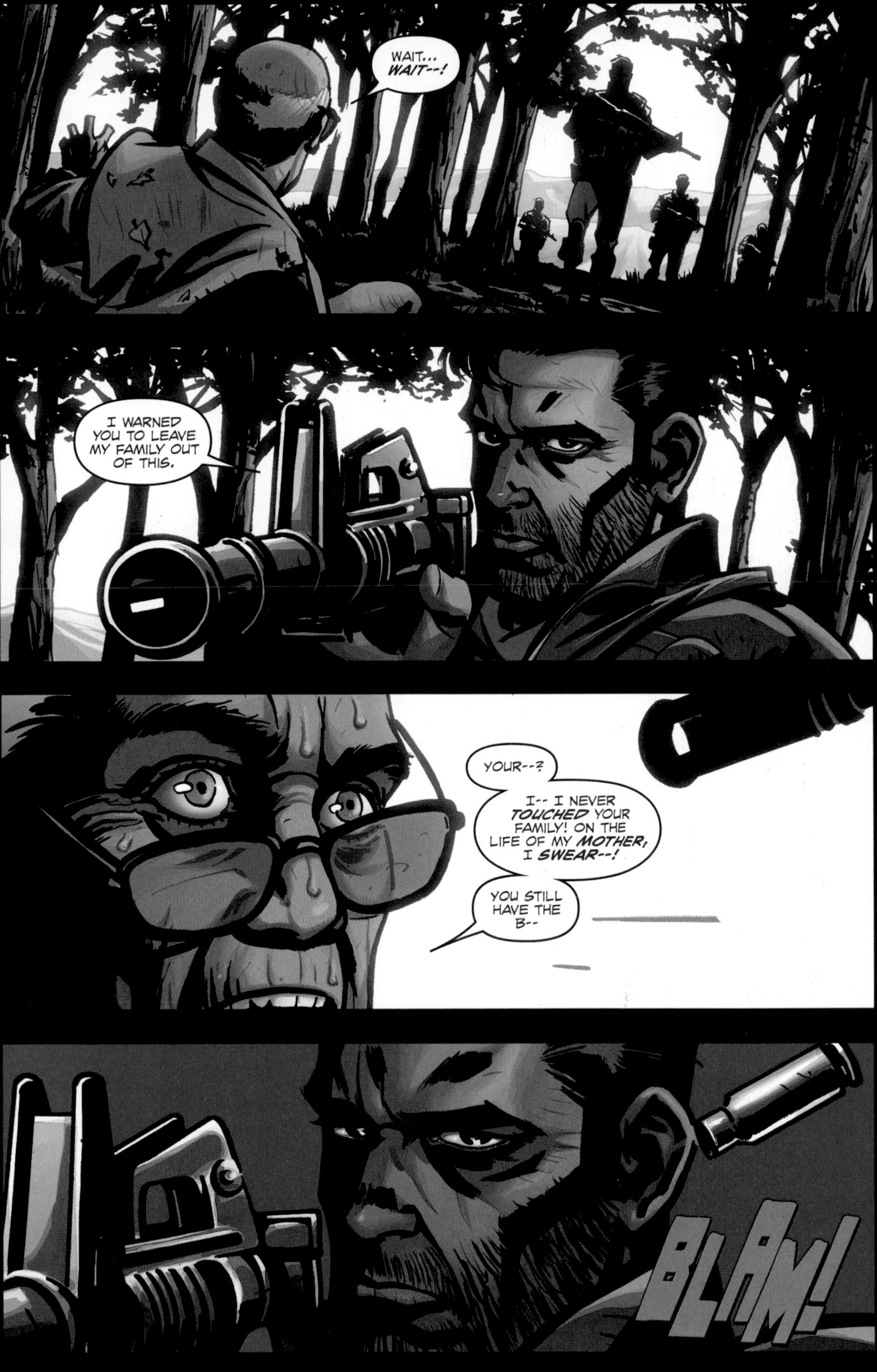
WAIT... WAIT--!
I WARNED YOU TO LEAVE MY FAMILY OUT OF THIS.
YOUR--?
I-- I NEVER TOUCHED YOUR FAMILY! ON THE LIFE OF MY MOTHER, I SWEAR--!
YOU STILL HAVE THE B--
BLAM!

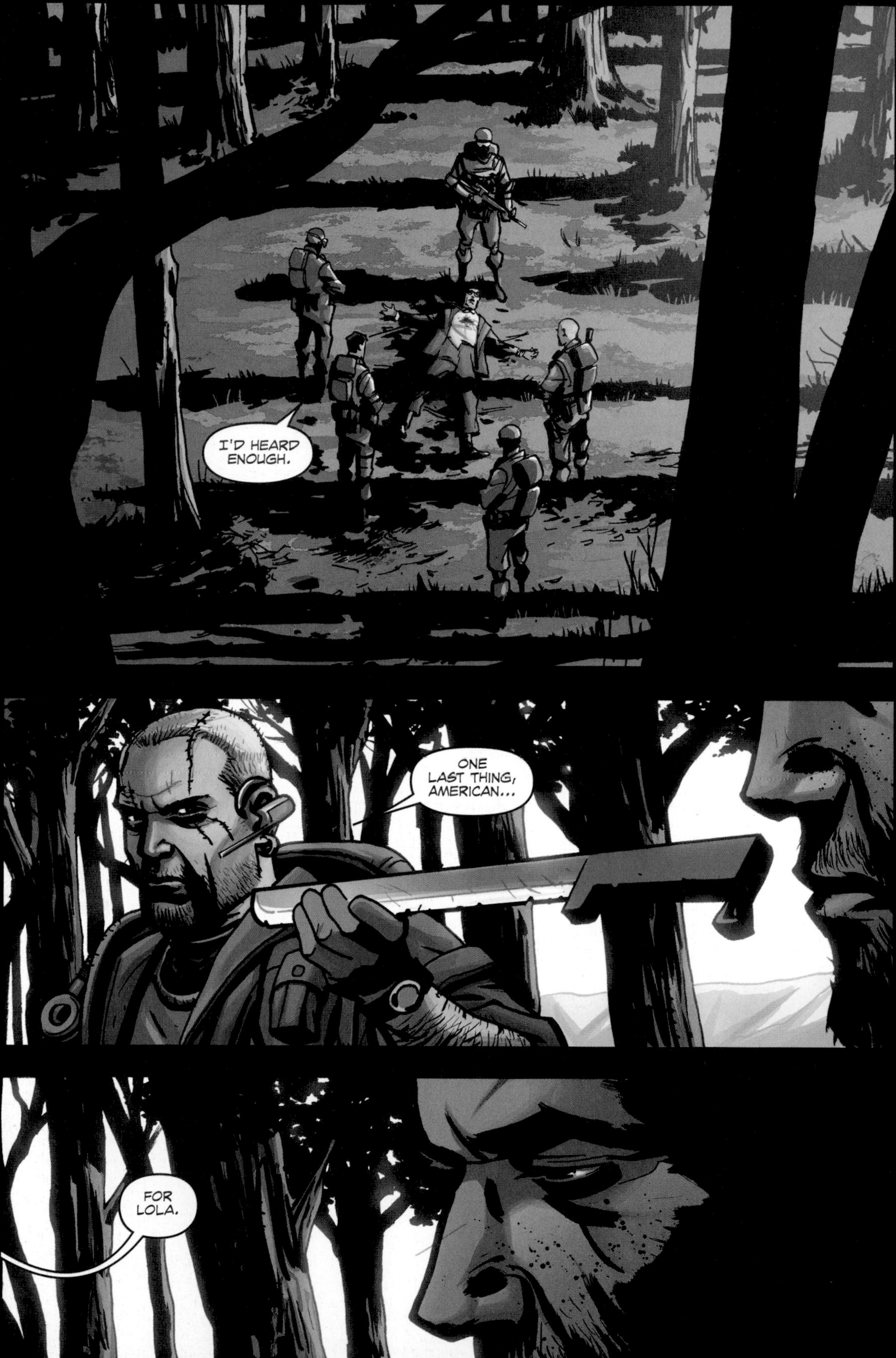
I'D HEARD ENOUGH.
ONE LAST THING, AMERICAN...
FOR LOLA.

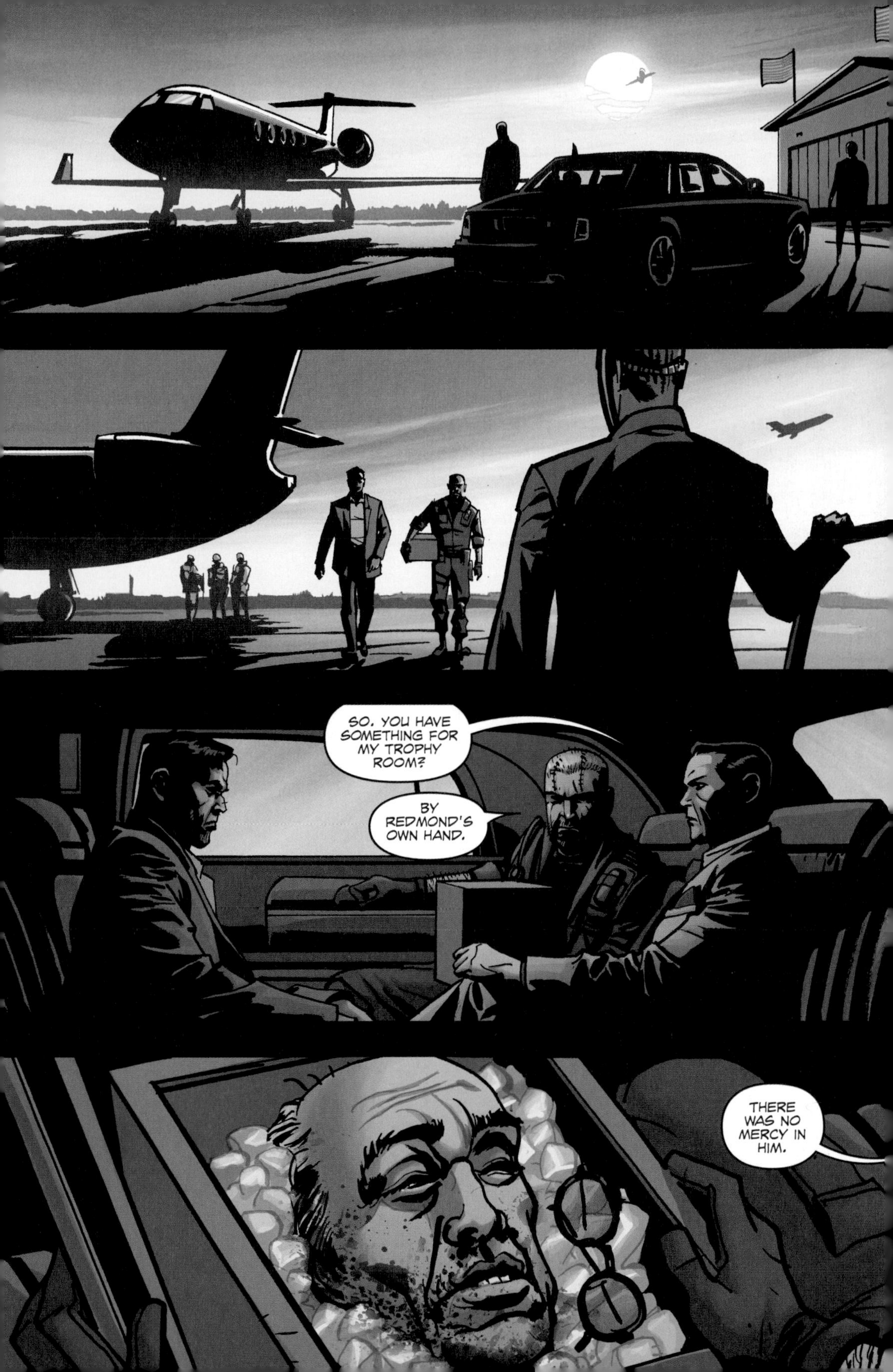
SO. YOU HAVE SOMETHING FOR MY TROPHY ROOM?
BY REDMOND'S OWN HAND.
THERE WAS NO MERCY IN HIM.

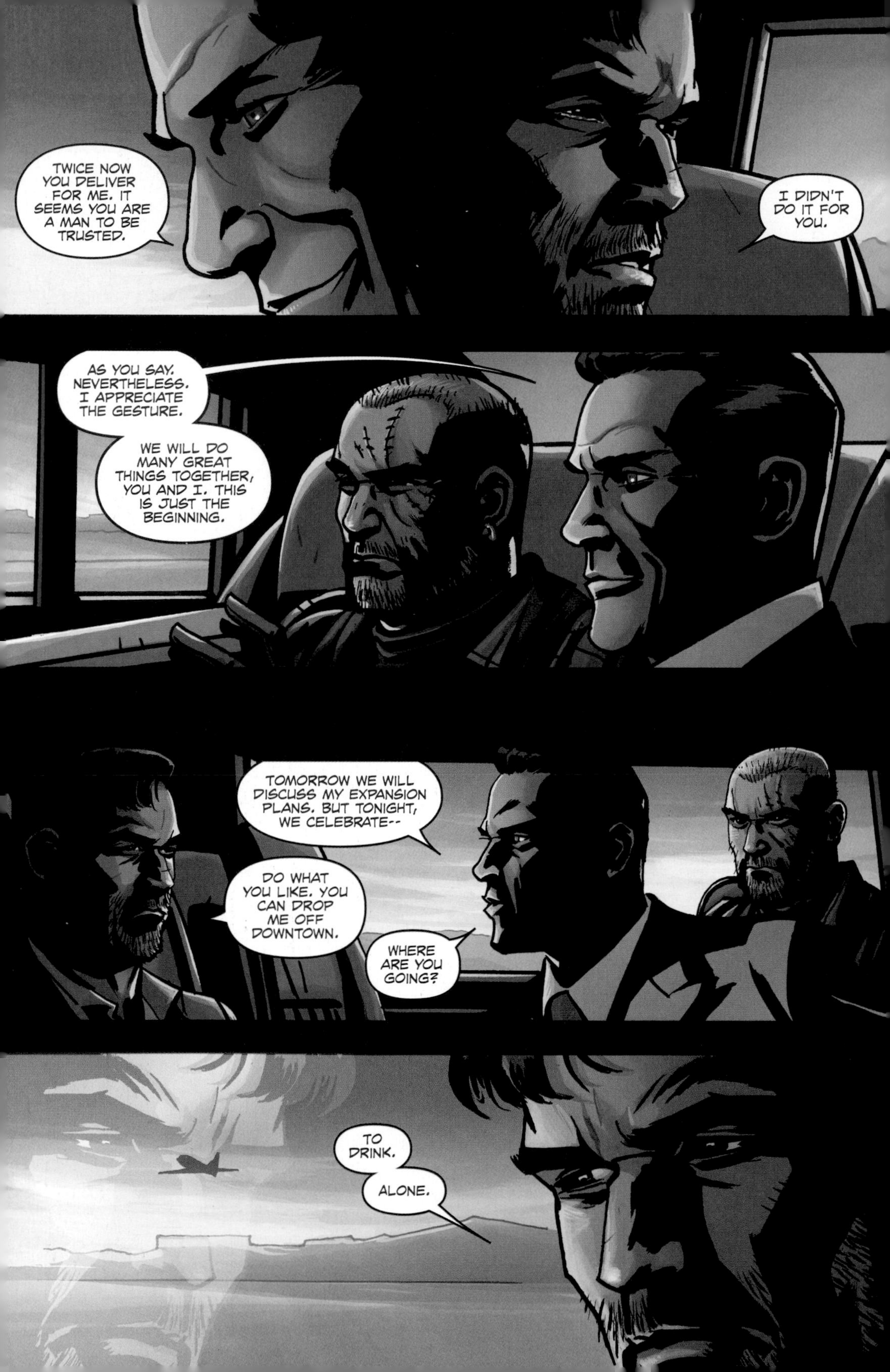
TWICE NOW YOU DELIVER FOR ME. IT SEEMS YOU ARE A MAN TO BE TRUSTED.
I DIDN'T DO IT FOR YOU.
AS YOU SAY. NEVERTHELESS. I APPRECIATE THE GESTURE.
WE WILL DO MANY GREAT THINGS TOGETHER, YOU AND I. THIS IS JUST THE BEGINNING.
TOMORROW WE WILL DISCUSS MY EXPANSION PLANS. BUT TONIGHT, WE CELEBRATE--
DO WHAT YOU LIKE. YOU CAN DROP ME OFF DOWNTOWN.
WHERE ARE YOU GOING?
TO DRINK.
ALONE.

HELLO, ARNO.

AAH--!

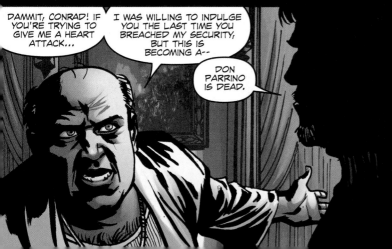

DAMMIT, CONRAD! IF YOU'RE TRYING TO GIVE ME A HEART ATTACK...

I WAS WILLING TO INDULGE YOU THE LAST TIME YOU BREACHED MY SECURITY, BUT THIS IS BECOMING A--

DON PARRINO IS DEAD.

I CUT HIS HEAD OFF WITH A MACHETE.

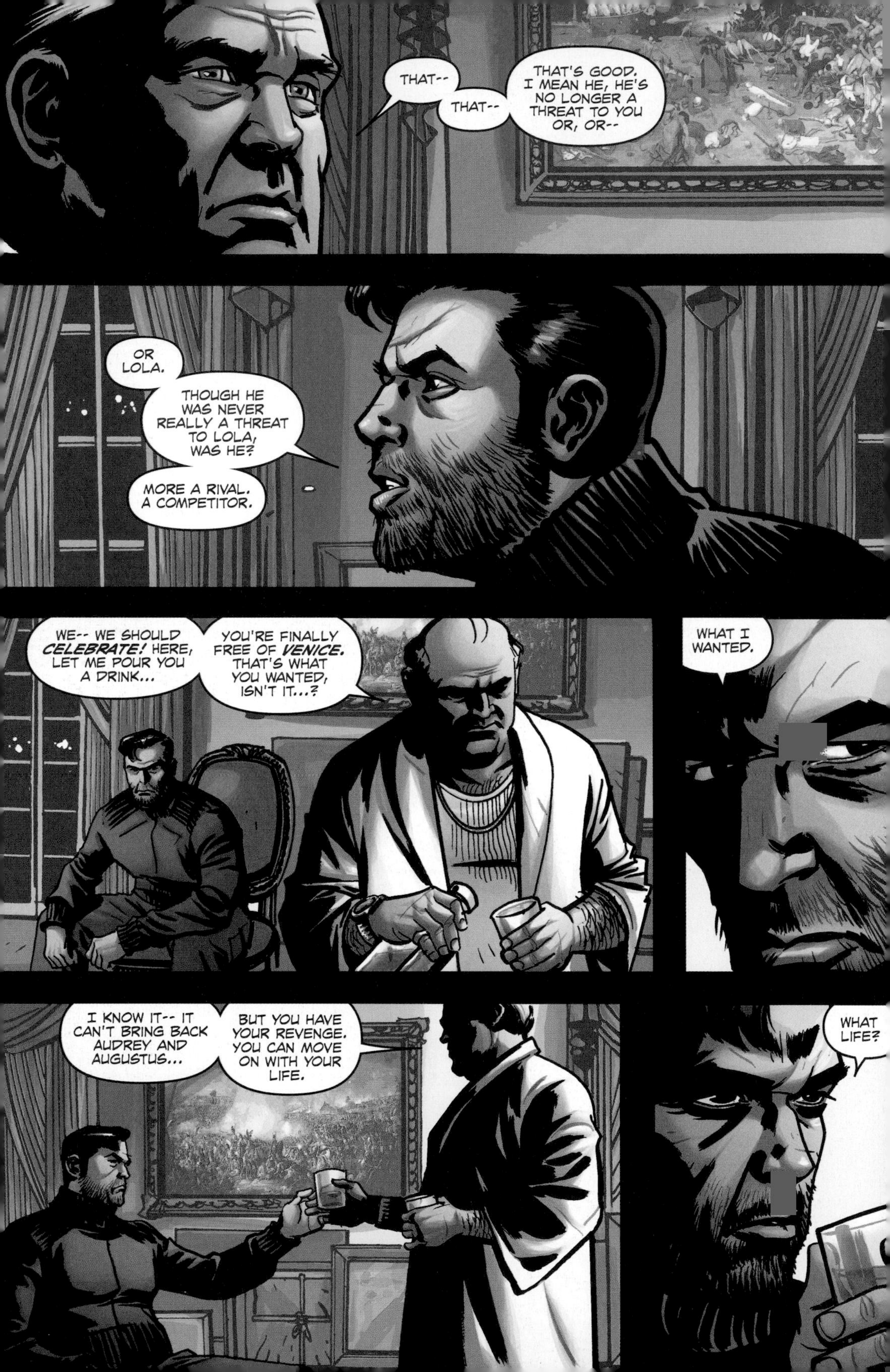
THAT--
THAT--
THAT'S GOOD. I MEAN HE, HE'S NO LONGER A THREAT TO YOU OR, OR--
OR LOLA.
THOUGH HE WAS NEVER REALLY A THREAT TO LOLA, WAS HE?
MORE A RIVAL. A COMPETITOR.
WE-- WE SHOULD CELEBRATE! HERE, LET ME POUR YOU A DRINK...
YOU'RE FINALLY FREE OF VENICE. THAT'S WHAT YOU WANTED, ISN'T IT...?
WHAT I WANTED.
I KNOW IT-- IT CAN'T BRING BACK AUDREY AND AUGUSTUS...
BUT YOU HAVE YOUR REVENGE. YOU CAN MOVE ON WITH YOUR LIFE.
WHAT LIFE?

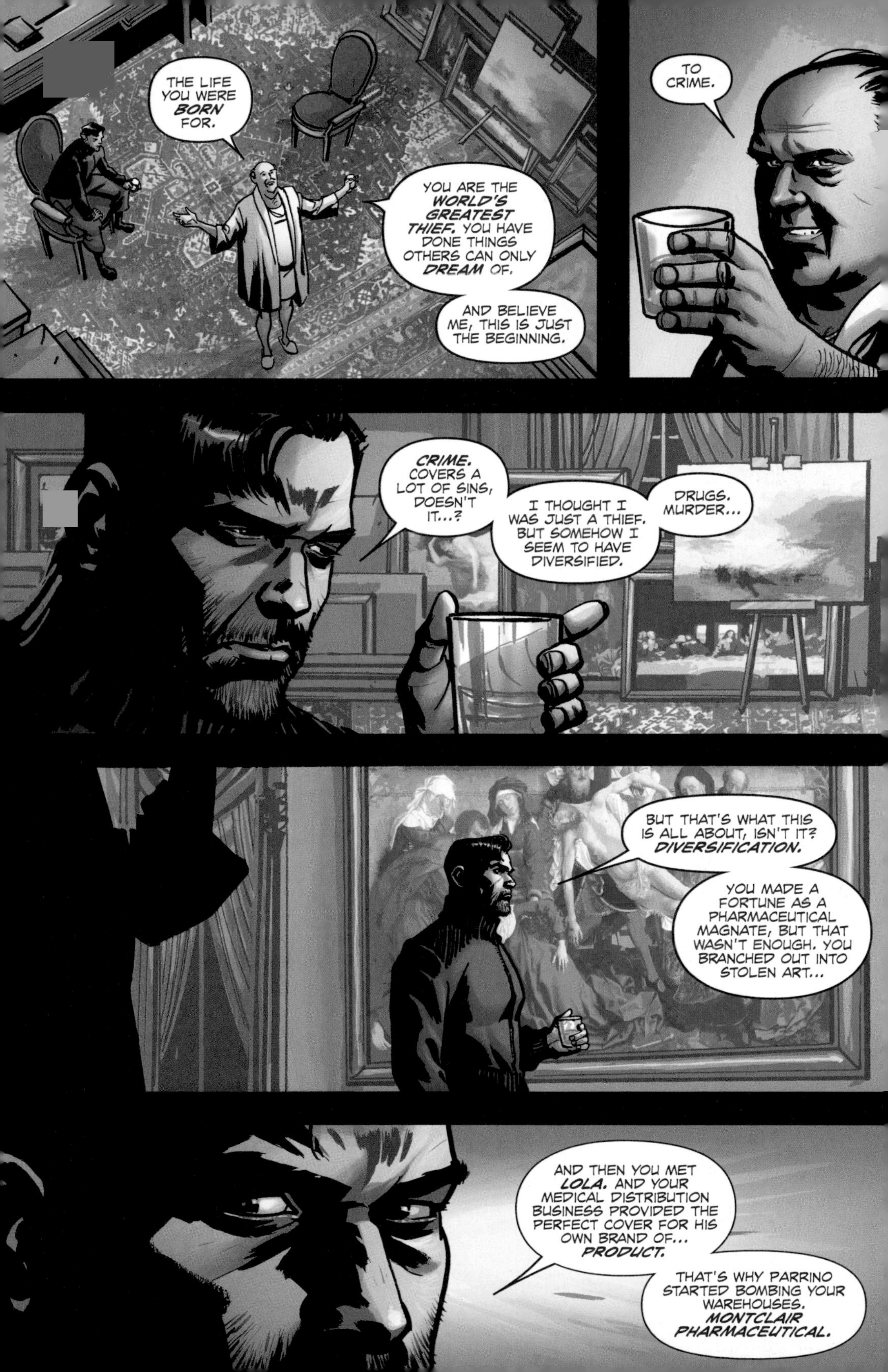
THE LIFE YOU WERE BORN FOR.
YOU ARE THE WORLD'S GREATEST THIEF. YOU HAVE DONE THINGS OTHERS CAN ONLY DREAM OF.
AND BELIEVE ME, THIS IS JUST THE BEGINNING.
TO CRIME.
CRIME. COVERS A LOT OF SINS, DOESN'T IT...?
I THOUGHT I WAS JUST A THIEF. BUT SOMEHOW I SEEM TO HAVE DIVERSIFIED.
DRUGS. MURDER...
BUT THAT'S WHAT THIS IS ALL ABOUT, ISN'T IT? DIVERSIFICATION.
YOU MADE A FORTUNE AS A PHARMACEUTICAL MAGNATE, BUT THAT WASN'T ENOUGH. YOU BRANCHED OUT INTO STOLEN ART...
AND THEN YOU MET LOLA. AND YOUR MEDICAL DISTRIBUTION BUSINESS PROVIDED THE PERFECT COVER FOR HIS OWN BRAND OF... PRODUCT.
THAT'S WHY PARRINO STARTED BOMBING YOUR WAREHOUSES. MONTCLAIR PHARMACEUTICAL.

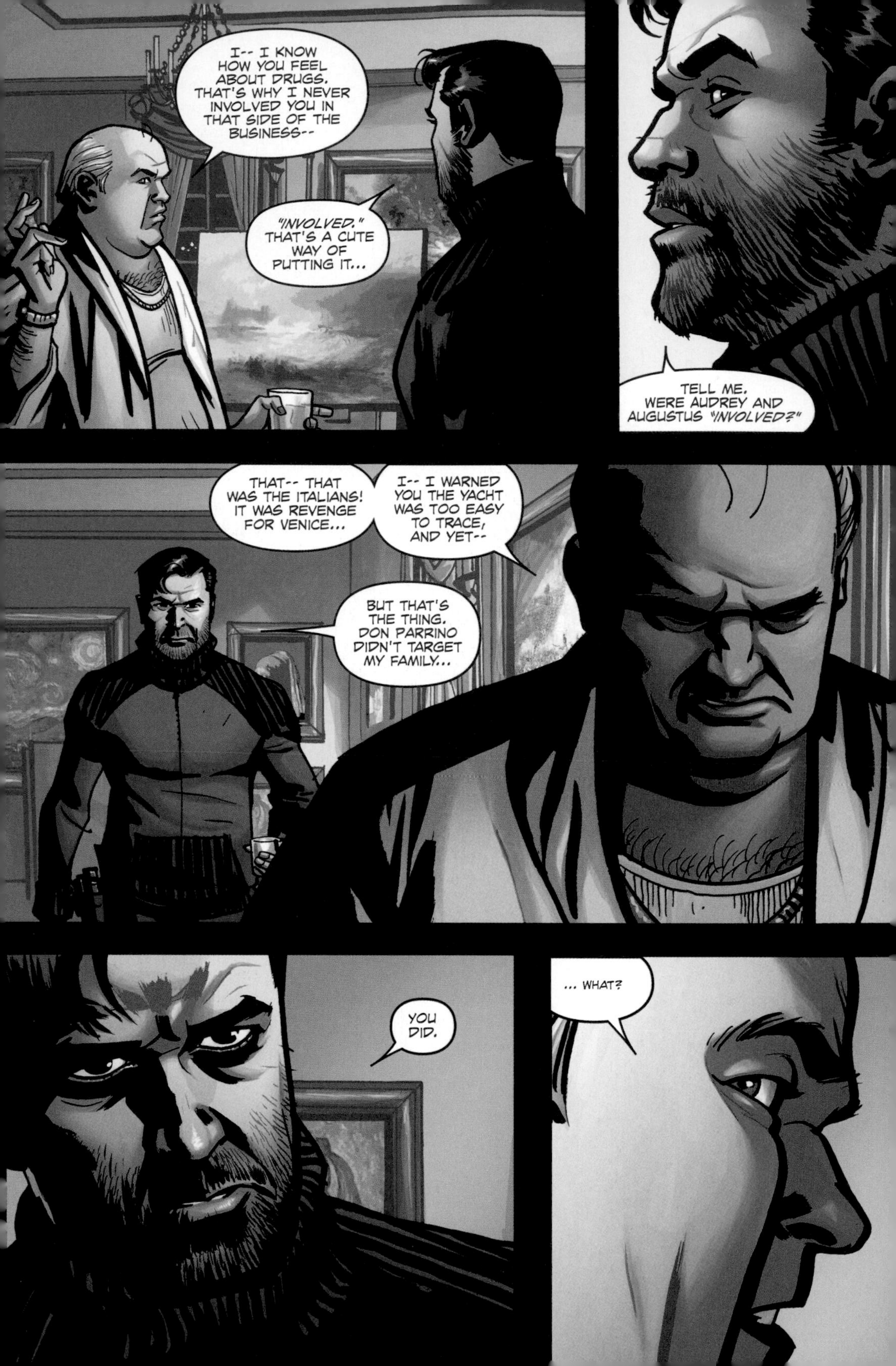
I-- I KNOW HOW YOU FEEL ABOUT DRUGS. THAT'S WHY I NEVER INVOLVED YOU IN THAT SIDE OF THE BUSINESS--
"INVOLVED." THAT'S A CUTE WAY OF PUTTING IT...
TELL ME. WERE AUDREY AND AUGUSTUS "INVOLVED?"
THAT-- THAT WAS THE ITALIANS! IT WAS REVENGE FOR VENICE...
I-- I WARNED YOU THE YACHT WAS TOO EASY TO TRACE, AND YET--
BUT THAT'S THE THING. DON PARRINO DIDN'T TARGET MY FAMILY...
YOU DID.
... WHAT?

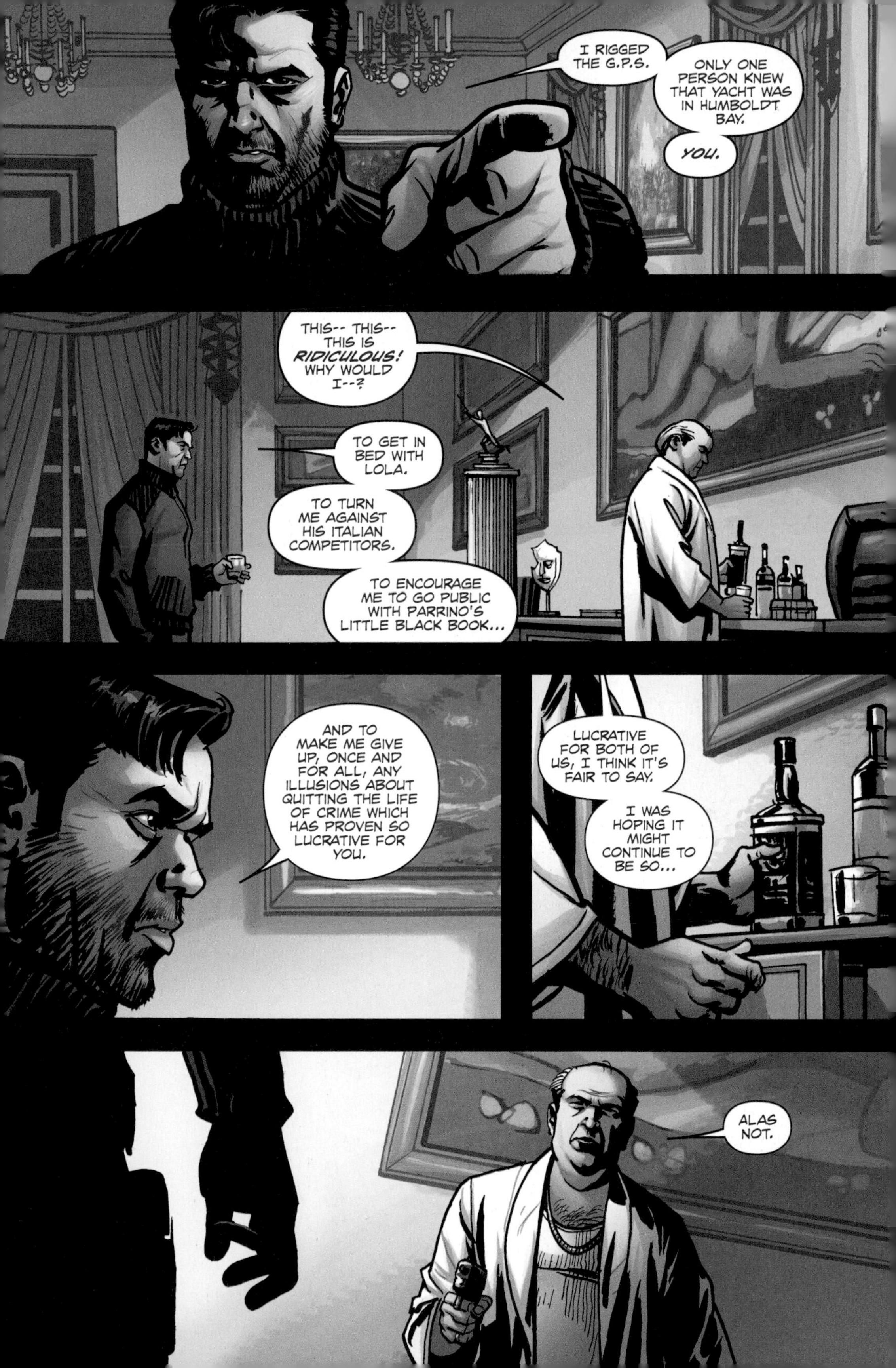
I RIGGED THE G.P.S.
ONLY ONE PERSON KNEW THAT YACHT WAS IN HUMBOLDT BAY.
YOU.
THIS-- THIS-- THIS IS RIDICULOUS! WHY WOULD I--?
TO GET IN BED WITH LOLA.
TO TURN ME AGAINST HIS ITALIAN COMPETITORS.
TO ENCOURAGE ME TO GO PUBLIC WITH PARRINO'S LITTLE BLACK BOOK...
AND TO MAKE ME GIVE UP, ONCE AND FOR ALL, ANY ILLUSIONS ABOUT QUITTING THE LIFE OF CRIME WHICH HAS PROVEN SO LUCRATIVE FOR YOU.
LUCRATIVE FOR BOTH OF US, I THINK IT'S FAIR TO SAY.
I WAS HOPING IT MIGHT CONTINUE TO BE SO...
ALAS NOT.

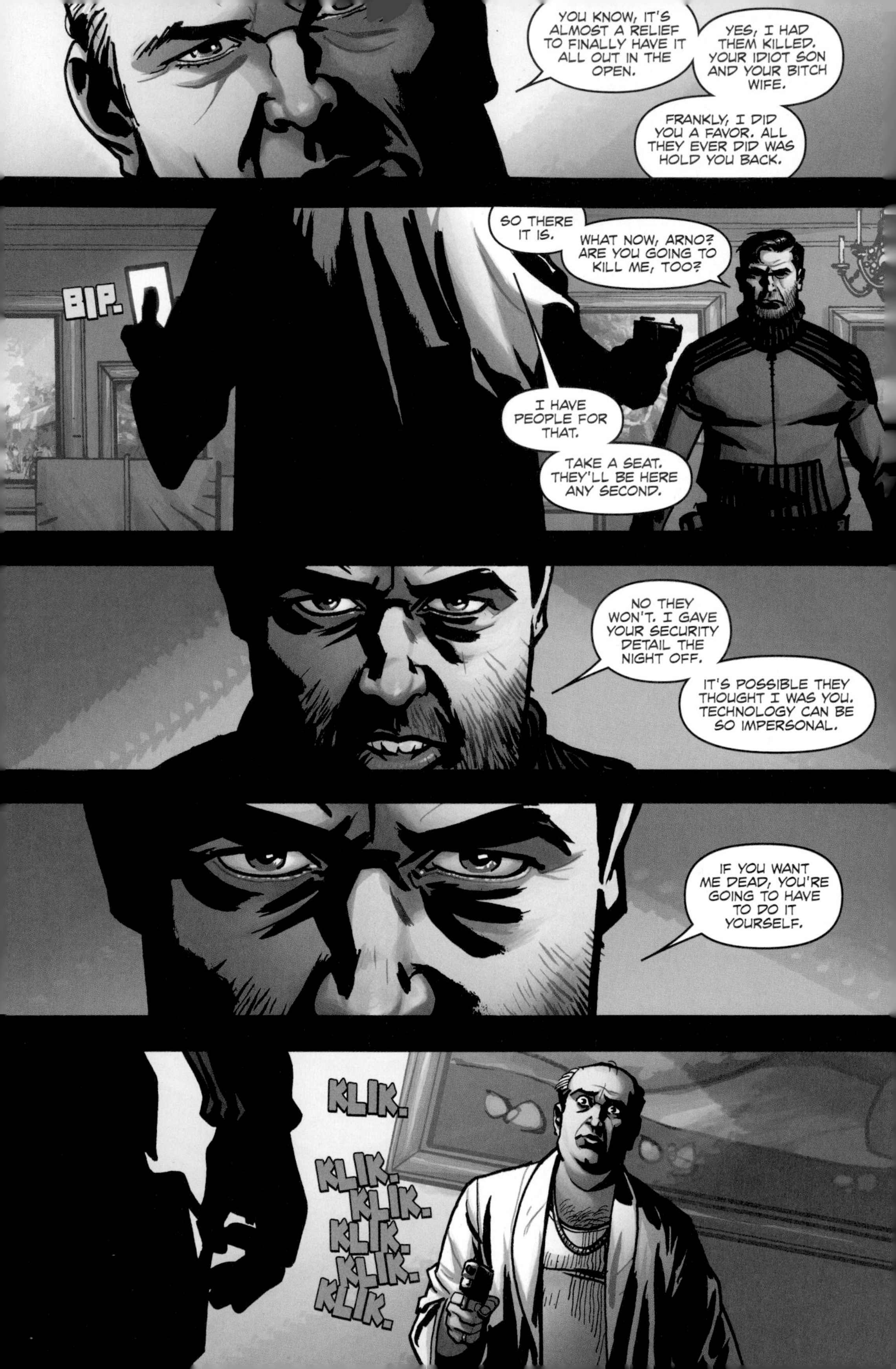
YOU KNOW, IT'S ALMOST A RELIEF TO FINALLY HAVE IT ALL OUT IN THE OPEN.
YES, I HAD THEM KILLED. YOUR IDIOT SON AND YOUR BITCH WIFE.
FRANKLY, I DID YOU A FAVOR. ALL THEY EVER DID WAS HOLD YOU BACK.
BIP.
SO THERE IT IS.
WHAT NOW, ARNO? ARE YOU GOING TO KILL ME, TOO?
I HAVE PEOPLE FOR THAT.
TAKE A SEAT. THEY'LL BE HERE ANY SECOND.
NO THEY WON'T. I GAVE YOUR SECURITY DETAIL THE NIGHT OFF.
IT'S POSSIBLE THEY THOUGHT I WAS YOU. TECHNOLOGY CAN BE SO IMPERSONAL.
IF YOU WANT ME DEAD, YOU'RE GOING TO HAVE TO DO IT YOURSELF.
KLIK.
KLIK. KLIK. KLIK. KLIK. KLIK.

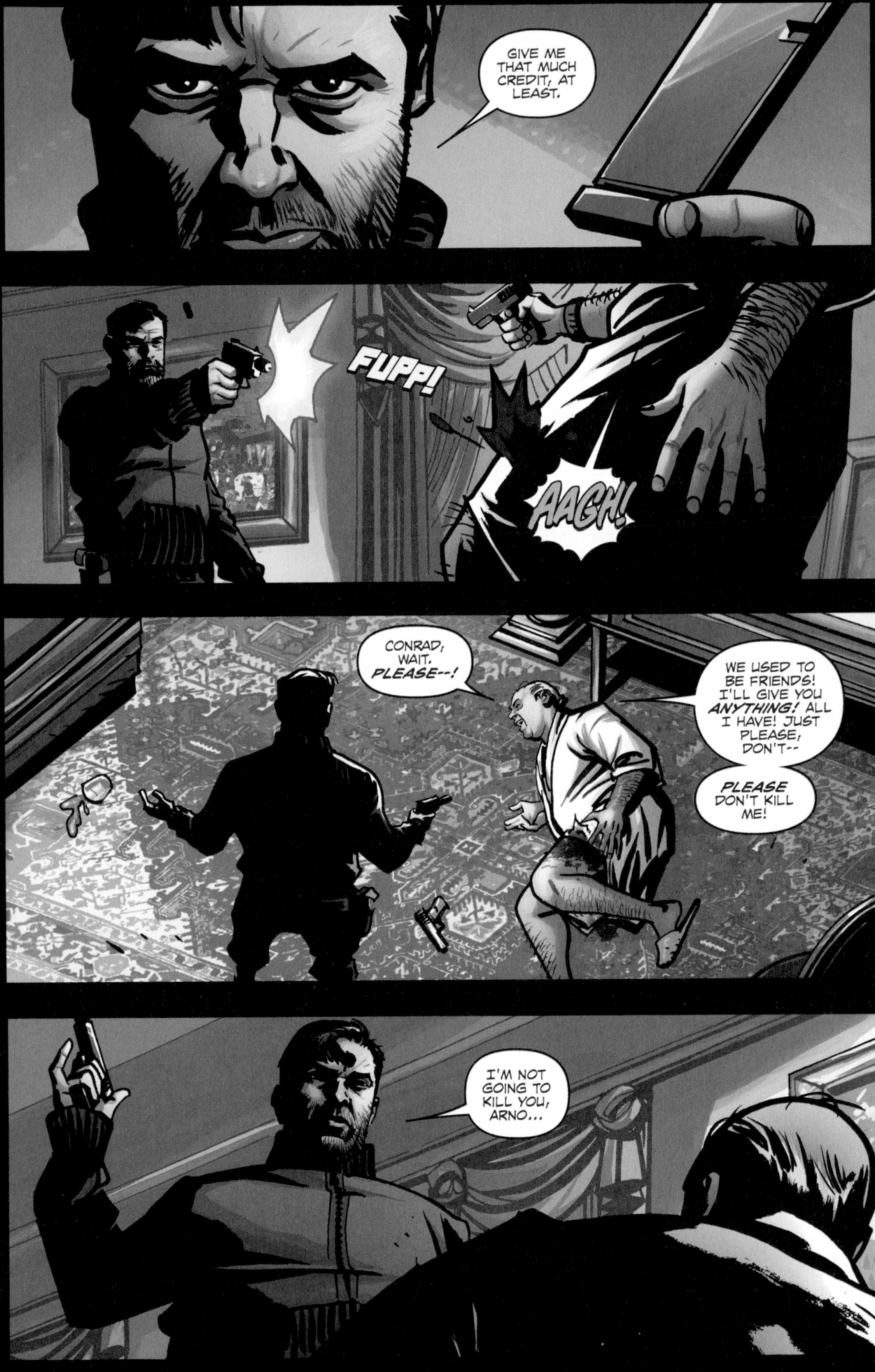
GIVE ME THAT MUCH CREDIT, AT LEAST.
FUPP!
AAGH!
CONRAD, WAIT. PLEASE--!
WE USED TO BE FRIENDS! I'LL GIVE YOU ANYTHING! ALL I HAVE! JUST PLEASE, DON'T--
PLEASE DON'T KILL ME!
I'M NOT GOING TO KILL YOU, ARNO...

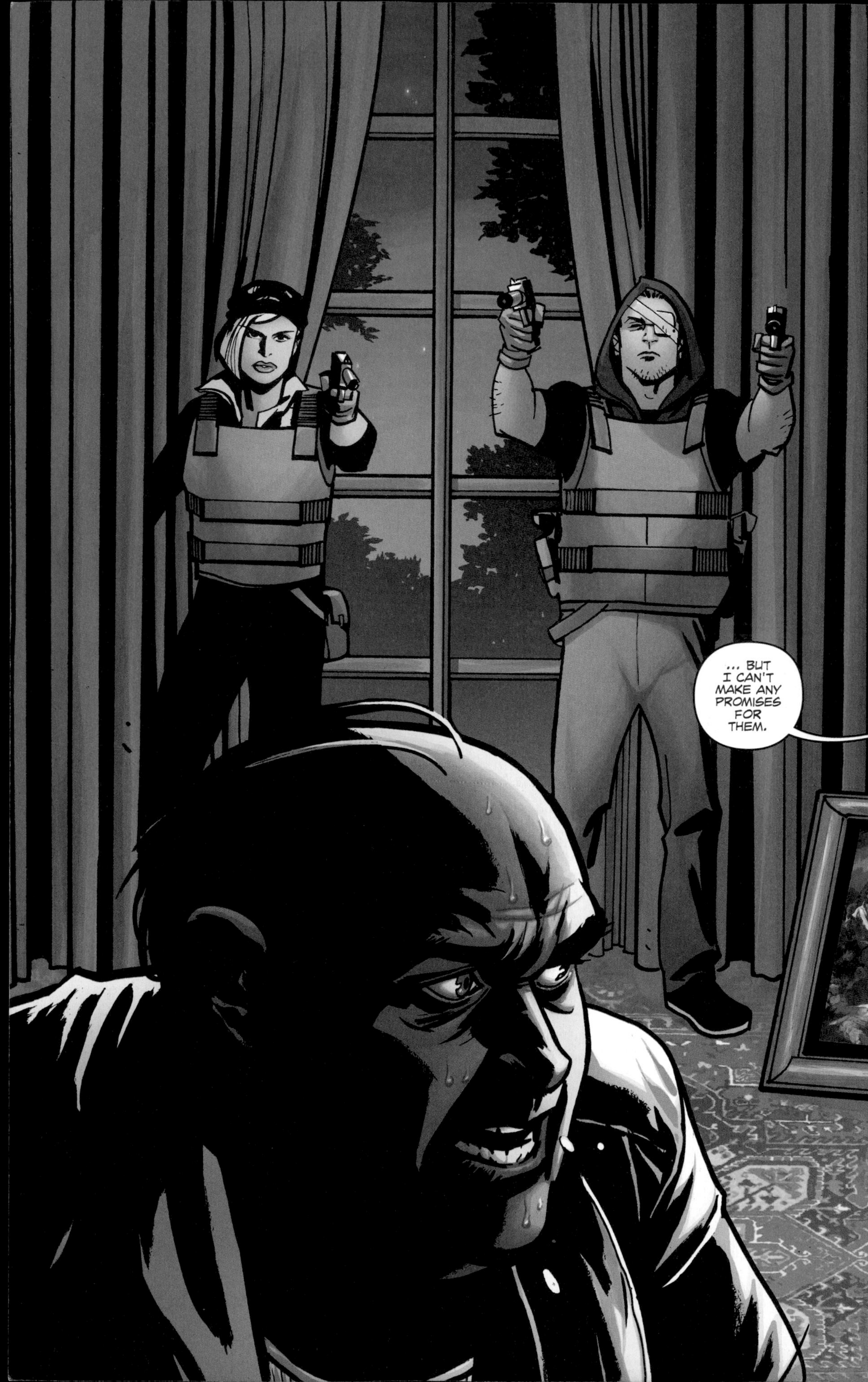
... BUT I CAN'T MAKE ANY PROMISES FOR THEM.

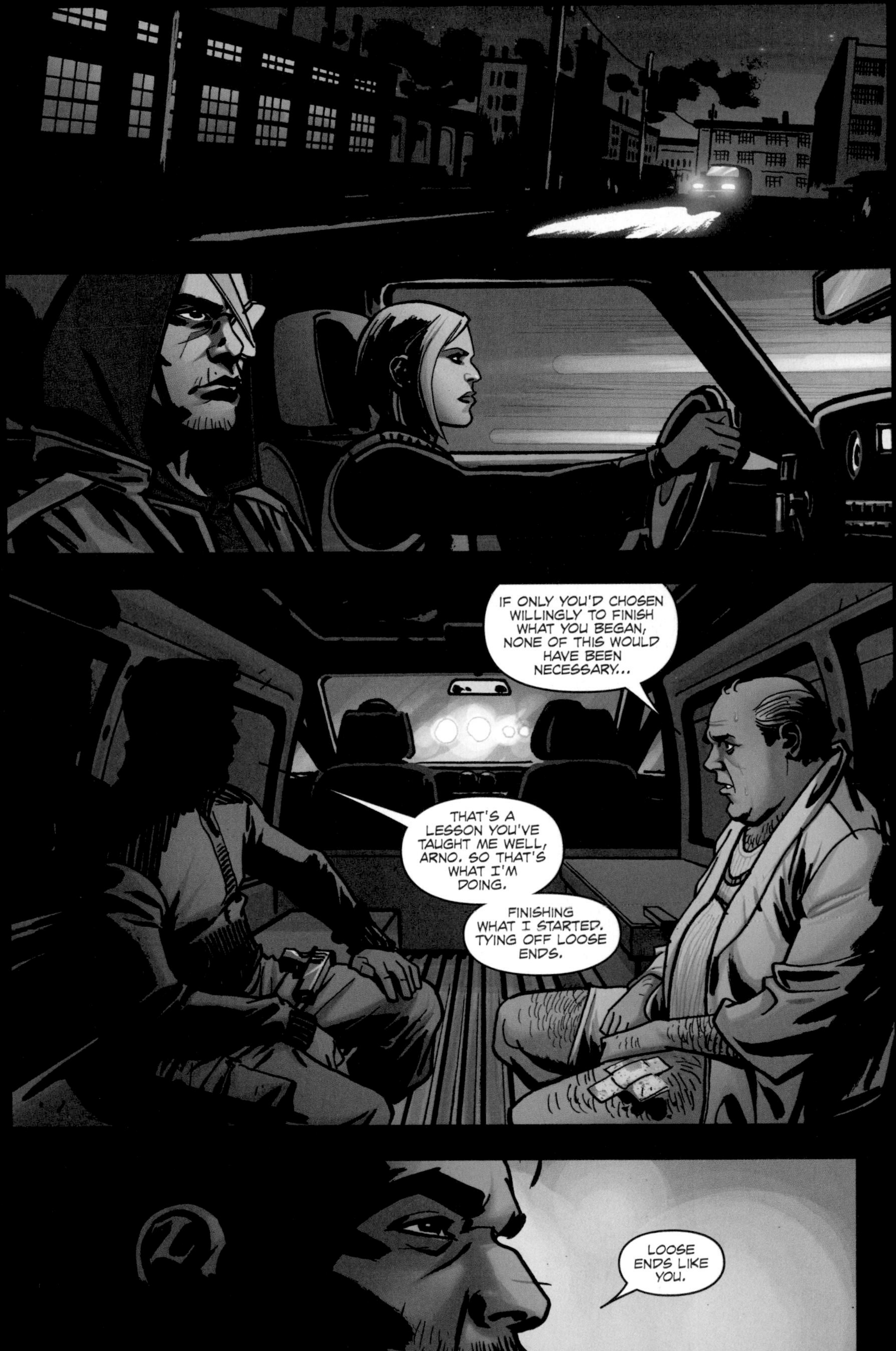
IF ONLY YOU'D CHOSEN WILLINGLY TO FINISH WHAT YOU BEGAN, NONE OF THIS WOULD HAVE BEEN NECESSARY...
THAT'S A LESSON YOU'VE TAUGHT ME WELL, ARNO. SO THAT'S WHAT I'M DOING.
FINISHING WHAT I STARTED. TYING OFF LOOSE ENDS.
LOOSE ENDS LIKE YOU.

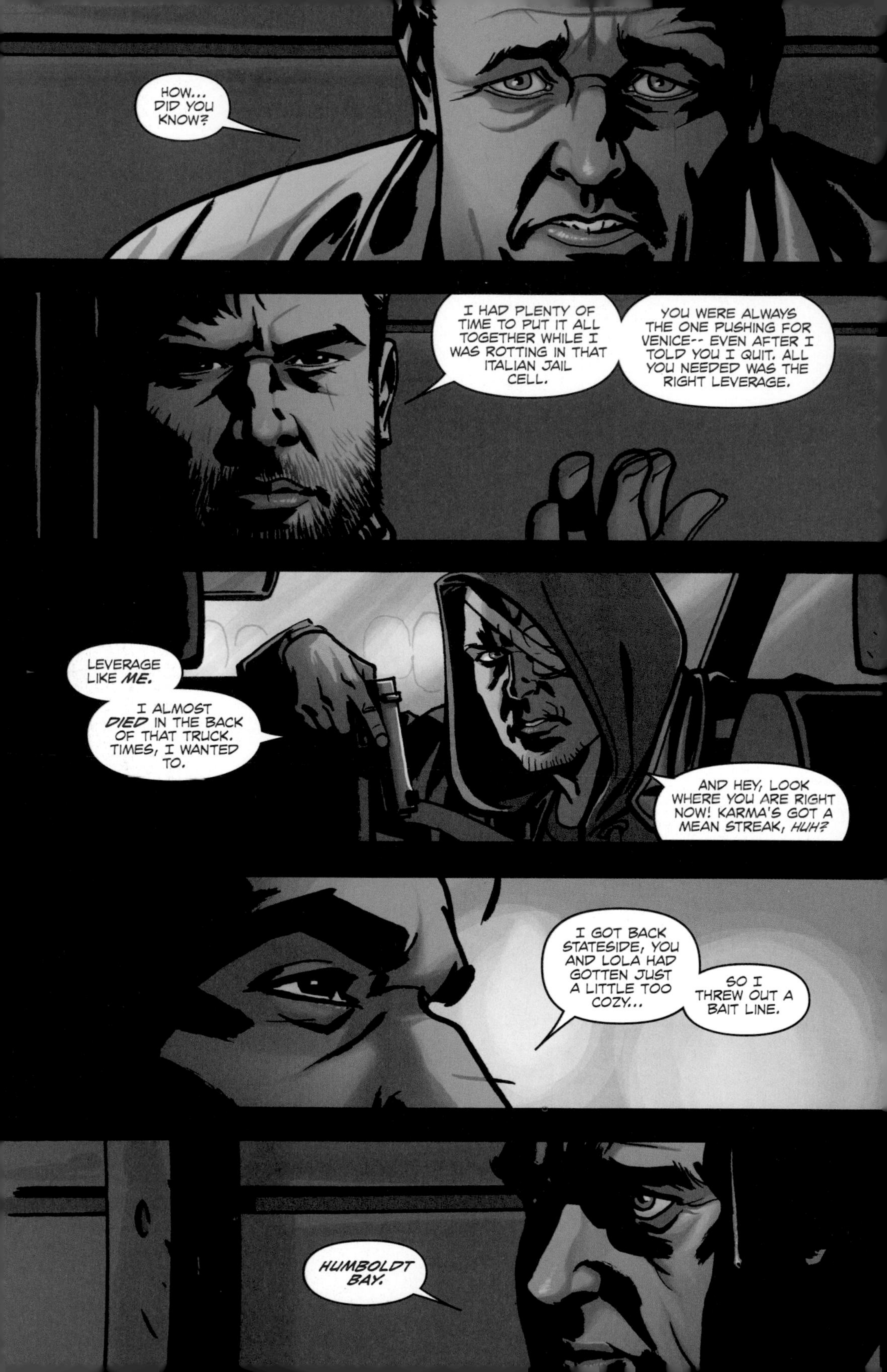
HOW... DID YOU KNOW?
I HAD PLENTY OF TIME TO PUT IT ALL TOGETHER WHILE I WAS ROTTING IN THAT ITALIAN JAIL CELL.
YOU WERE ALWAYS THE ONE PUSHING FOR VENICE-- EVEN AFTER I TOLD YOU I QUIT. ALL YOU NEEDED WAS THE RIGHT LEVERAGE.
LEVERAGE LIKE *ME.*
I ALMOST *DIED* IN THE BACK OF THAT TRUCK. TIMES, I WANTED TO.
AND HEY, LOOK WHERE YOU ARE RIGHT NOW! KARMA'S GOT A MEAN STREAK, *HUH?*
I GOT BACK STATESIDE, YOU AND LOLA HAD GOTTEN JUST A LITTLE TOO COZY...
SO I THREW OUT A BAIT LINE.
HUMBOLDT BAY.

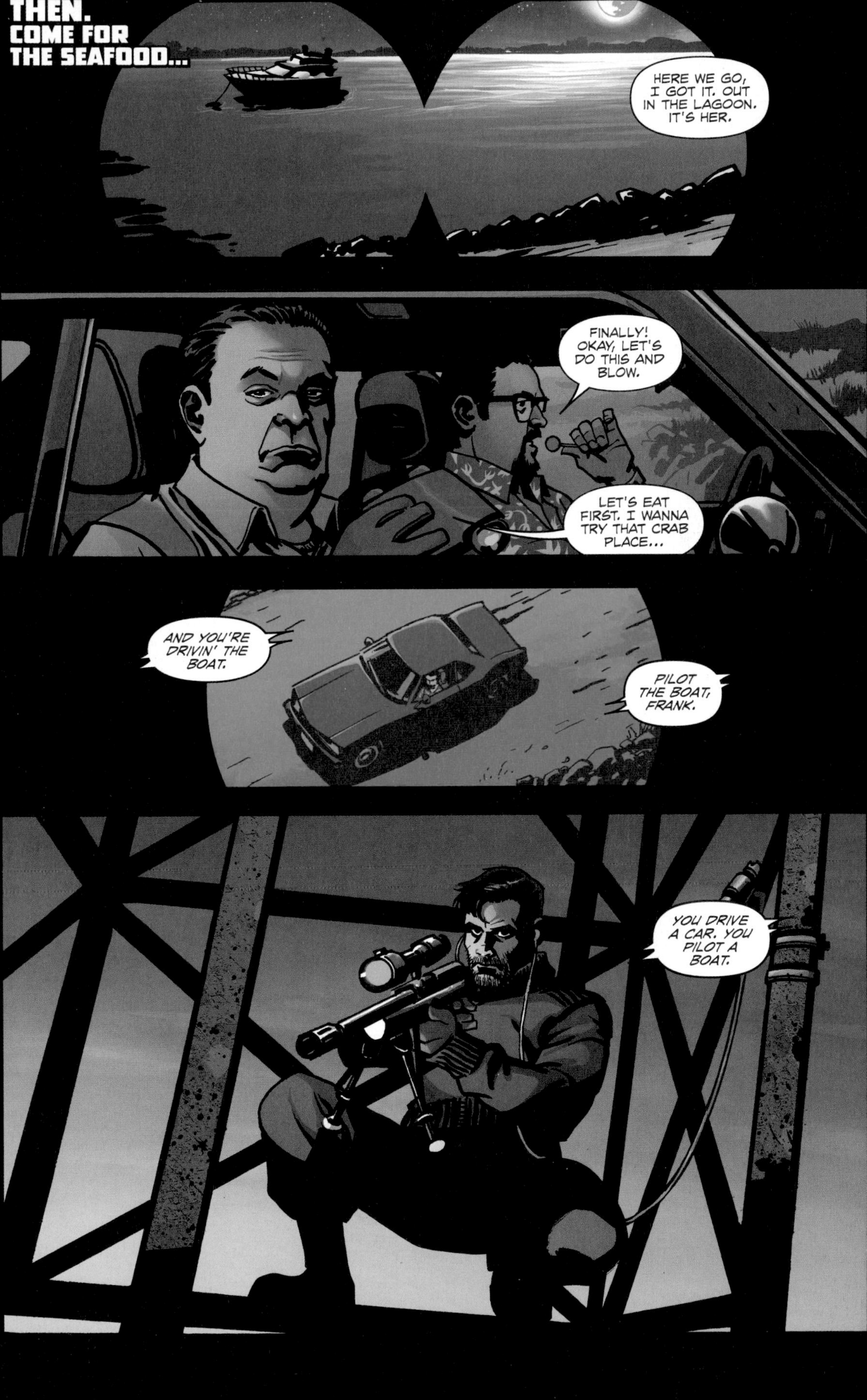
THEN. COME FOR THE SEAFOOD...
HERE WE GO, I GOT IT. OUT IN THE LAGOON. IT'S HER.
FINALLY! OKAY, LET'S DO THIS AND BLOW.
LET'S EAT FIRST. I WANNA TRY THAT CRAB PLACE...
AND YOU'RE DRIVIN' THE BOAT.
PILOT THE BOAT, FRANK.
YOU DRIVE A CAR. YOU PILOT A BOAT.

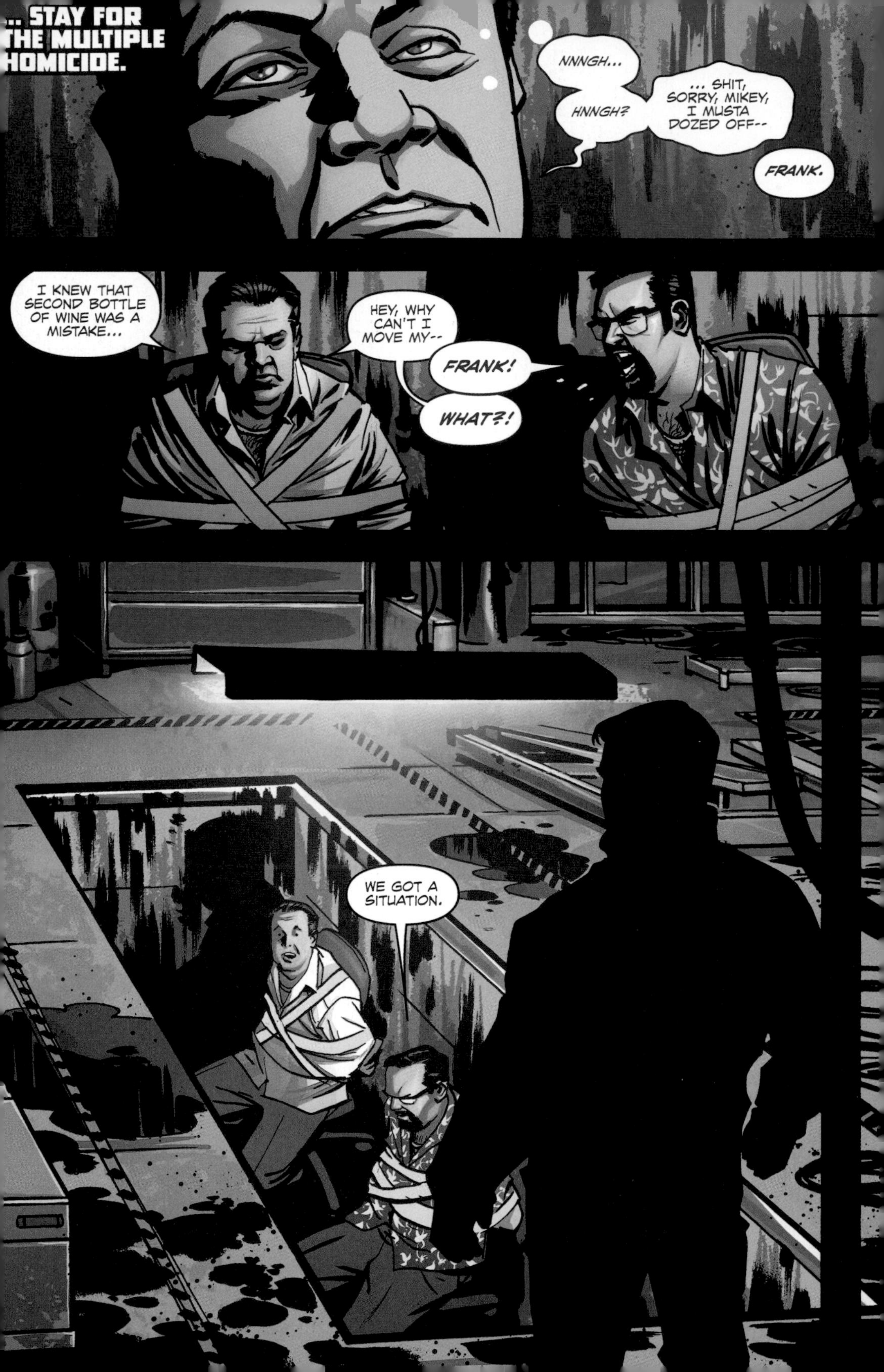
.. STAY FOR THE MULTIPLE HOMICIDE.
NNNGH...
HNNGH?
... SHIT, SORRY, MIKEY, I MUSTA DOZED OFF--
FRANK.
I KNEW THAT SECOND BOTTLE OF WINE WAS A MISTAKE...
HEY, WHY CAN'T I MOVE MY--
FRANK!
WHAT?!
WE GOT A SITUATION.

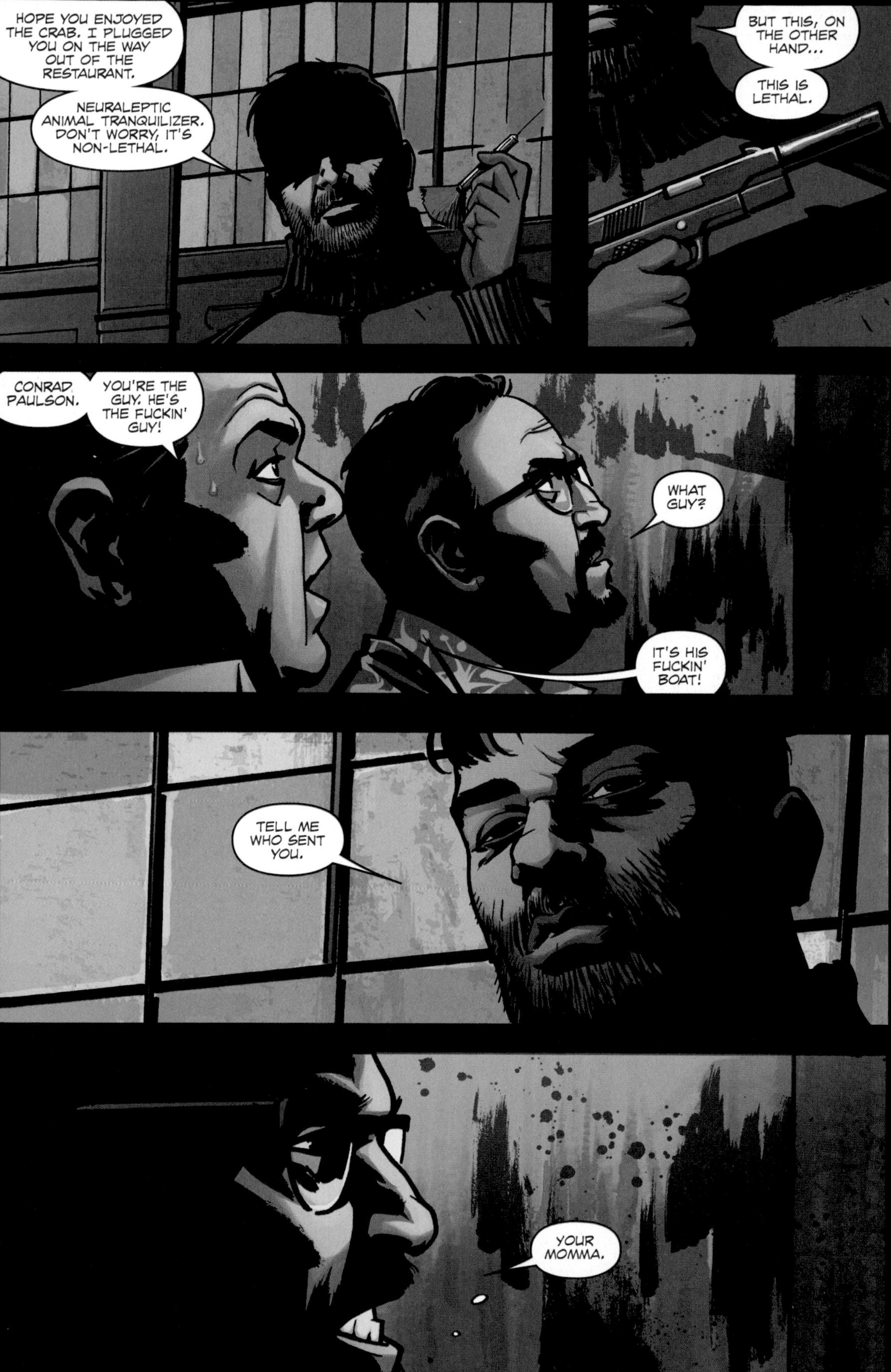
HOPE YOU ENJOYED THE CRAB. I PLUGGED YOU ON THE WAY OUT OF THE RESTAURANT.
NEURALEPTIC ANIMAL TRANQUILIZER. DON'T WORRY, IT'S NON-LETHAL.
BUT THIS, ON THE OTHER HAND...
THIS IS LETHAL.
CONRAD PAULSON.
YOU'RE THE GUY. HE'S THE FUCKIN' GUY!
WHAT GUY?
IT'S HIS FUCKIN' BOAT!
TELL ME WHO SENT YOU.
YOUR MOMMA.

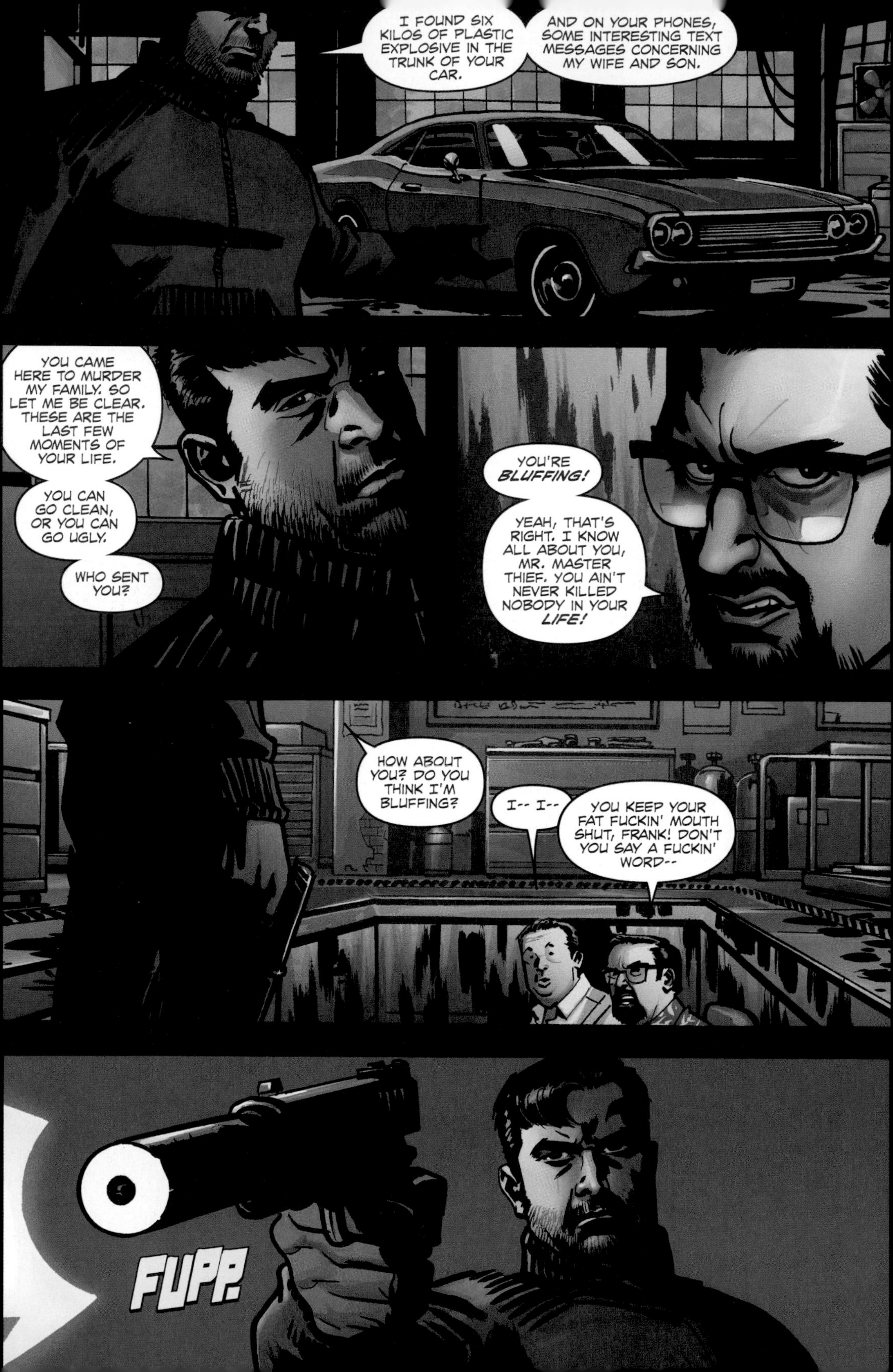
I FOUND SIX KILOS OF PLASTIC EXPLOSIVE IN THE TRUNK OF YOUR CAR.
AND ON YOUR PHONES, SOME INTERESTING TEXT MESSAGES CONCERNING MY WIFE AND SON.
YOU CAME HERE TO MURDER MY FAMILY. SO LET ME BE CLEAR. THESE ARE THE LAST FEW MOMENTS OF YOUR LIFE.
YOU CAN GO CLEAN, OR YOU CAN GO UGLY.
WHO SENT YOU?
YOU'RE *BLUFFING!*
YEAH, THAT'S RIGHT. I KNOW ALL ABOUT YOU, MR. MASTER THIEF. YOU AIN'T NEVER KILLED NOBODY IN YOUR *LIFE!*
HOW ABOUT YOU? DO YOU THINK I'M BLUFFING?
I-- I--
YOU KEEP YOUR FAT FUCKIN' MOUTH SHUT, FRANK! DON'T YOU SAY A FUCKIN' WORD--
FUPP.

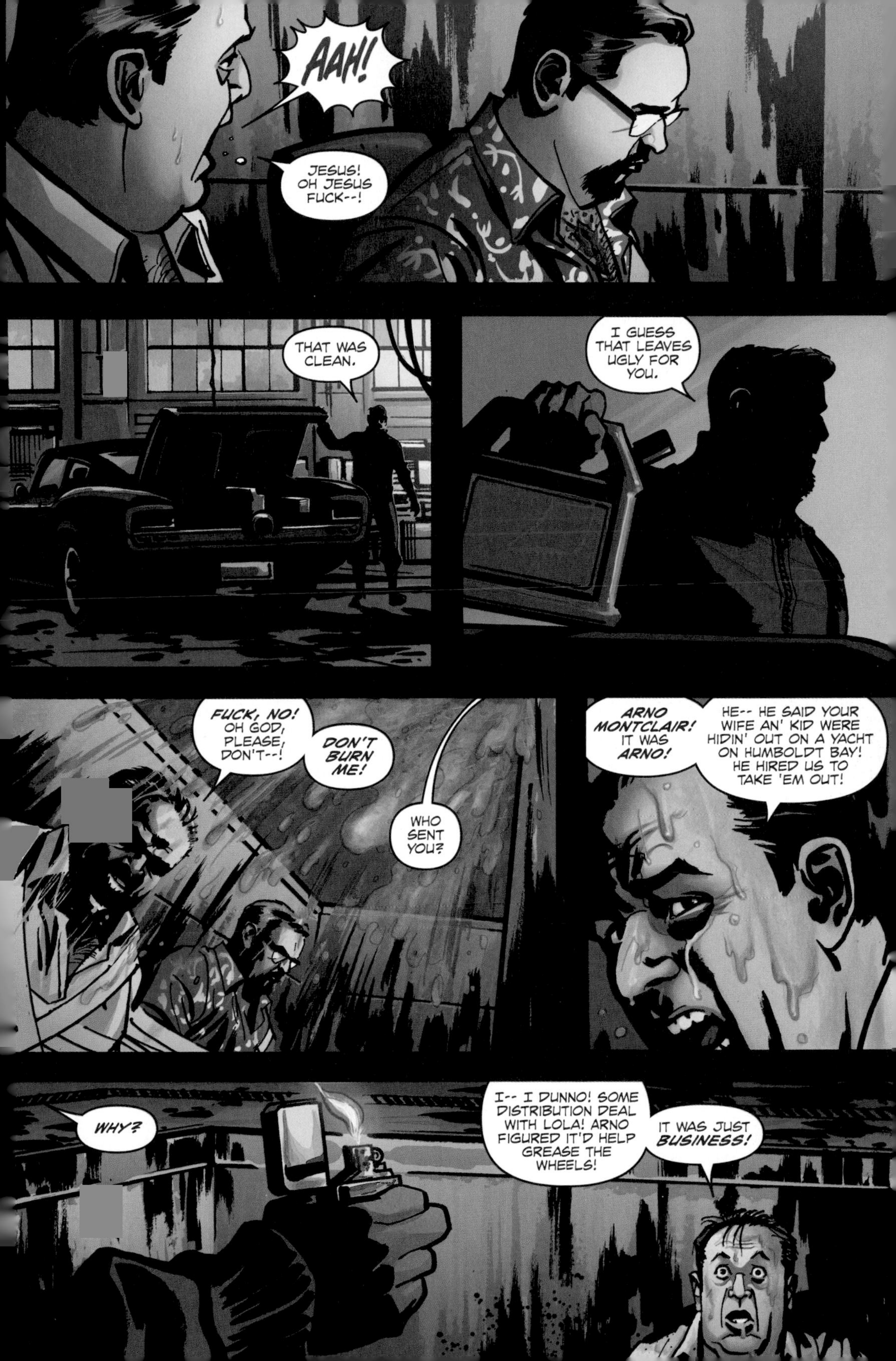
AAH!
JESUS! OH JESUS FUCK--!
THAT WAS CLEAN.
I GUESS THAT LEAVES UGLY FOR YOU.
FUCK, NO! OH GOD, PLEASE, DON'T--!
DON'T BURN ME!
WHO SENT YOU?
ARNO MONTCLAIR! IT WAS ARNO!
HE-- HE SAID YOUR WIFE AN' KID WERE HIDIN' OUT ON A YACHT ON HUMBOLDT BAY! HE HIRED US TO TAKE 'EM OUT!
WHY?
I-- I DUNNO! SOME DISTRIBUTION DEAL WITH LOLA! ARNO FIGURED IT'D HELP GREASE THE WHEELS!
IT WAS JUST BUSINESS!

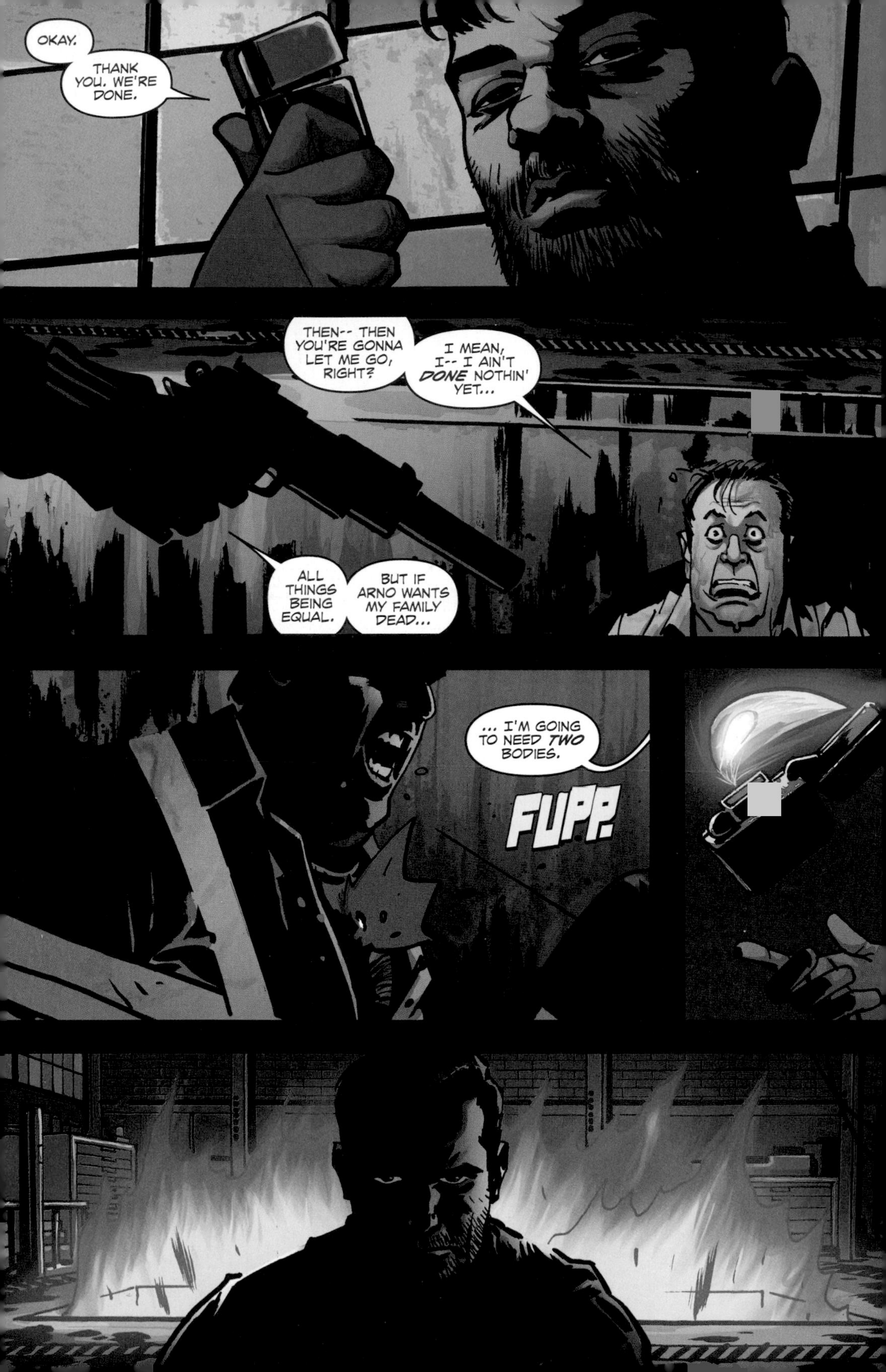
OKAY.
THANK YOU. WE'RE DONE.
THEN-- THEN YOU'RE GONNA LET ME GO, RIGHT?
I MEAN, I-- I AIN'T DONE NOTHIN' YET...
ALL THINGS BEING EQUAL.
BUT IF ARNO WANTS MY FAMILY DEAD...
... I'M GOING TO NEED TWO BODIES.
FUPP.

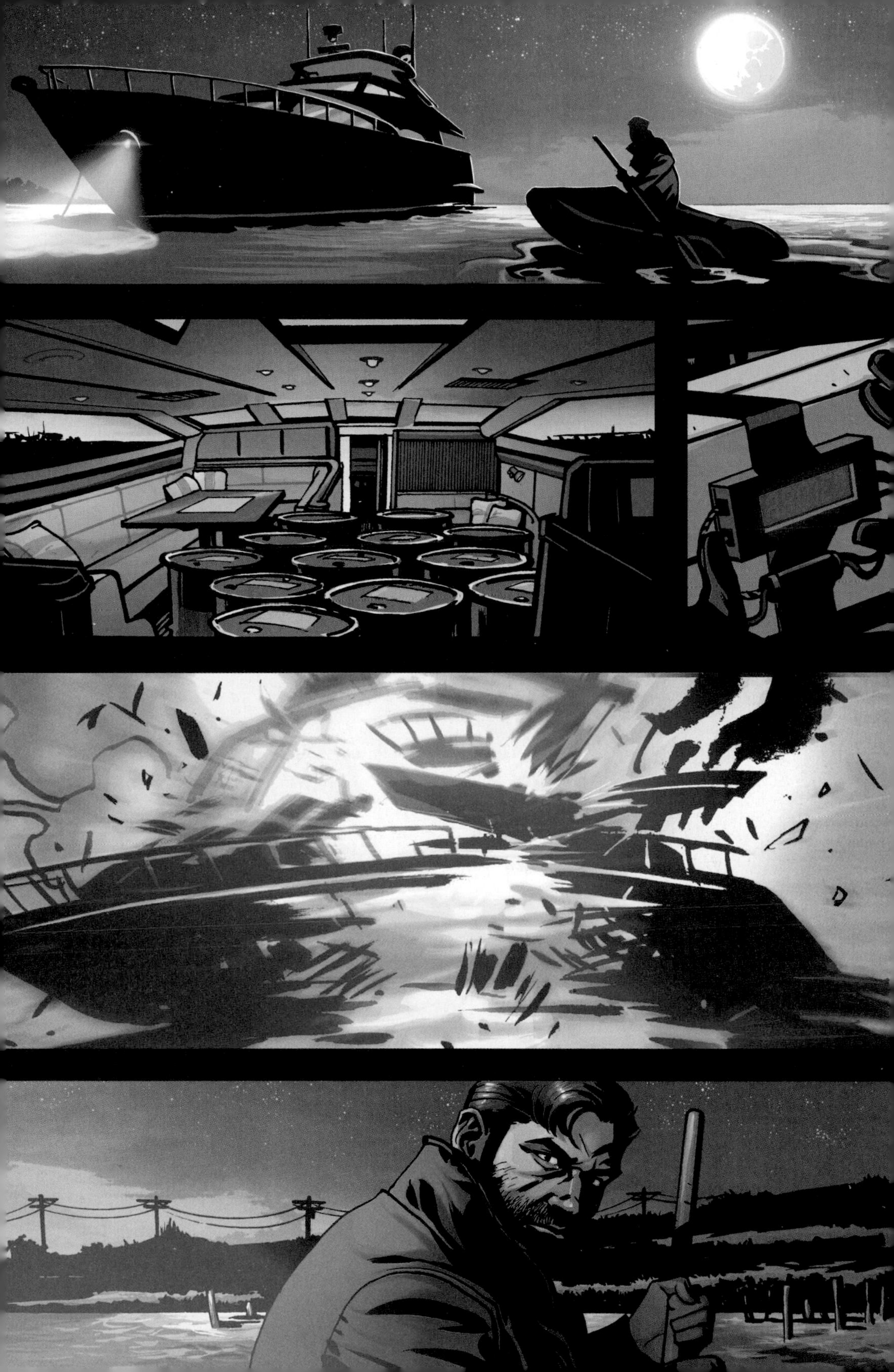

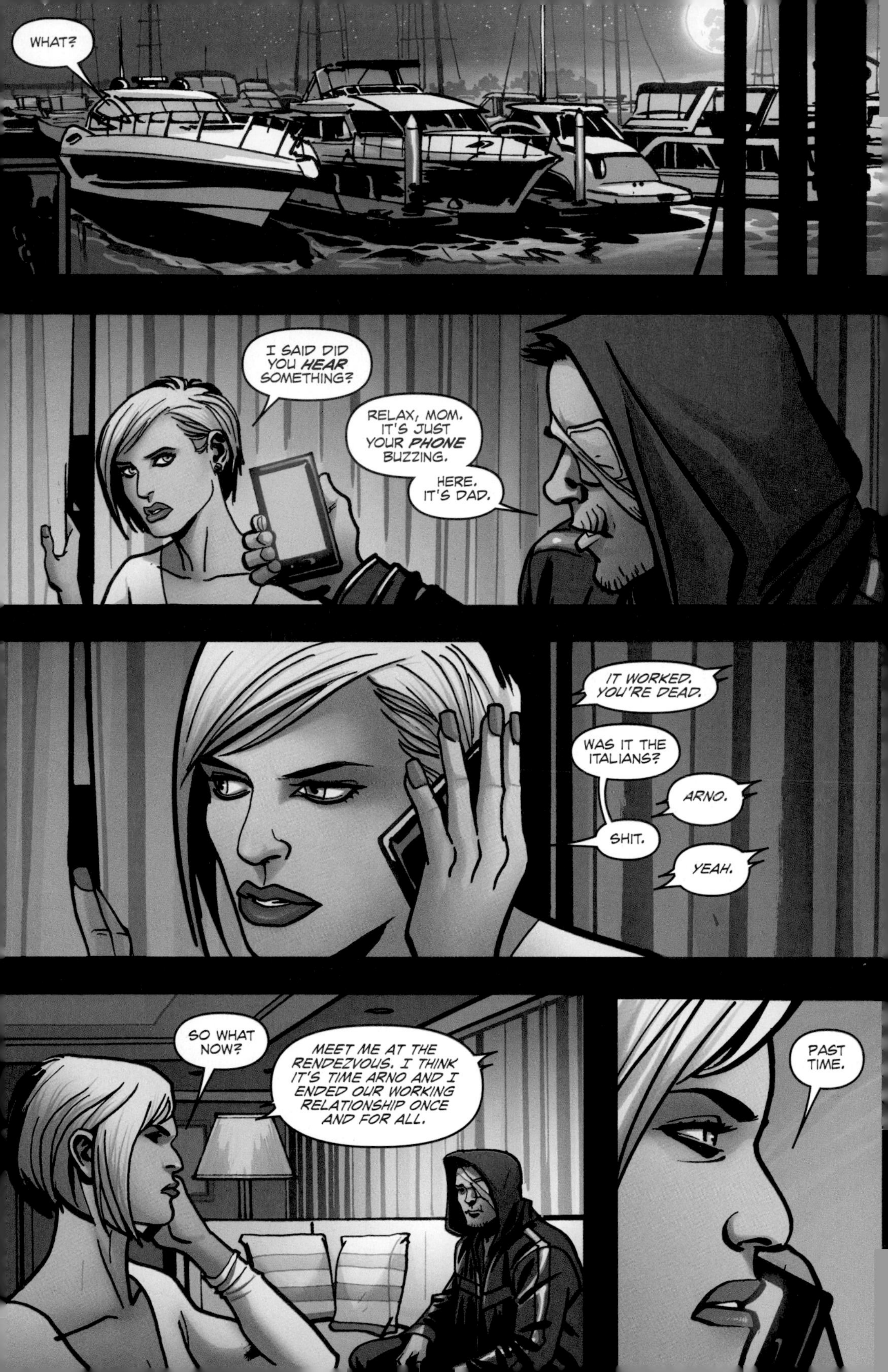
WHAT?
I SAID DID YOU *HEAR* SOMETHING?
RELAX, MOM. IT'S JUST YOUR *PHONE* BUZZING.
HERE. IT'S DAD.
IT WORKED. YOU'RE DEAD.
WAS IT THE ITALIANS?
ARNO.
SHIT.
YEAH.
SO WHAT NOW?
MEET ME AT THE RENDEZVOUS. I THINK IT'S TIME ARNO AND I ENDED OUR WORKING RELATIONSHIP ONCE AND FOR ALL.
PAST TIME.

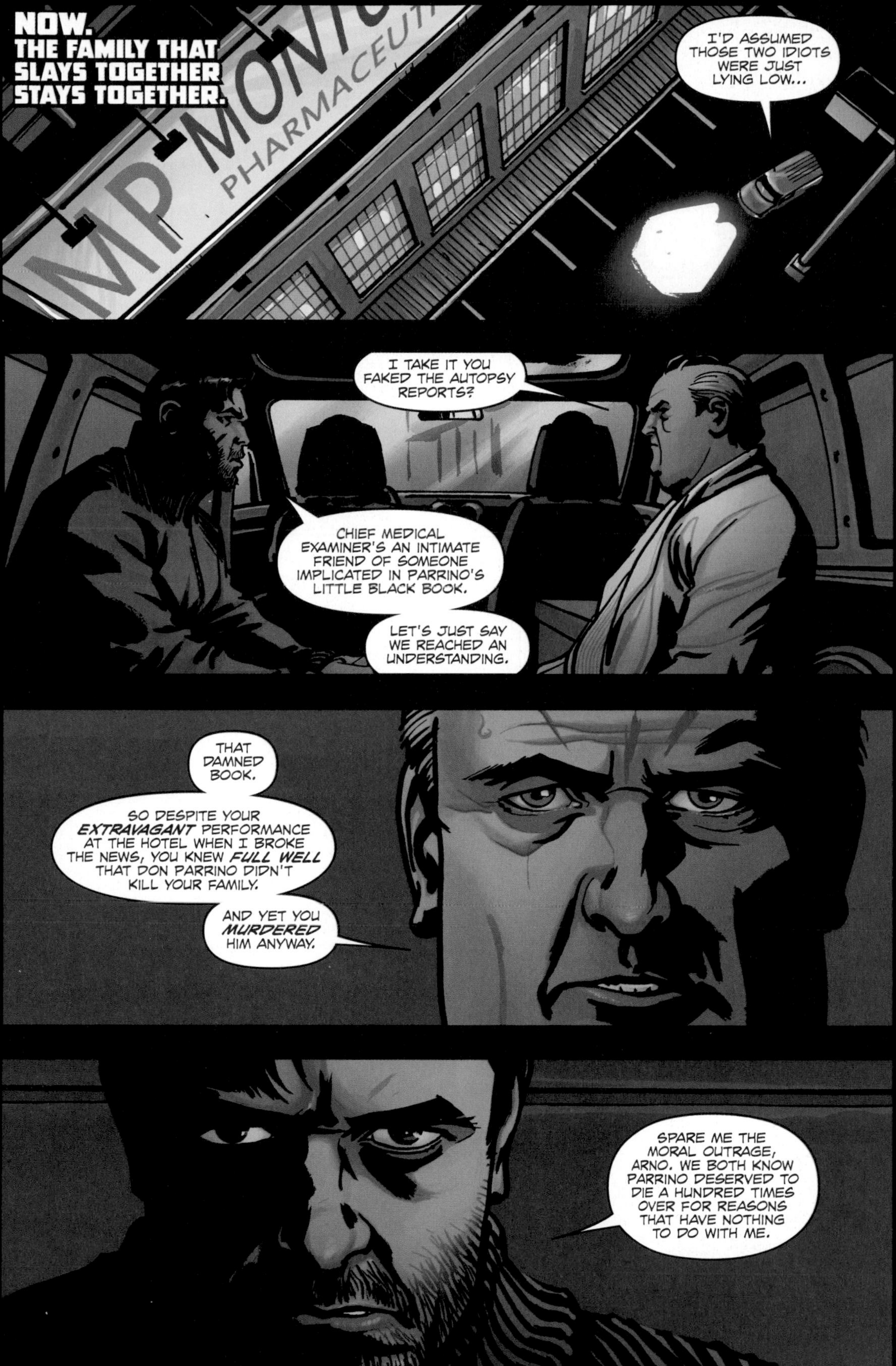
NOW.
THE FAMILY THAT SLAYS TOGETHER STAYS TOGETHER.
MP MONT PHARMACEUTI
I'D ASSUMED THOSE TWO IDIOTS WERE JUST LYING LOW...
I TAKE IT YOU FAKED THE AUTOPSY REPORTS?
CHIEF MEDICAL EXAMINER'S AN INTIMATE FRIEND OF SOMEONE IMPLICATED IN PARRINO'S LITTLE BLACK BOOK.
LET'S JUST SAY WE REACHED AN UNDERSTANDING.
THAT DAMNED BOOK.
SO DESPITE YOUR EXTRAVAGANT PERFORMANCE AT THE HOTEL WHEN I BROKE THE NEWS, YOU KNEW FULL WELL THAT DON PARRINO DIDN'T KILL YOUR FAMILY.
AND YET YOU MURDERED HIM ANYWAY.
SPARE ME THE MORAL OUTRAGE, ARNO. WE BOTH KNOW PARRINO DESERVED TO DIE A HUNDRED TIMES OVER FOR REASONS THAT HAVE NOTHING TO DO WITH ME.

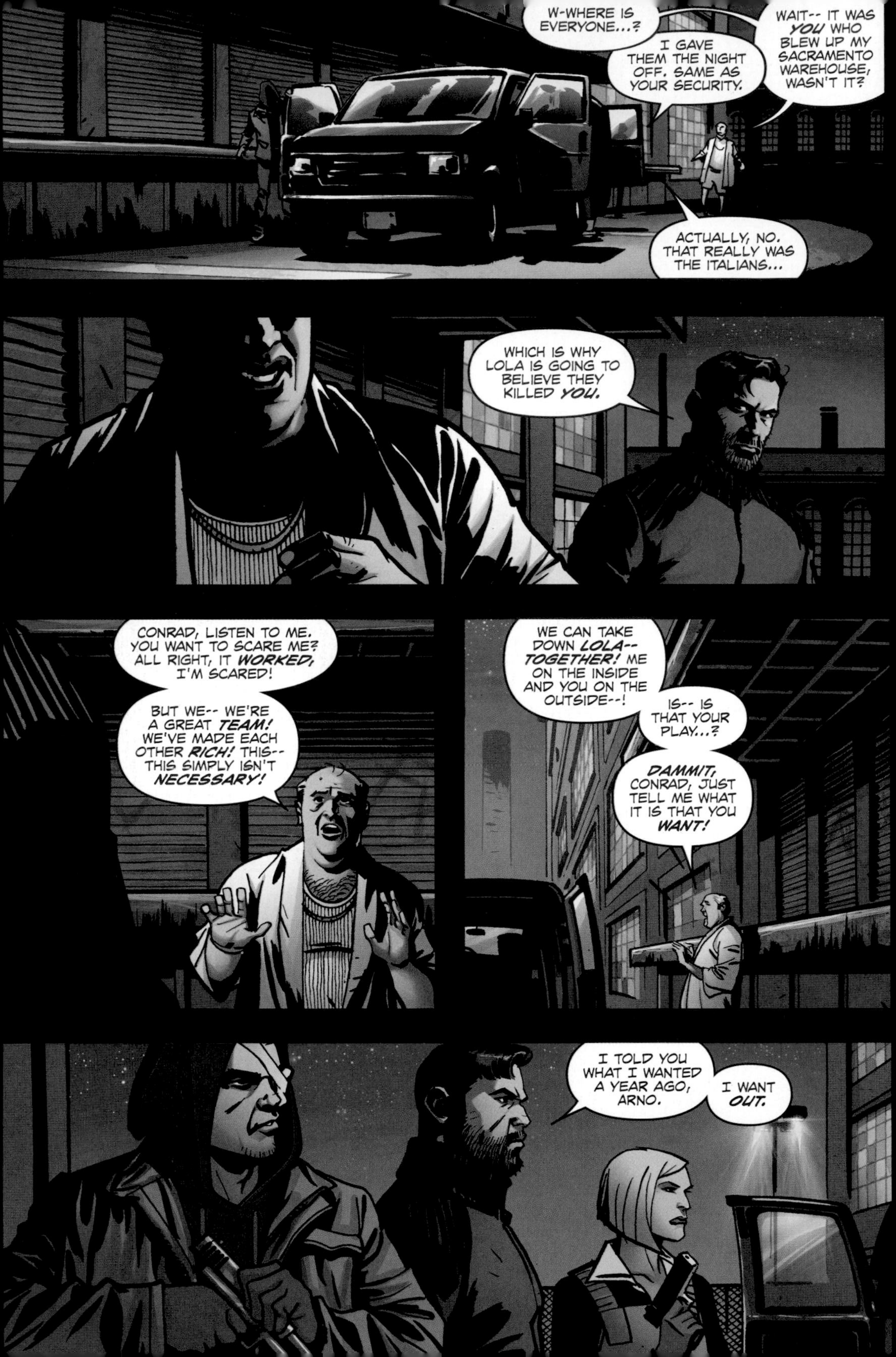
W-WHERE IS EVERYONE...?
I GAVE THEM THE NIGHT OFF. SAME AS YOUR SECURITY.
WAIT-- IT WAS *YOU* WHO BLEW UP MY SACRAMENTO WAREHOUSE, WASN'T IT?
ACTUALLY, NO. THAT REALLY WAS THE ITALIANS...
WHICH IS WHY LOLA IS GOING TO BELIEVE THEY KILLED *YOU.*
CONRAD, LISTEN TO ME. YOU WANT TO SCARE ME? ALL RIGHT, IT *WORKED,* I'M SCARED!
BUT WE-- WE'RE A GREAT *TEAM!* WE'VE MADE EACH OTHER *RICH!* THIS-- THIS SIMPLY ISN'T *NECESSARY!*
WE CAN TAKE DOWN *LOLA-- TOGETHER!* ME ON THE INSIDE AND YOU ON THE OUTSIDE--!
IS-- IS THAT YOUR PLAY...?
DAMMIT, CONRAD, JUST TELL ME WHAT IT IS THAT YOU *WANT!*
I TOLD YOU WHAT I WANTED A YEAR AGO, ARNO.
I WANT *OUT.*

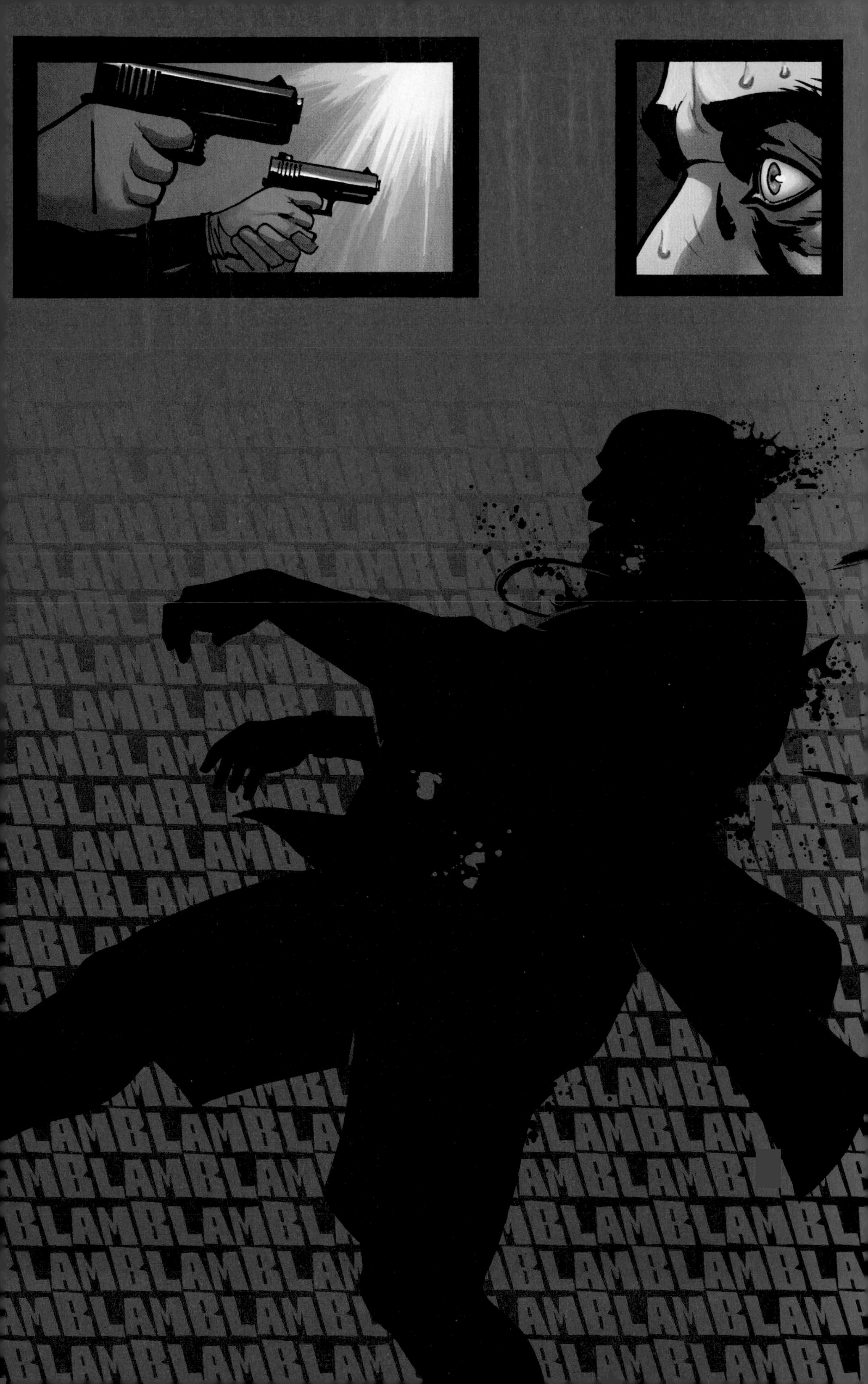
BLAMBLAMBLAMBLAM

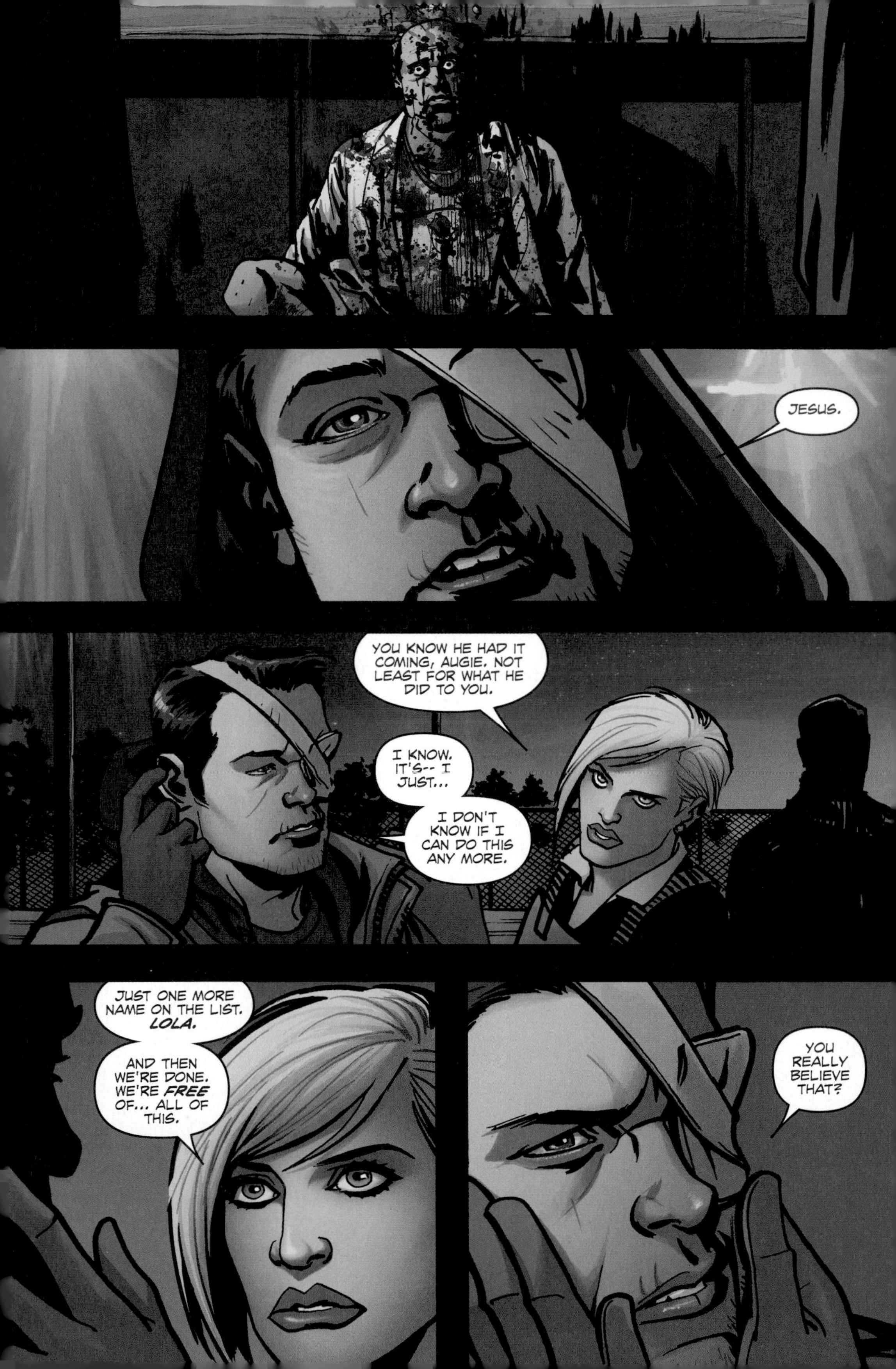
JESUS.
YOU KNOW HE HAD IT COMING, AUGIE. NOT LEAST FOR WHAT HE DID TO YOU.
I KNOW. IT'S-- I JUST...
I DON'T KNOW IF I CAN DO THIS ANY MORE.
JUST ONE MORE NAME ON THE LIST. LOLA.
AND THEN WE'RE DONE. WE'RE FREE OF... ALL OF THIS.
YOU REALLY BELIEVE THAT?

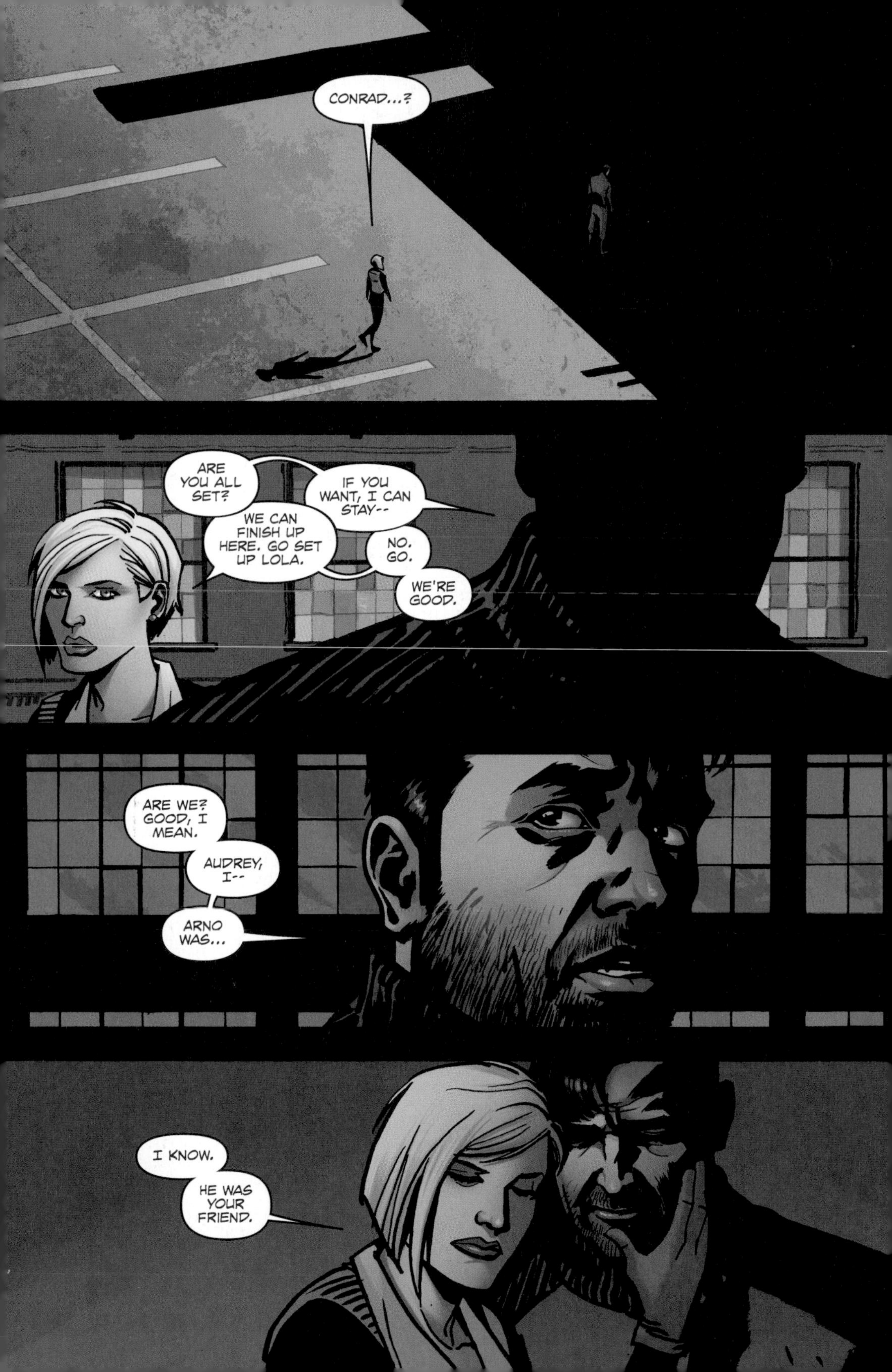
CONRAD...?
ARE YOU ALL SET?
IF YOU WANT, I CAN STAY--
WE CAN FINISH UP HERE. GO SET UP LOLA.
NO. GO.
WE'RE GOOD.
ARE WE? GOOD, I MEAN.
AUDREY, I--
ARNO WAS...
I KNOW.
HE WAS YOUR FRIEND.

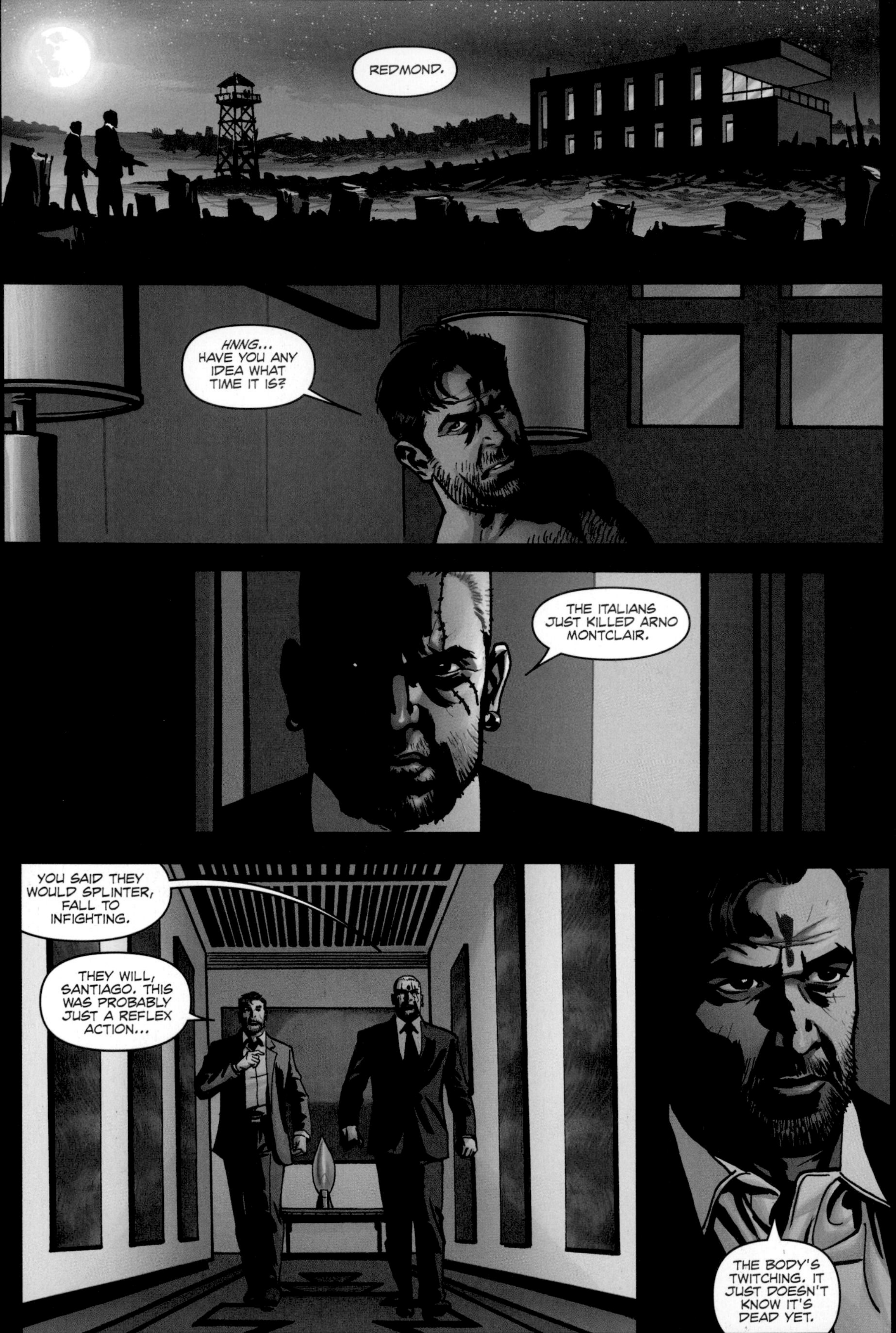
REDMOND.
HNNG... HAVE YOU ANY IDEA WHAT TIME IT IS?
THE ITALIANS JUST KILLED ARNO MONTCLAIR.
YOU SAID THEY WOULD SPLINTER, FALL TO INFIGHTING.
THEY WILL, SANTIAGO. THIS WAS PROBABLY JUST A REFLEX ACTION...
THE BODY'S TWITCHING. IT JUST DOESN'T KNOW IT'S DEAD YET.

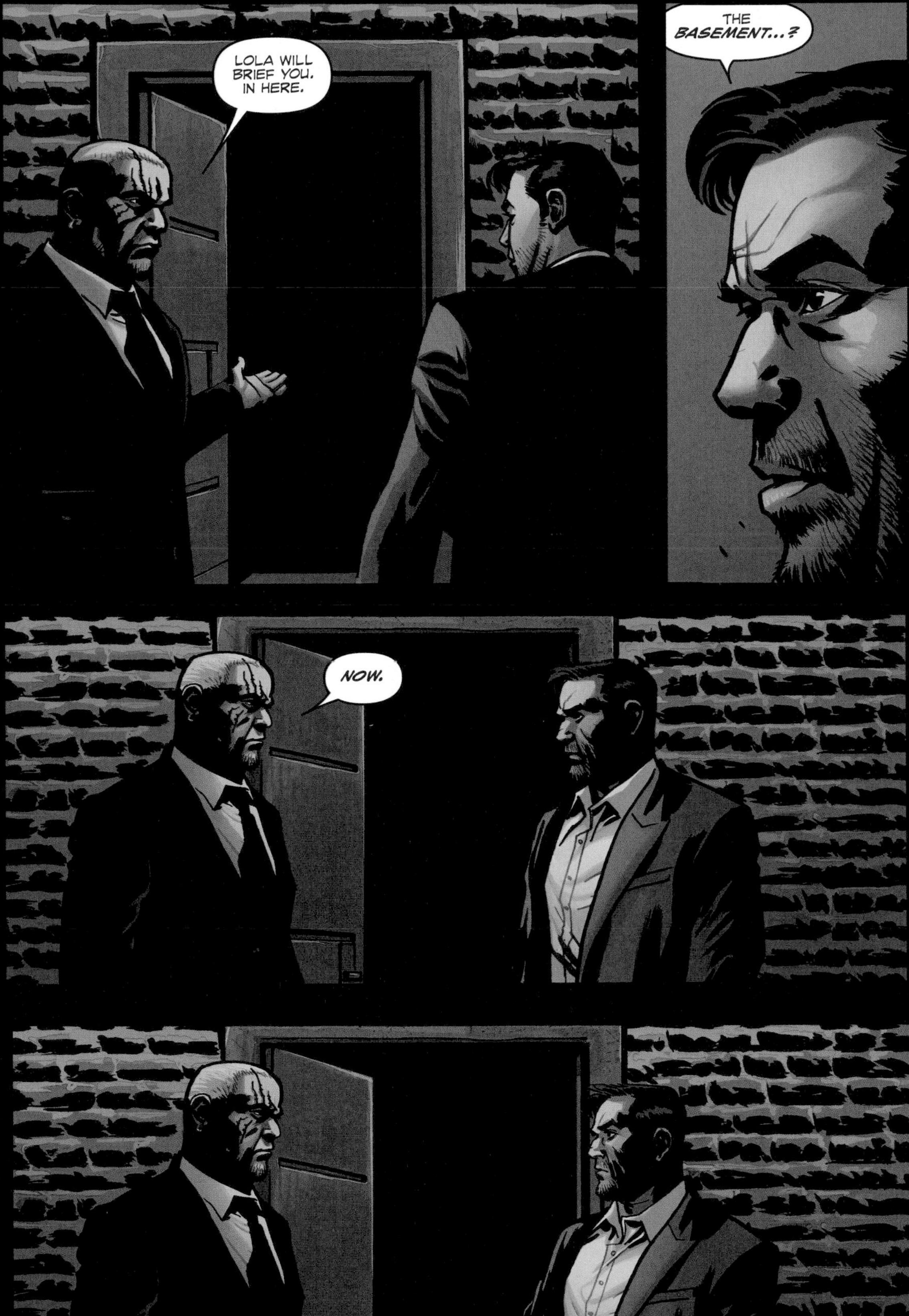
LOLA WILL BRIEF YOU. IN HERE.
THE BASEMENT...?
NOW.

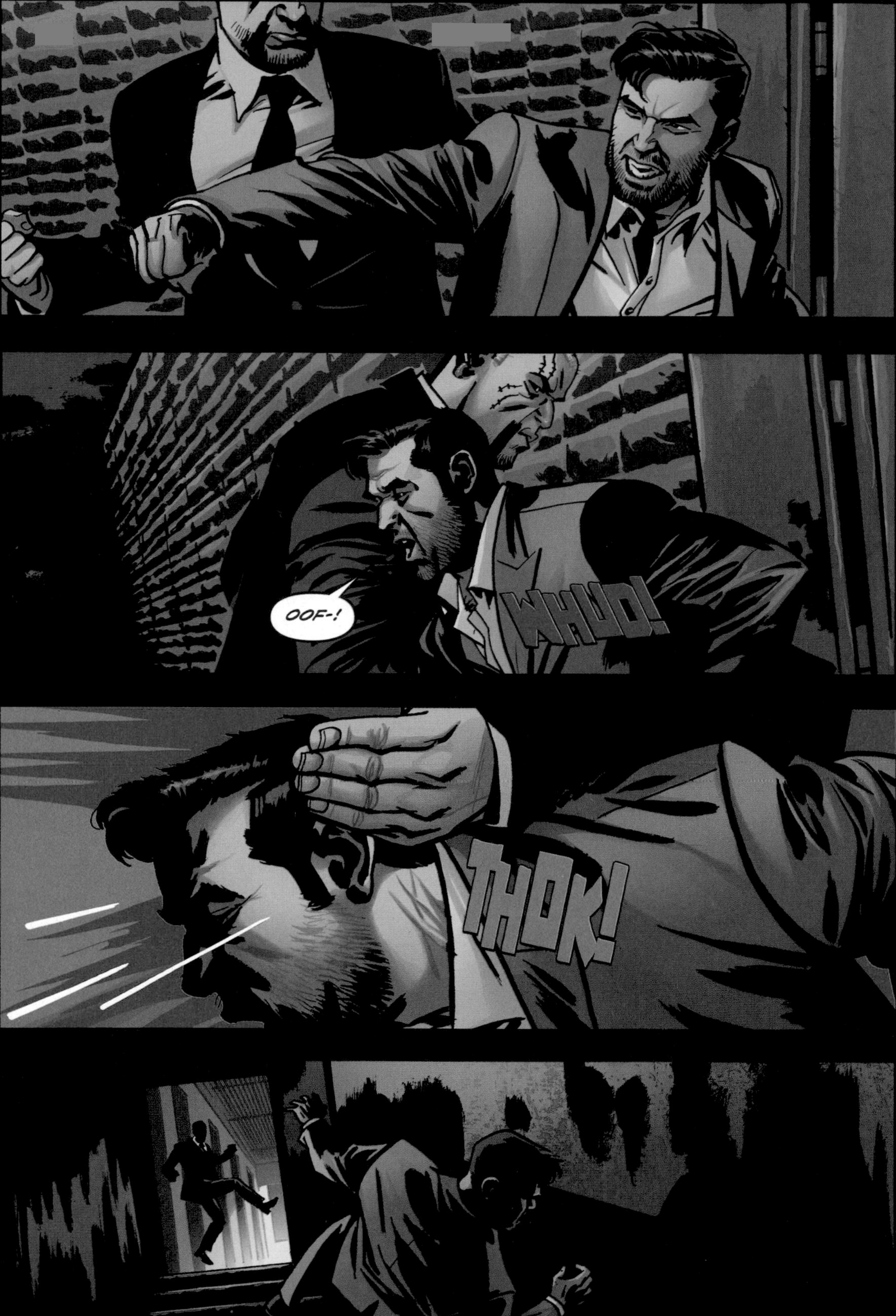
OOF-!
WHUD!
THOK!

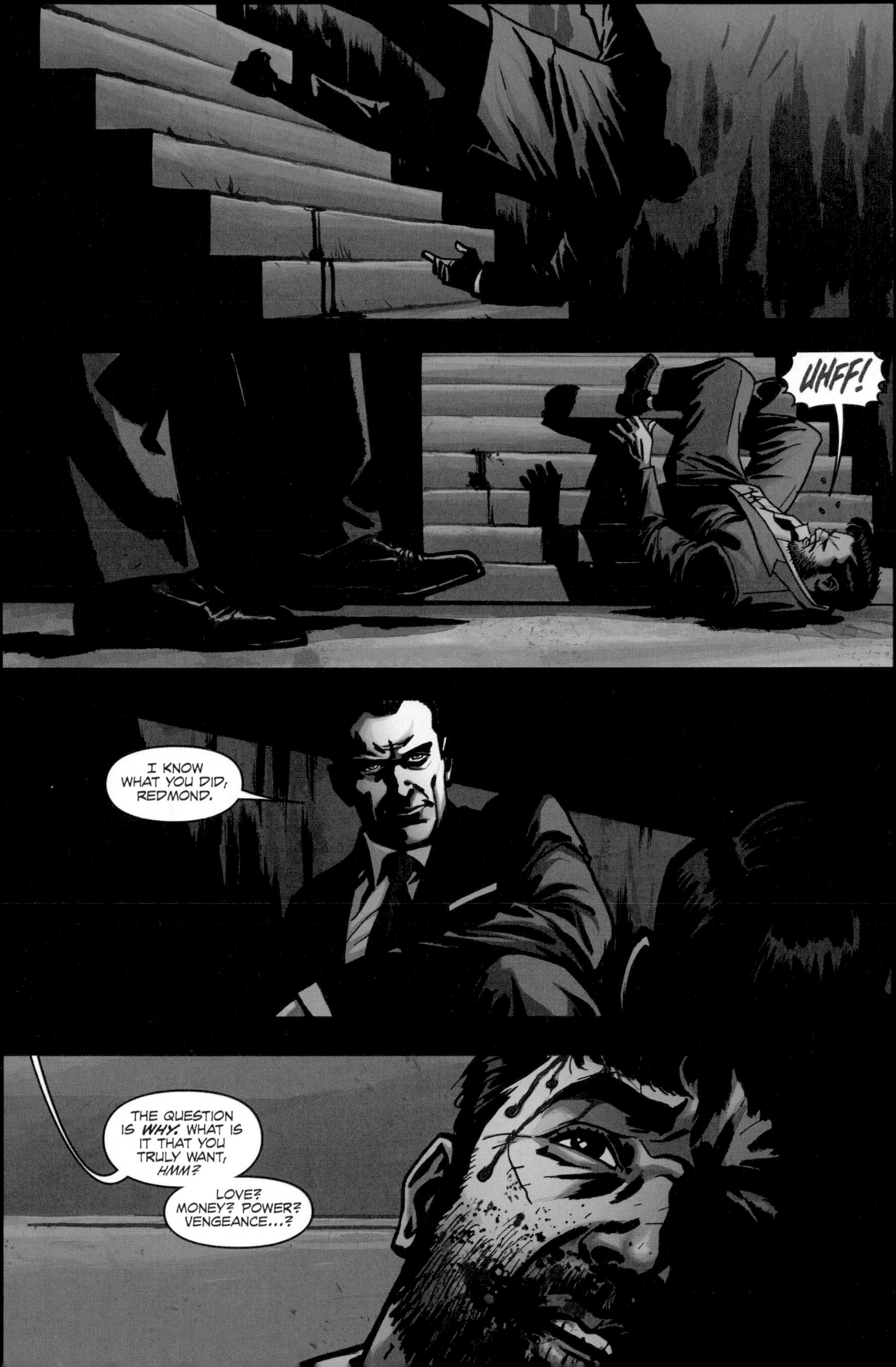
UHFF!
I KNOW WHAT YOU DID, REDMOND.
THE QUESTION IS WHY. WHAT IS IT THAT YOU TRULY WANT, HMM?
LOVE? MONEY? POWER? VENGEANCE...?

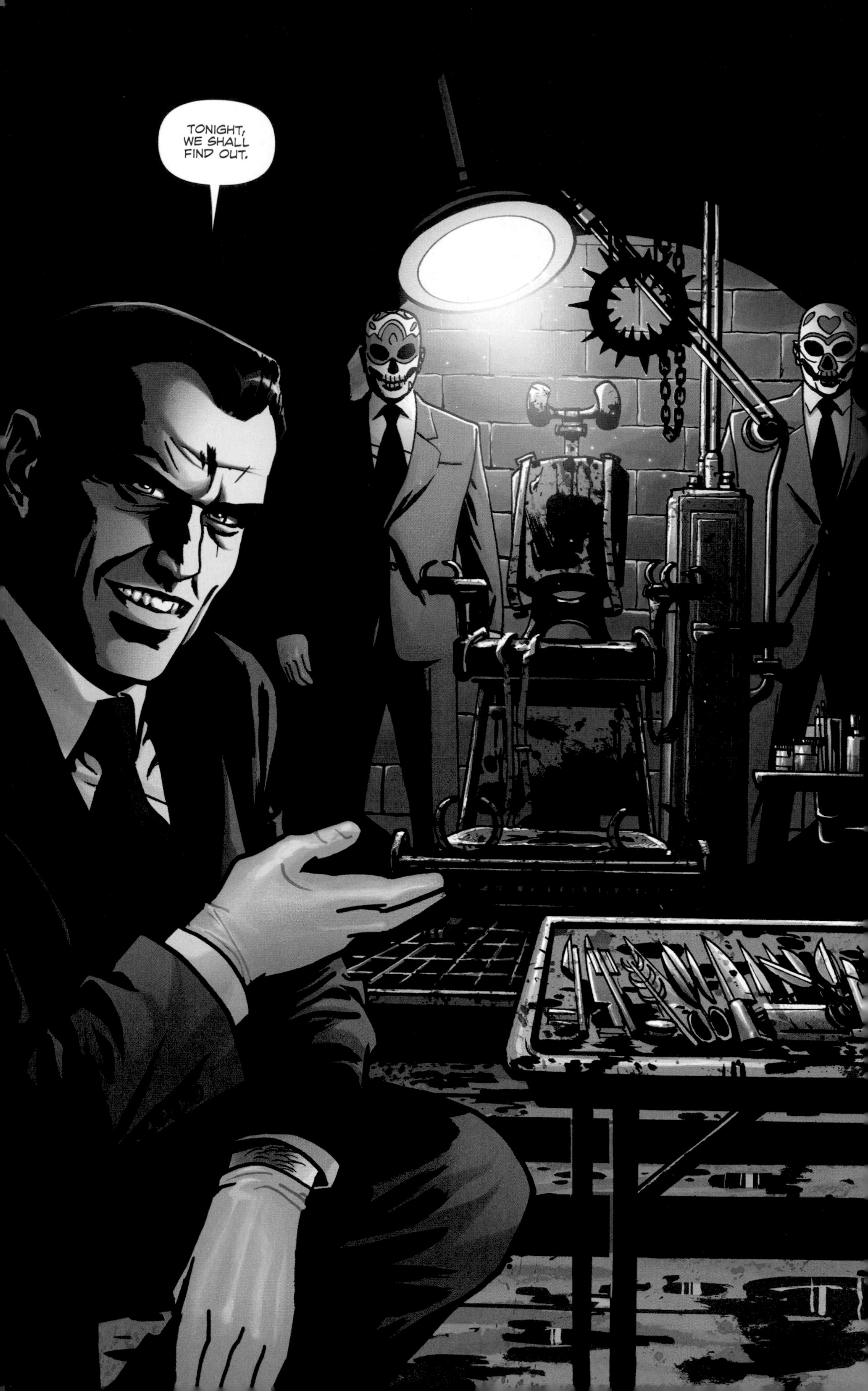
TONIGHT, WE SHALL FIND OUT.

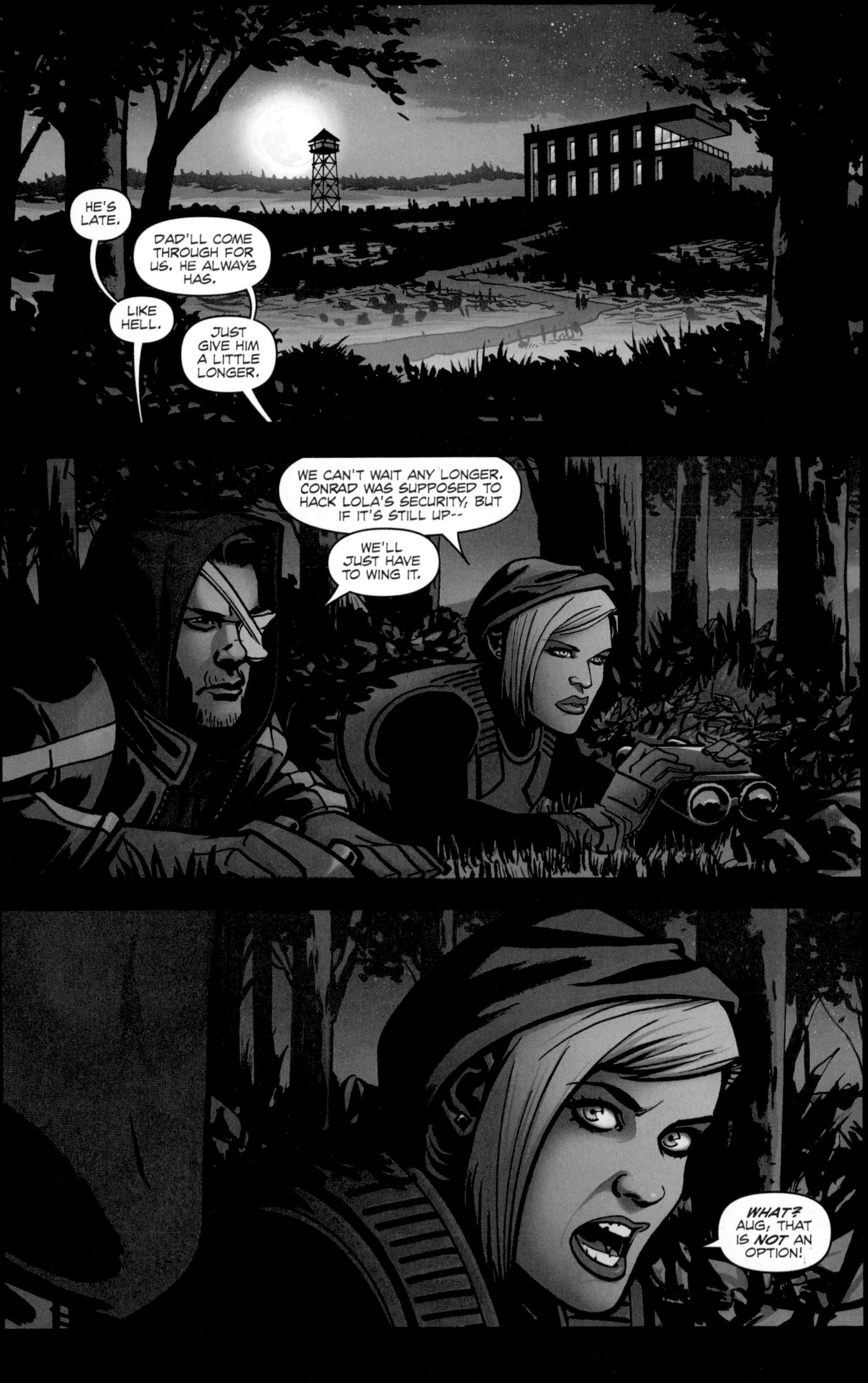
HE'S LATE.
DAD'LL COME THROUGH FOR US. HE ALWAYS HAS.
LIKE HELL.
JUST GIVE HIM A LITTLE LONGER.
WE CAN'T WAIT ANY LONGER. CONRAD WAS SUPPOSED TO HACK LOLA'S SECURITY, BUT IF IT'S STILL UP--
WE'LL JUST HAVE TO WING IT.
WHAT? AUG, THAT IS NOT AN OPTION!

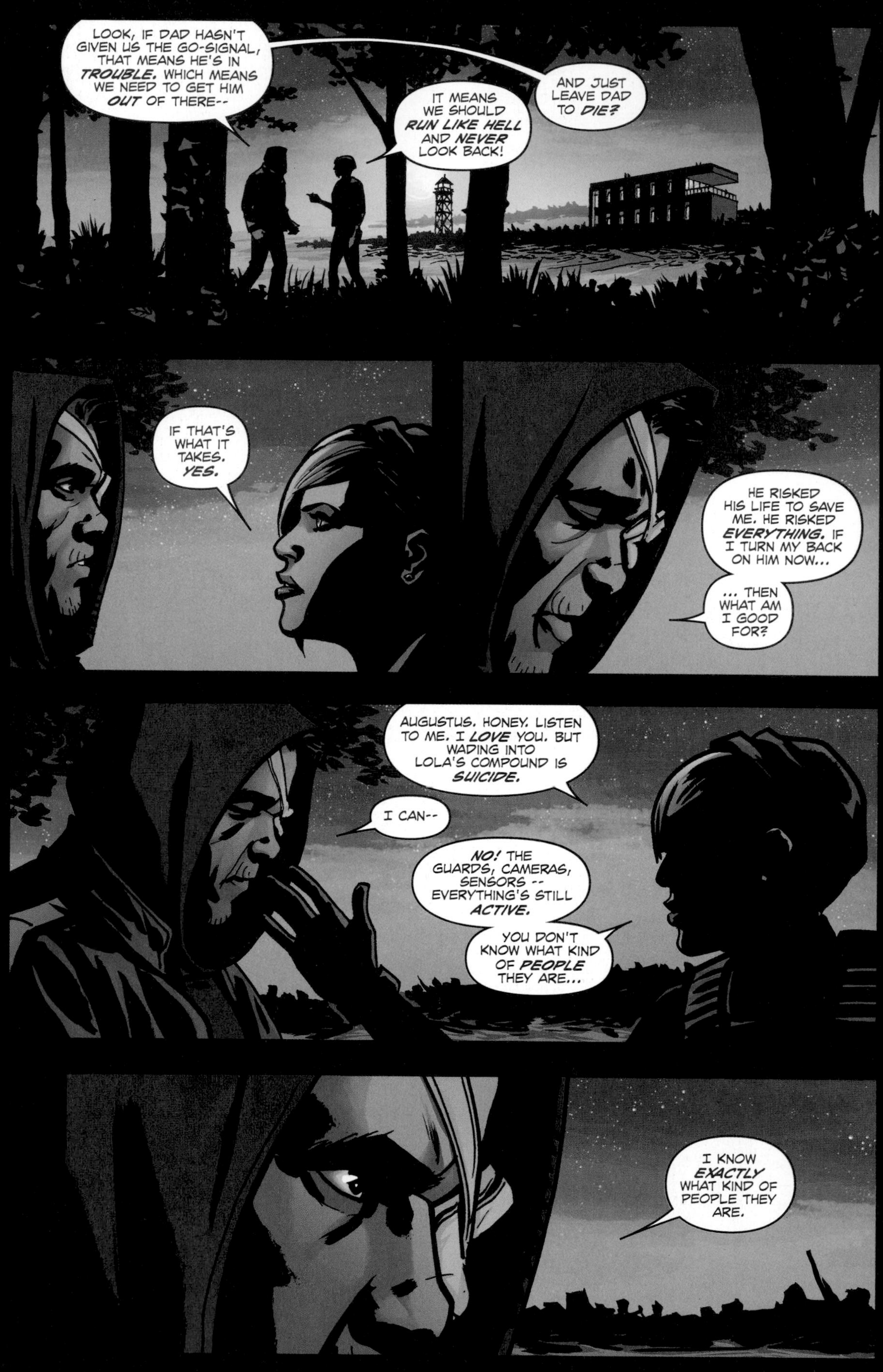
LOOK, IF DAD HASN'T GIVEN US THE GO-SIGNAL, THAT MEANS HE'S IN *TROUBLE.* WHICH MEANS WE NEED TO GET HIM *OUT* OF THERE--
IT MEANS WE SHOULD *RUN LIKE HELL* AND *NEVER* LOOK BACK!
AND JUST LEAVE DAD TO *DIE?*
IF THAT'S WHAT IT TAKES. *YES.*
HE RISKED HIS LIFE TO SAVE ME. HE RISKED *EVERYTHING.* IF I TURN MY BACK ON HIM NOW...
... THEN WHAT AM I GOOD FOR?
AUGUSTUS. HONEY. LISTEN TO ME. I *LOVE* YOU. BUT WADING INTO LOLA'S COMPOUND IS *SUICIDE.*
I CAN--
NO! THE GUARDS, CAMERAS, SENSORS -- EVERYTHING'S STILL *ACTIVE.*
YOU DON'T KNOW WHAT KIND OF *PEOPLE* THEY ARE...
I KNOW *EXACTLY* WHAT KIND OF PEOPLE THEY ARE.

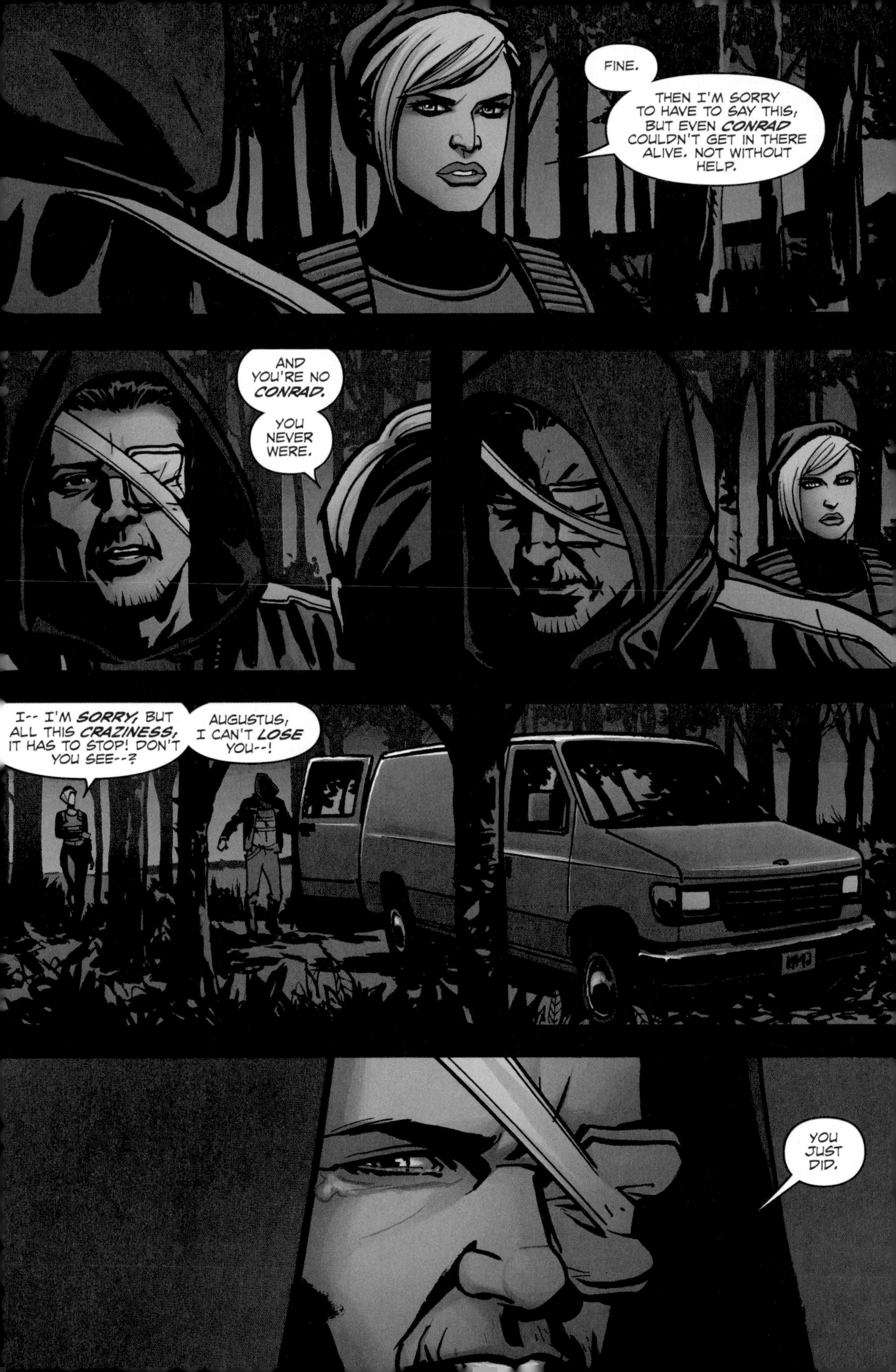
FINE.
THEN I'M SORRY TO HAVE TO SAY THIS, BUT EVEN CONRAD COULDN'T GET IN THERE ALIVE. NOT WITHOUT HELP.
AND YOU'RE NO CONRAD.
YOU NEVER WERE.
I-- I'M SORRY, BUT ALL THIS CRAZINESS, IT HAS TO STOP! DON'T YOU SEE--?
AUGUSTUS, I CAN'T LOSE YOU--!
YOU JUST DID.

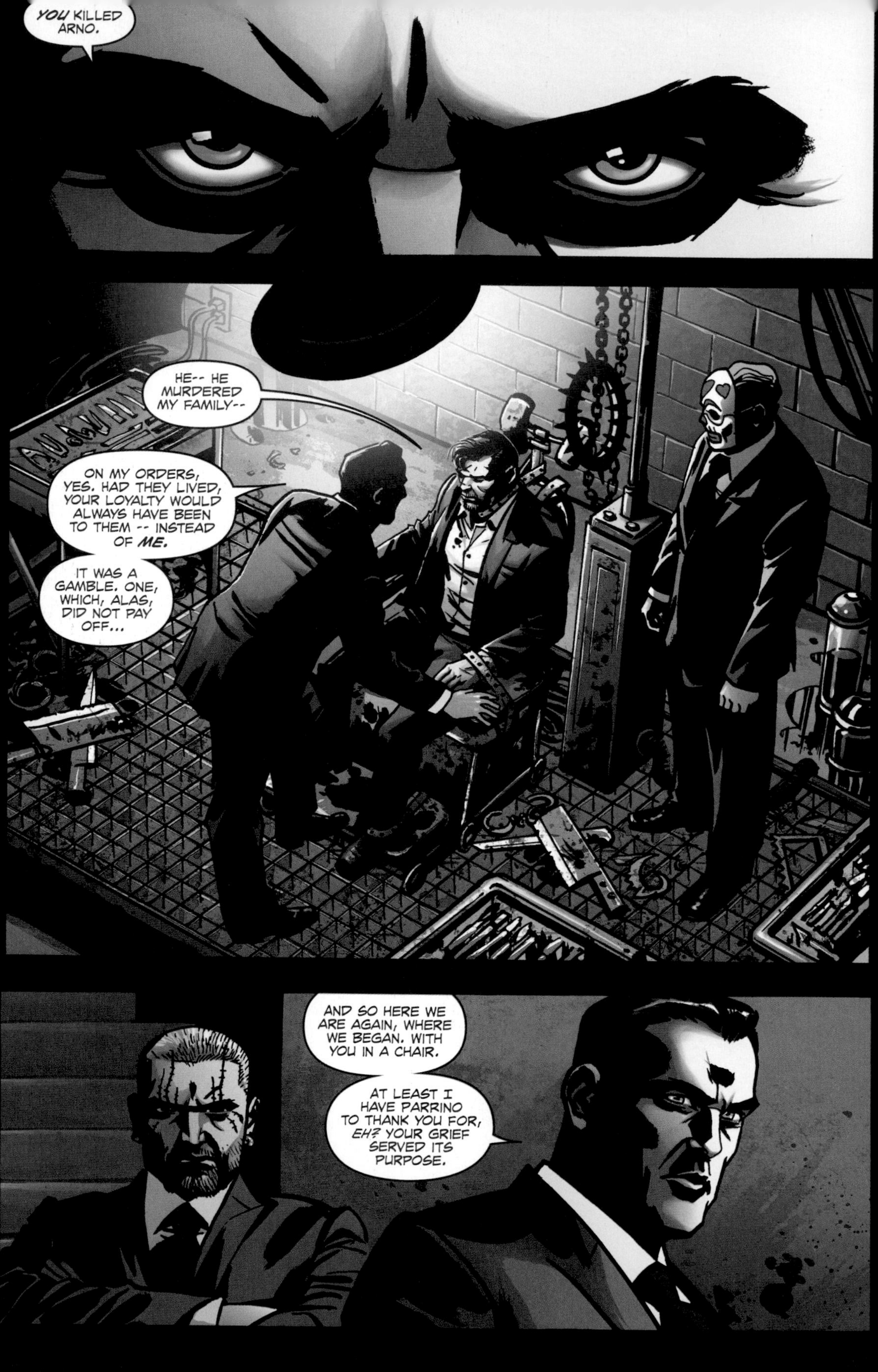
YOU KILLED ARNO.
HE-- HE MURDERED MY FAMILY--
ON MY ORDERS, YES. HAD THEY LIVED, YOUR LOYALTY WOULD ALWAYS HAVE BEEN TO THEM -- INSTEAD OF ME.
IT WAS A GAMBLE. ONE, WHICH, ALAS, DID NOT PAY OFF...
AND SO HERE WE ARE AGAIN, WHERE WE BEGAN. WITH YOU IN A CHAIR.
AT LEAST I HAVE PARRINO TO THANK YOU FOR, EH? YOUR GRIEF SERVED ITS PURPOSE.

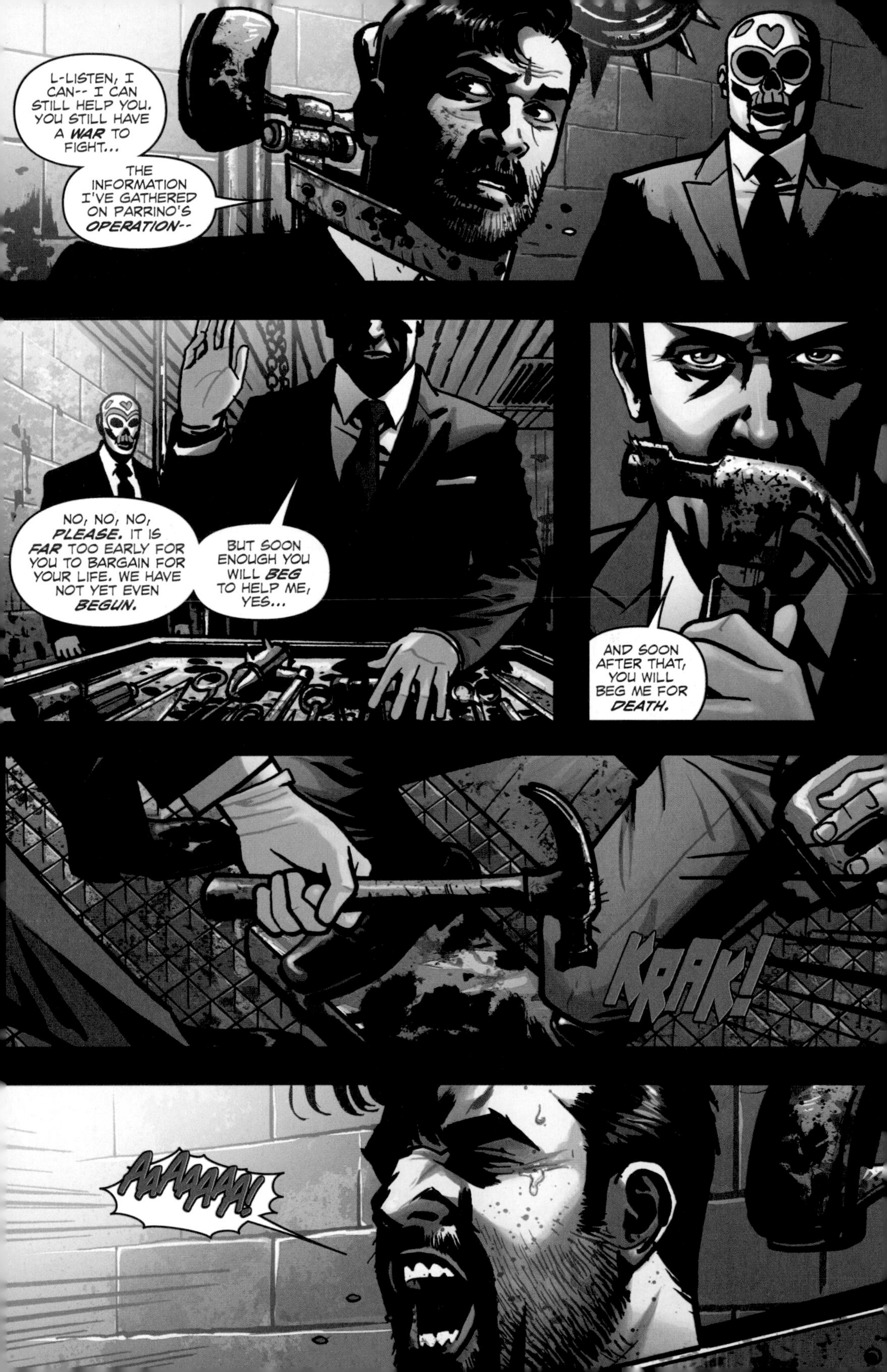
L-LISTEN, I CAN-- I CAN STILL HELP YOU. YOU STILL HAVE A WAR TO FIGHT...
THE INFORMATION I'VE GATHERED ON PARRINO'S OPERATION--
NO, NO, NO, PLEASE. IT IS FAR TOO EARLY FOR YOU TO BARGAIN FOR YOUR LIFE. WE HAVE NOT YET EVEN BEGUN.
BUT SOON ENOUGH YOU WILL BEG TO HELP ME, YES...
AND SOON AFTER THAT, YOU WILL BEG ME FOR DEATH.
KRAK!
AAAAAAA!

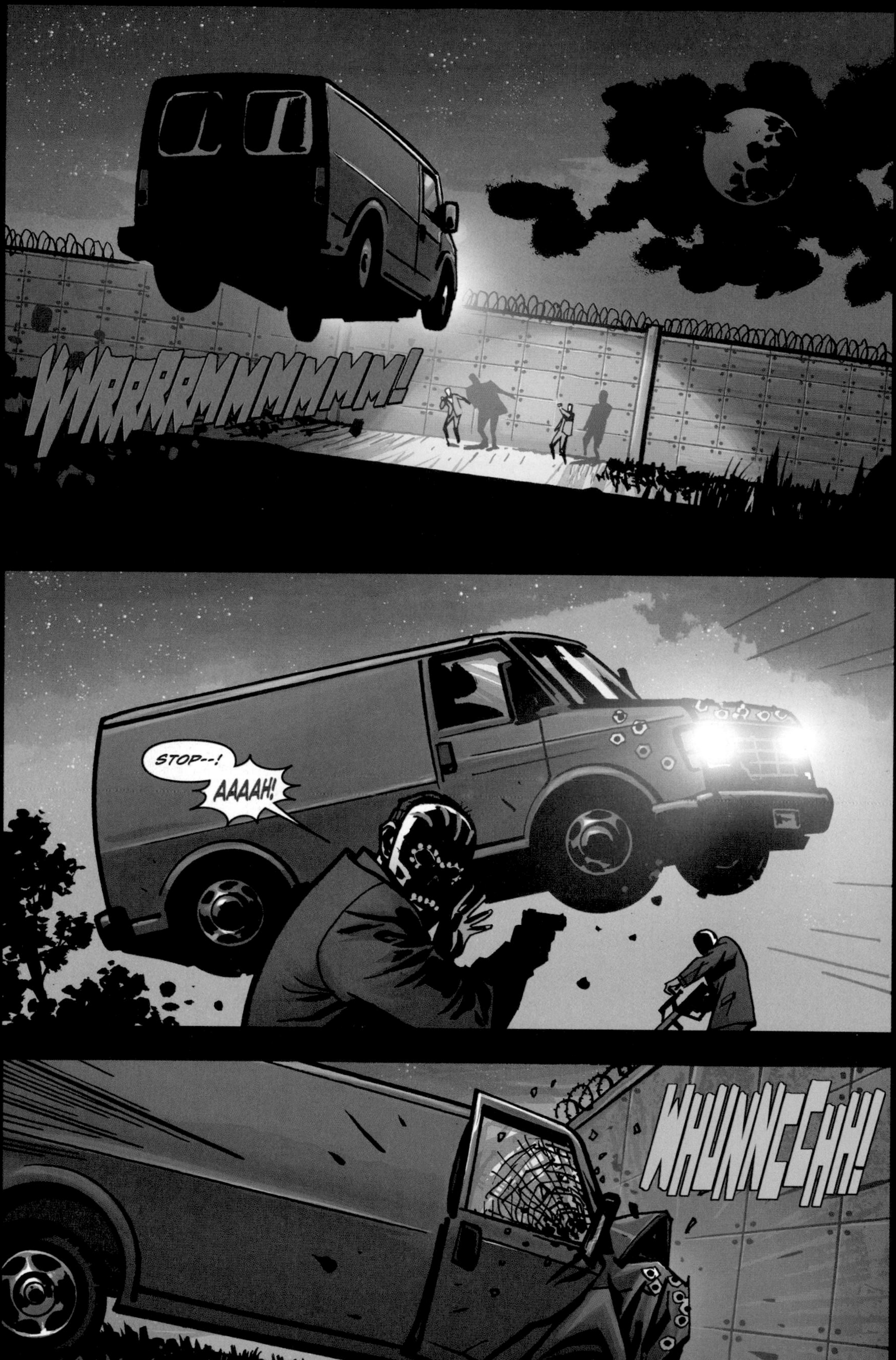
WHRRRRMMMMMMM!
STOP--!
AAAAH!
WHUNNCHH!

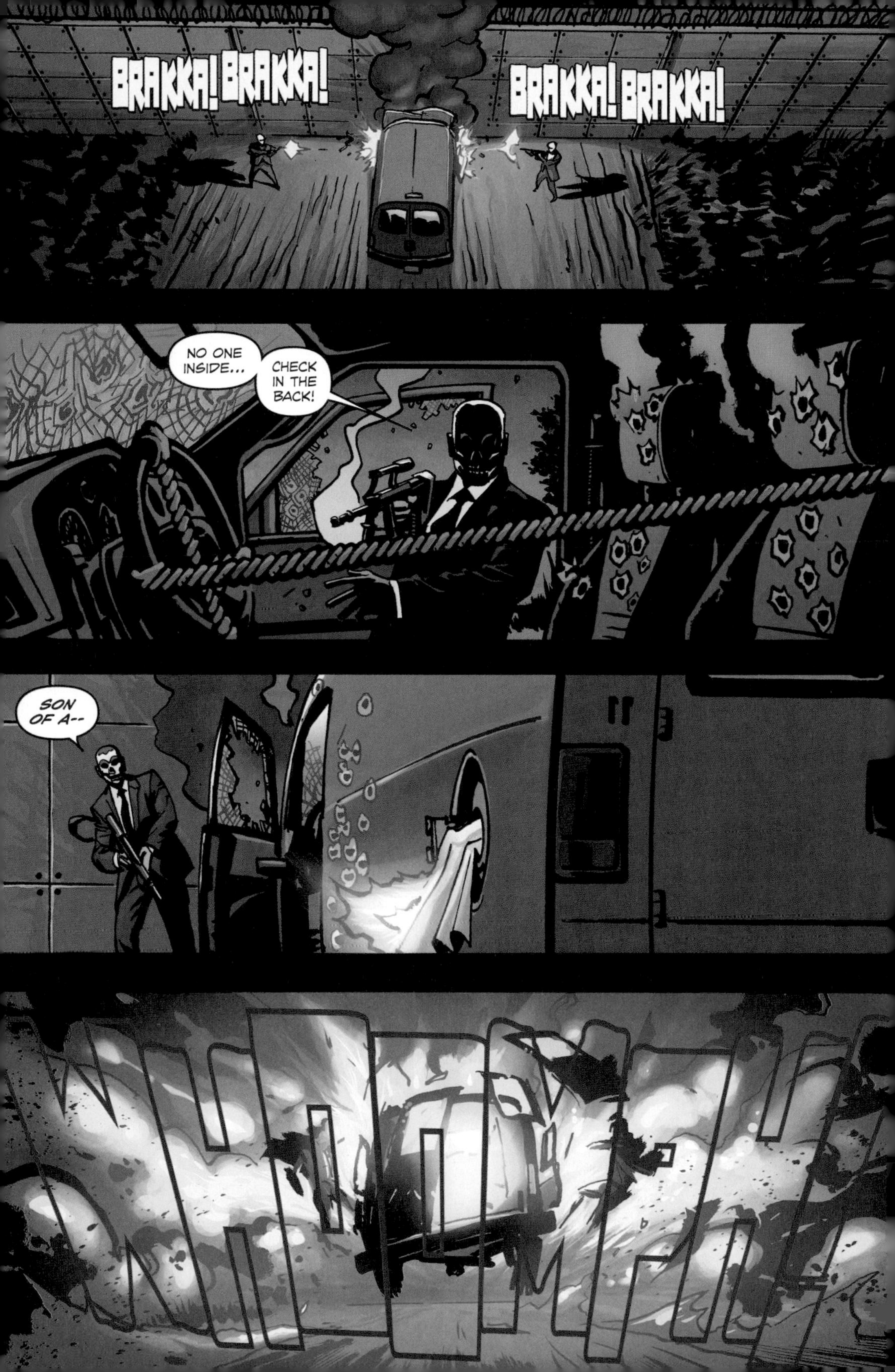
BRAKKA! BRAKKA!
BRAKKA! BRAKKA!
NO ONE INSIDE...
CHECK IN THE BACK!
SON OF A--

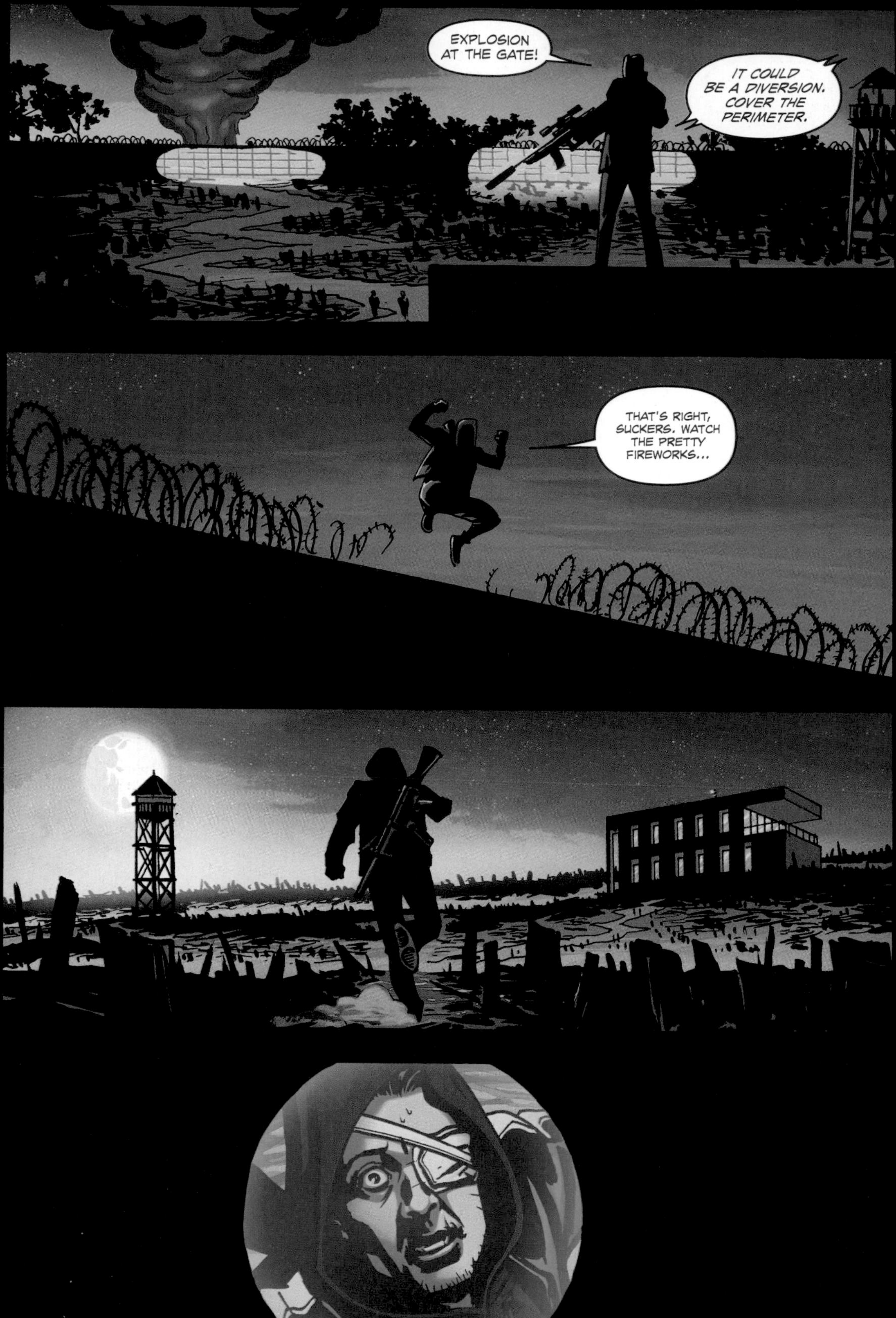
EXPLOSION AT THE GATE!
IT COULD BE A DIVERSION. COVER THE PERIMETER.
THAT'S RIGHT, SUCKERS. WATCH THE PRETTY FIREWORKS...

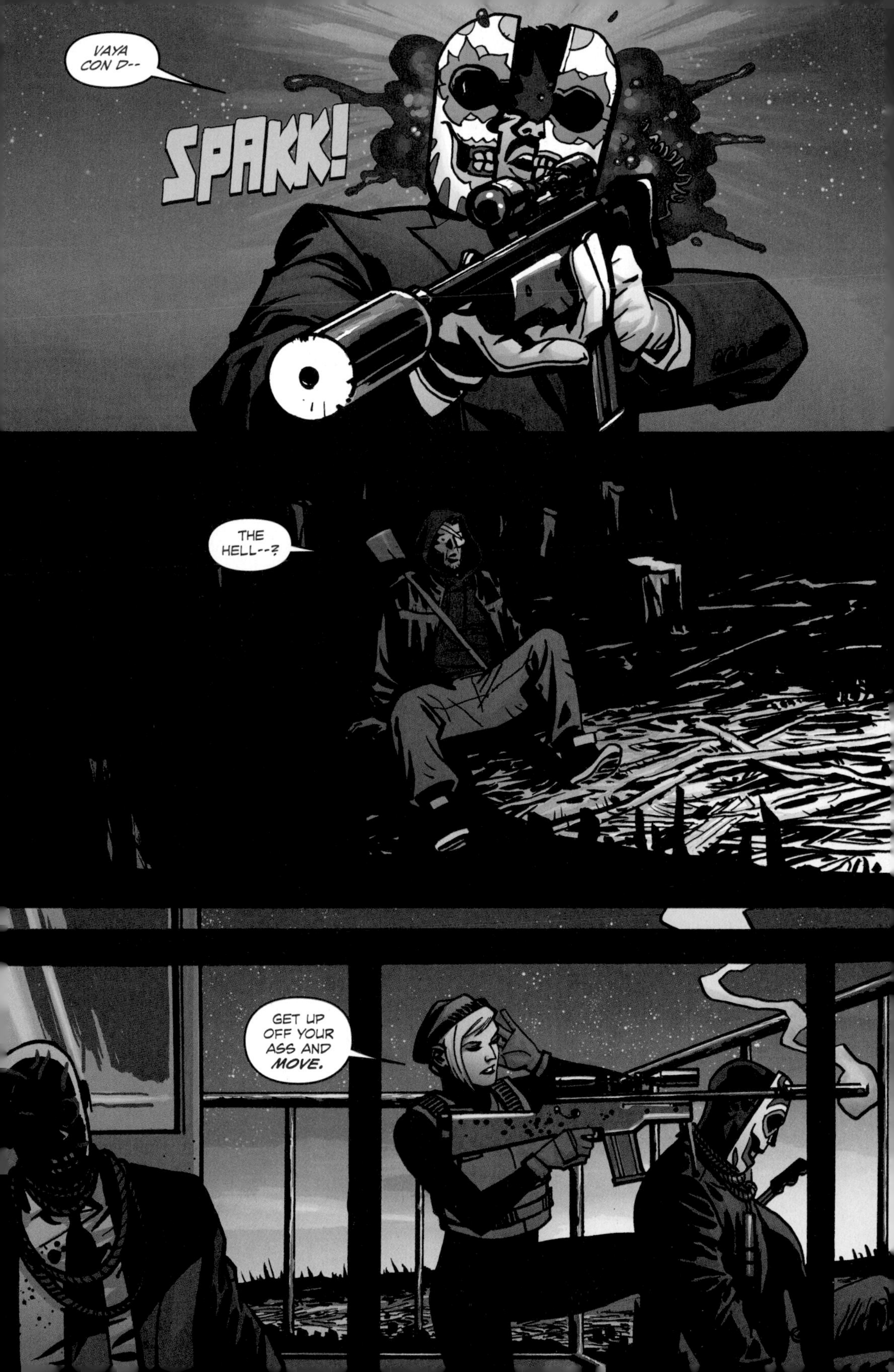
VAYA CON D--
SPAKK!
THE HELL--?
GET UP OFF YOUR ASS AND MOVE.

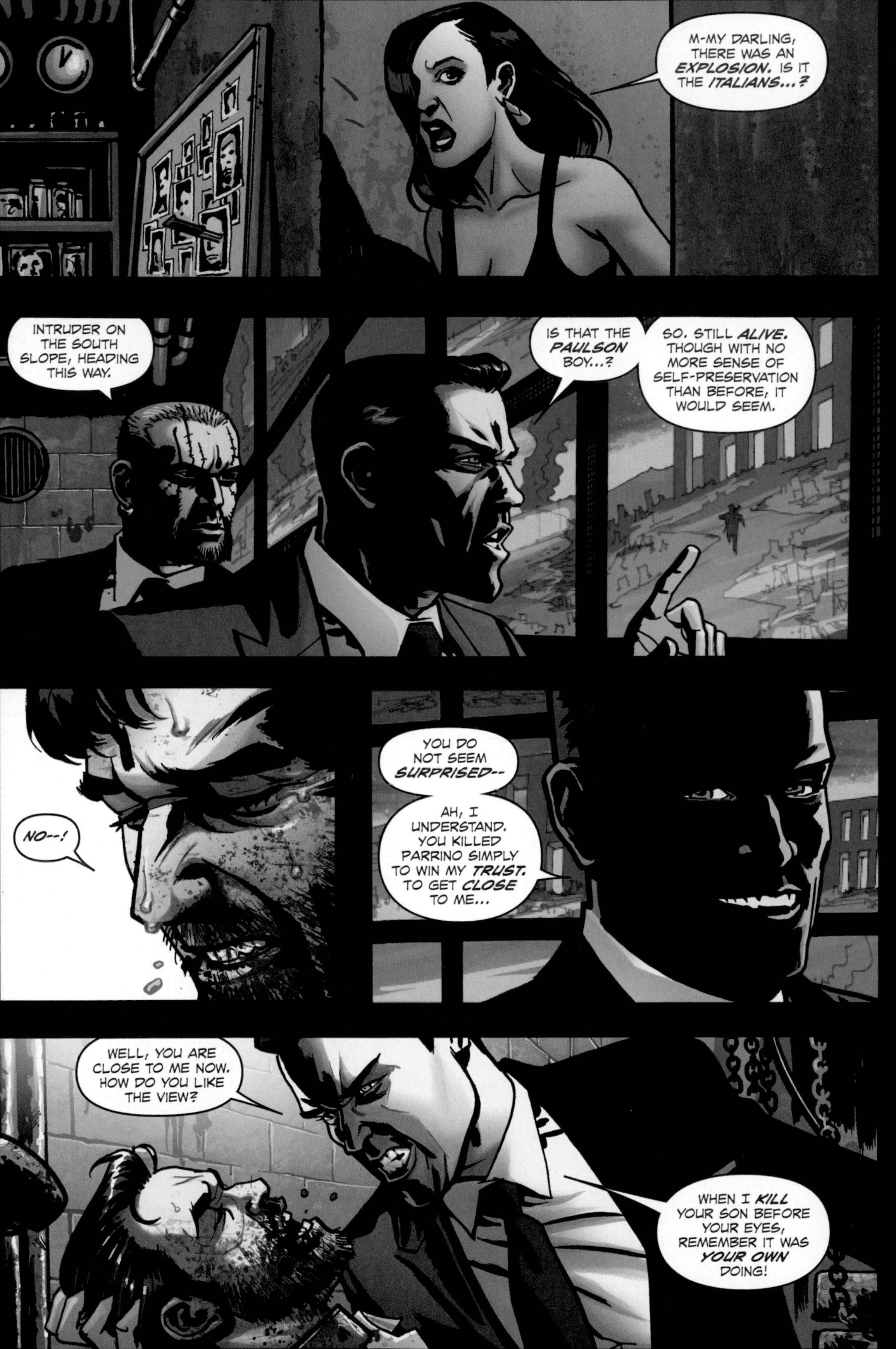
M-MY DARLING, THERE WAS AN EXPLOSION. IS IT THE ITALIANS...?
INTRUDER ON THE SOUTH SLOPE, HEADING THIS WAY.
IS THAT THE PAULSON BOY...?
SO. STILL ALIVE. THOUGH WITH NO MORE SENSE OF SELF-PRESERVATION THAN BEFORE, IT WOULD SEEM.
YOU DO NOT SEEM SURPRISED--
NO--!
AH, I UNDERSTAND. YOU KILLED PARRINO SIMPLY TO WIN MY TRUST. TO GET CLOSE TO ME...
WELL, YOU ARE CLOSE TO ME NOW. HOW DO YOU LIKE THE VIEW?
WHEN I KILL YOUR SON BEFORE YOUR EYES, REMEMBER IT WAS YOUR OWN DOING!

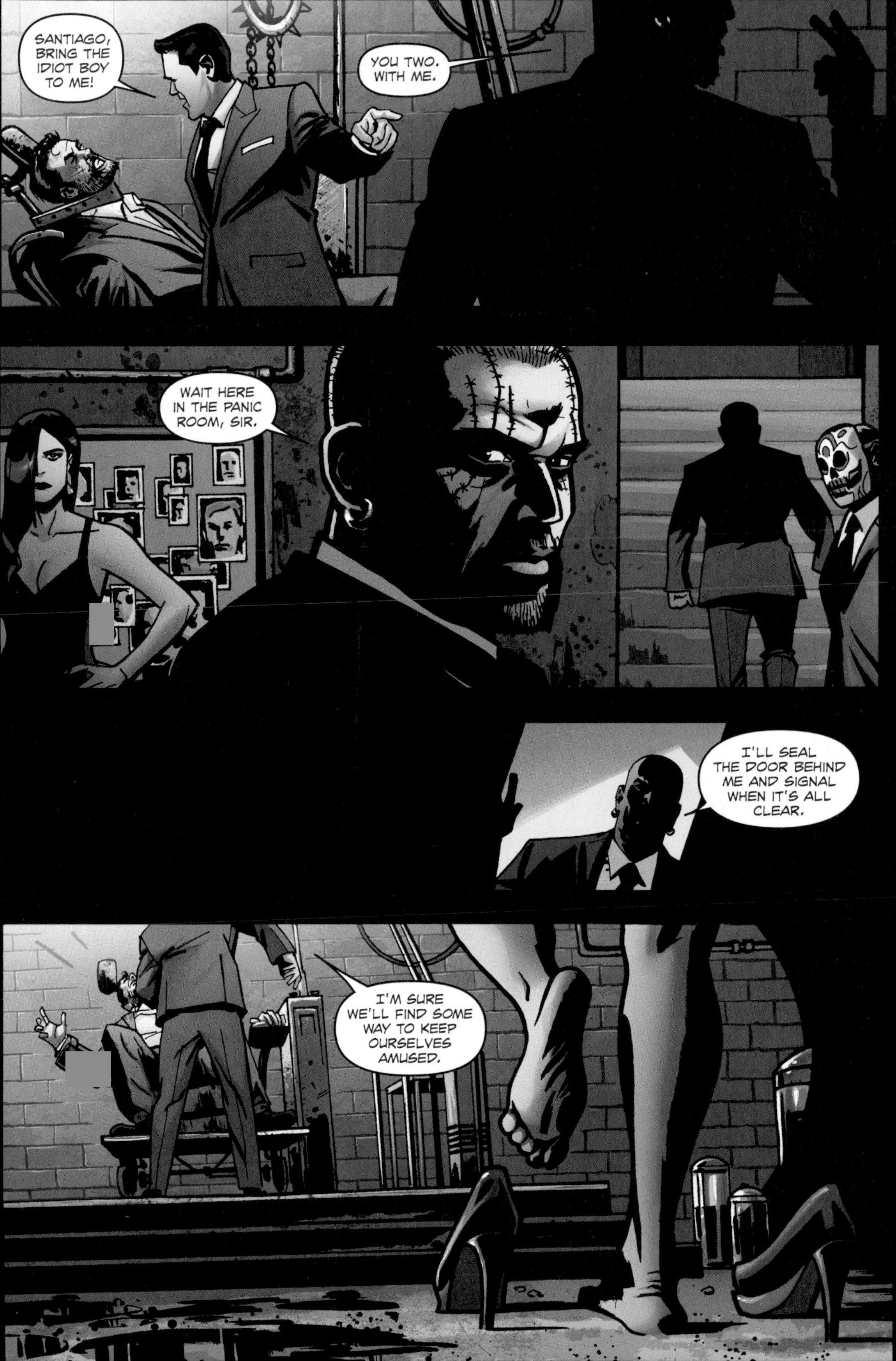
SANTIAGO, BRING THE IDIOT BOY TO ME!
YOU TWO. WITH ME.
WAIT HERE IN THE PANIC ROOM, SIR.
I'LL SEAL THE DOOR BEHIND ME AND SIGNAL WHEN IT'S ALL CLEAR.
I'M SURE WE'LL FIND SOME WAY TO KEEP OURSELVES AMUSED.

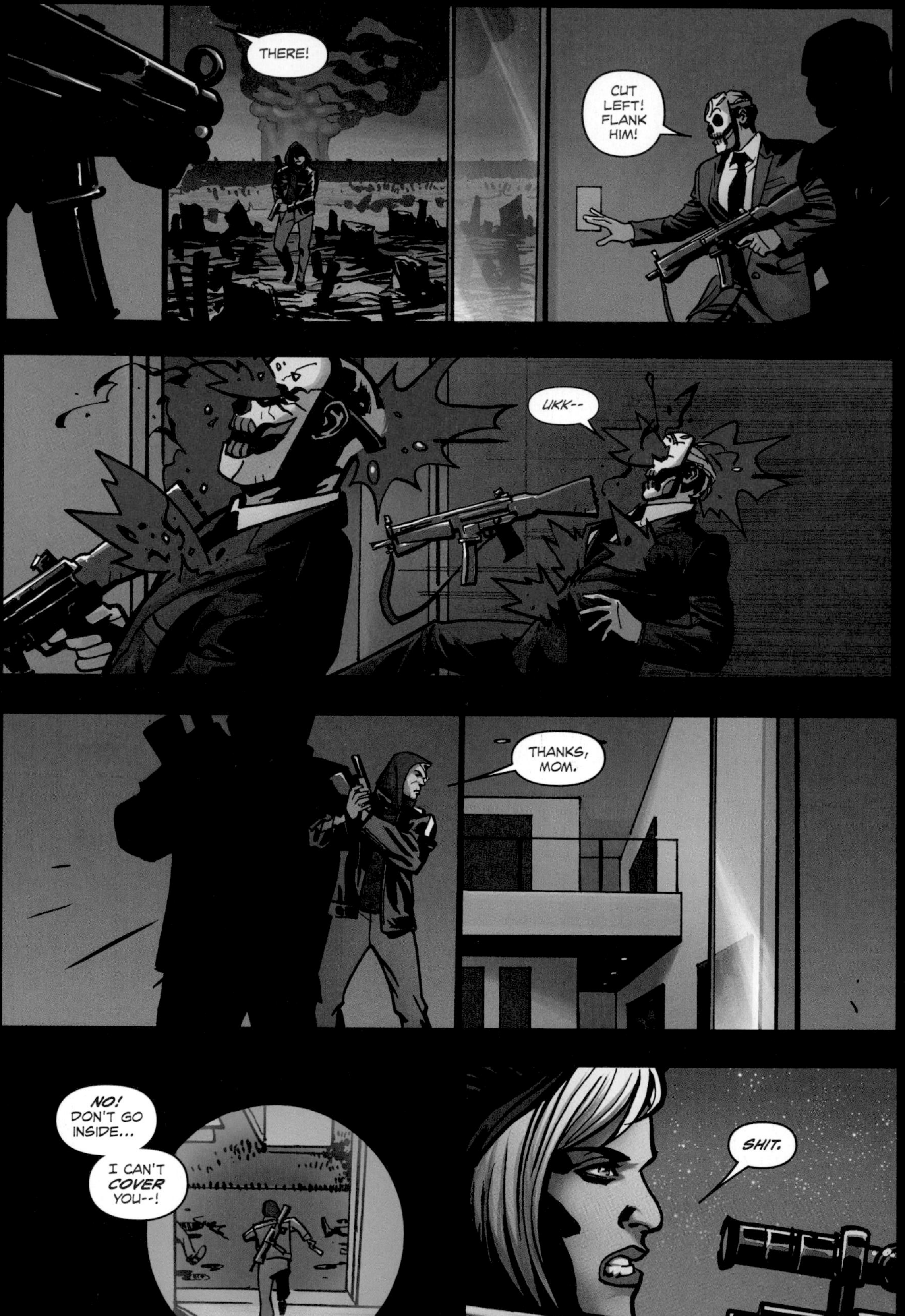
THERE!
CUT LEFT! FLANK HIM!
UKK--
THANKS, MOM.
NO! DON'T GO INSIDE...
I CAN'T COVER YOU--!
SHIT.

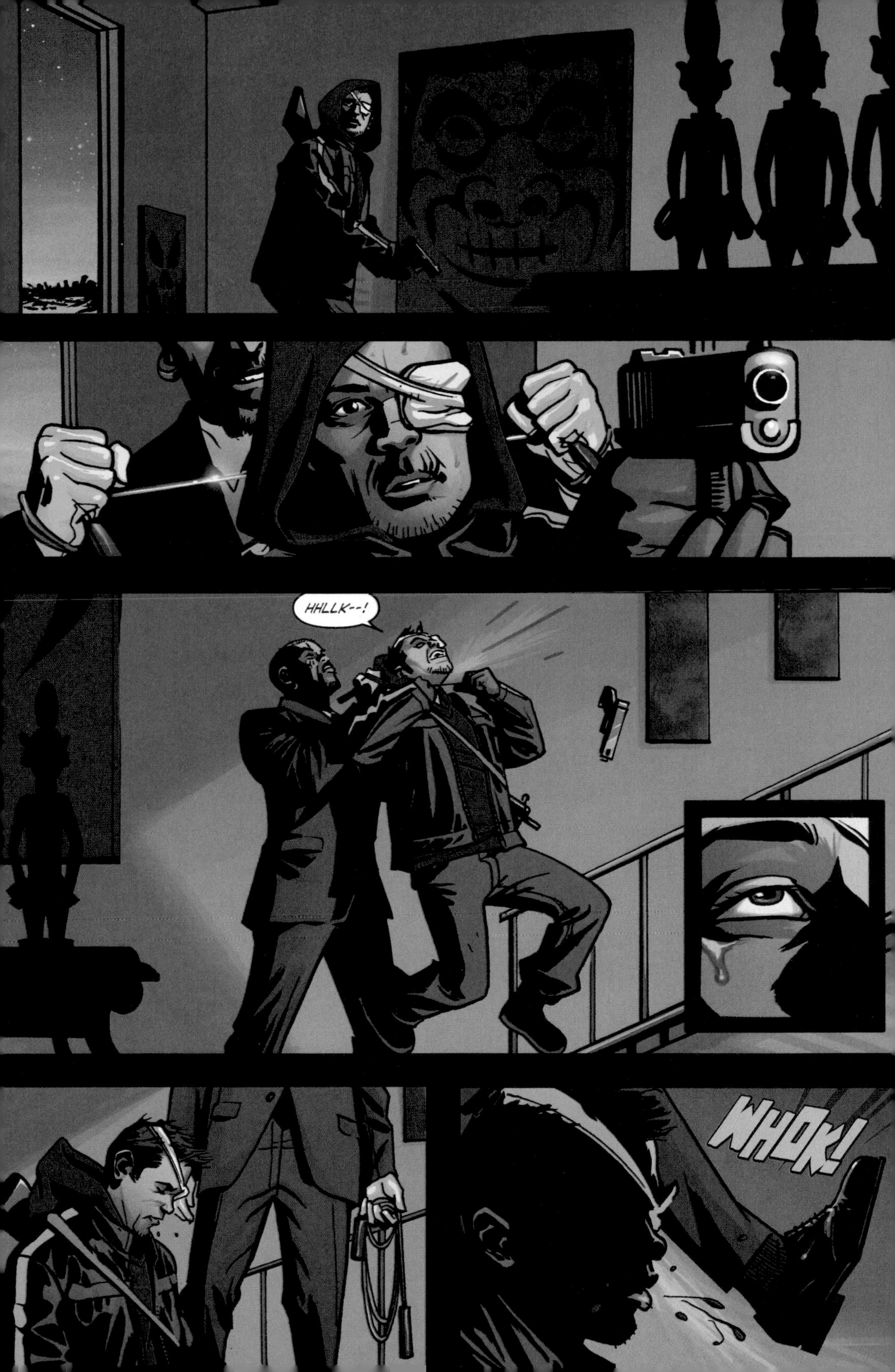
HHLLK--!
WHOK!

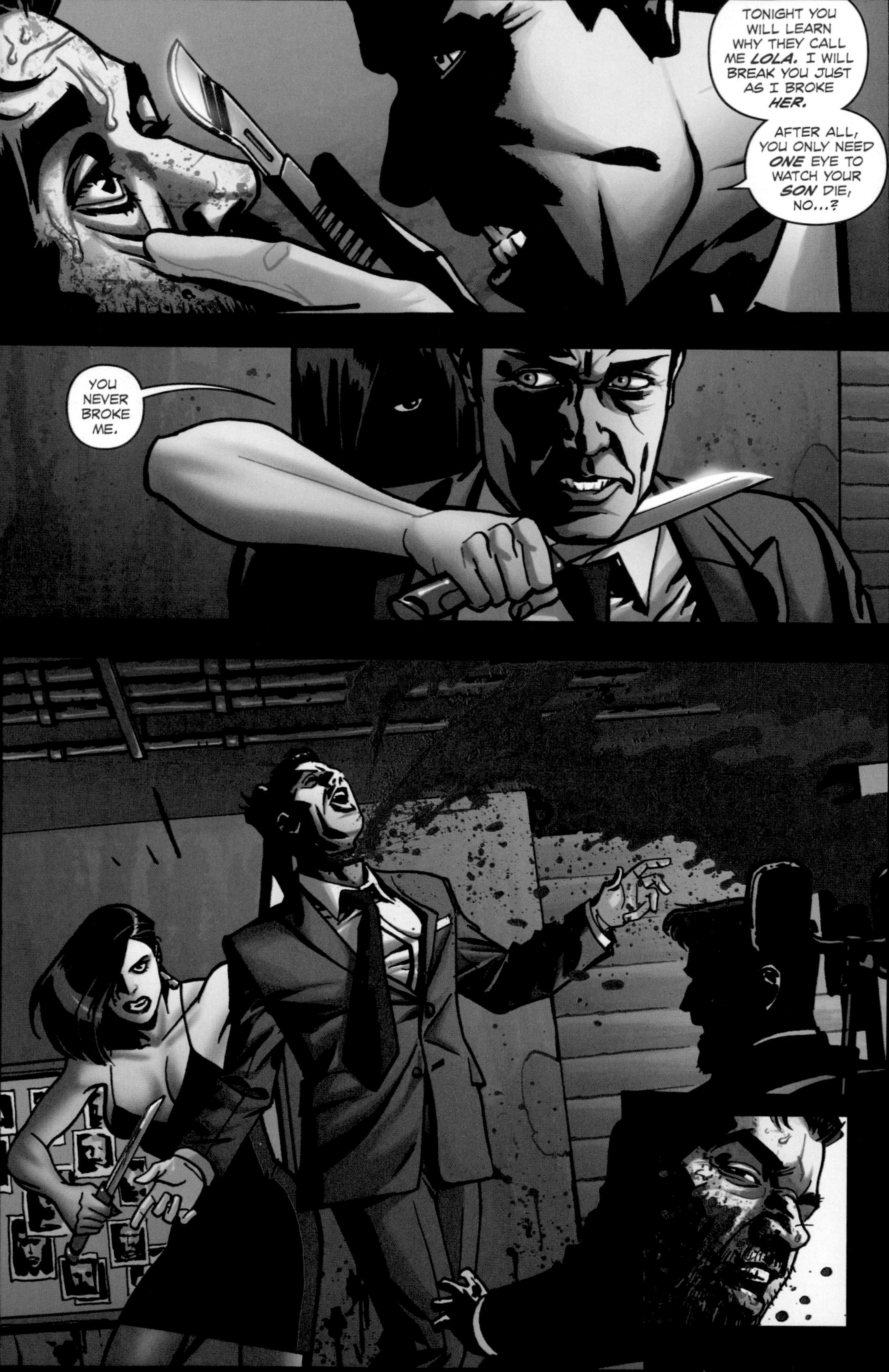
TONIGHT YOU WILL LEARN WHY THEY CALL ME LOLA. I WILL BREAK YOU JUST AS I BROKE HER.
AFTER ALL, YOU ONLY NEED ONE EYE TO WATCH YOUR SON DIE, NO...?
YOU NEVER BROKE ME.

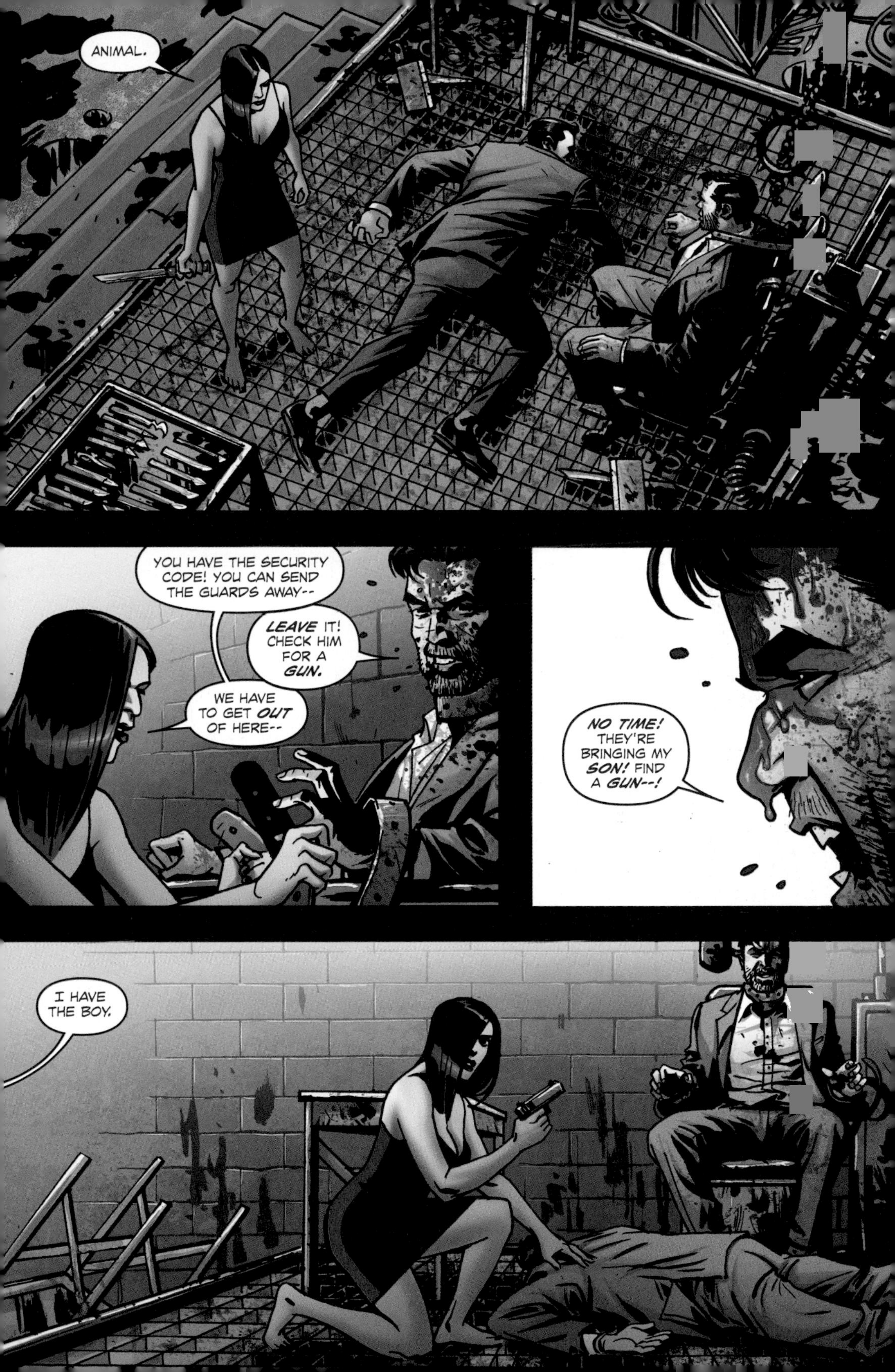
ANIMAL.
YOU HAVE THE SECURITY CODE! YOU CAN SEND THE GUARDS AWAY--
LEAVE IT! CHECK HIM FOR A GUN.
WE HAVE TO GET OUT OF HERE--
NO TIME! THEY'RE BRINGING MY SON! FIND A GUN--!
I HAVE THE BOY.

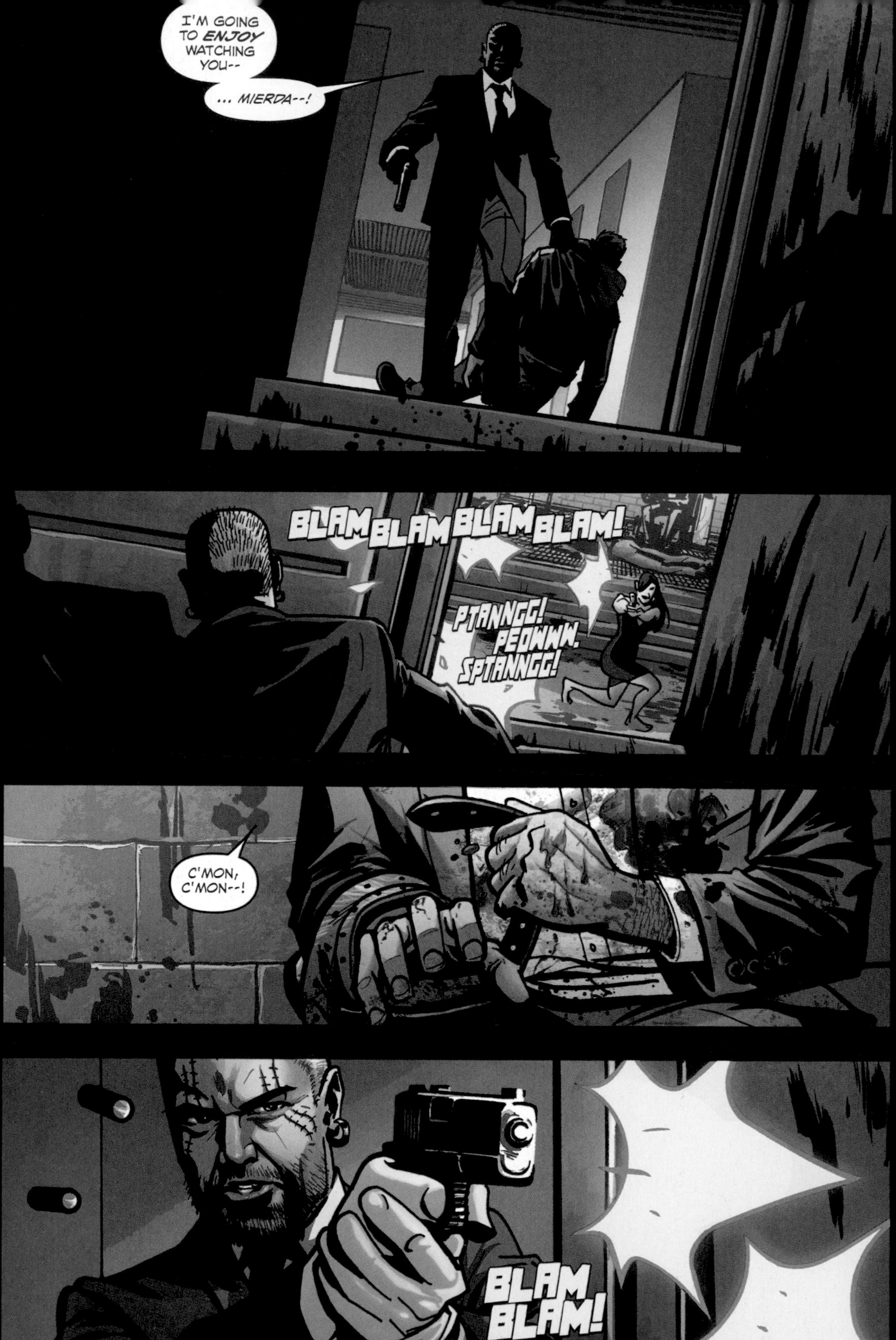

I'M GOING TO ENJOY WATCHING YOU--
... MIERDA--!
BLAM BLAM BLAM BLAM!
PTANNGG! PEOWW. SPTANNGG!
C'MON, C'MON--!
BLAM BLAM!

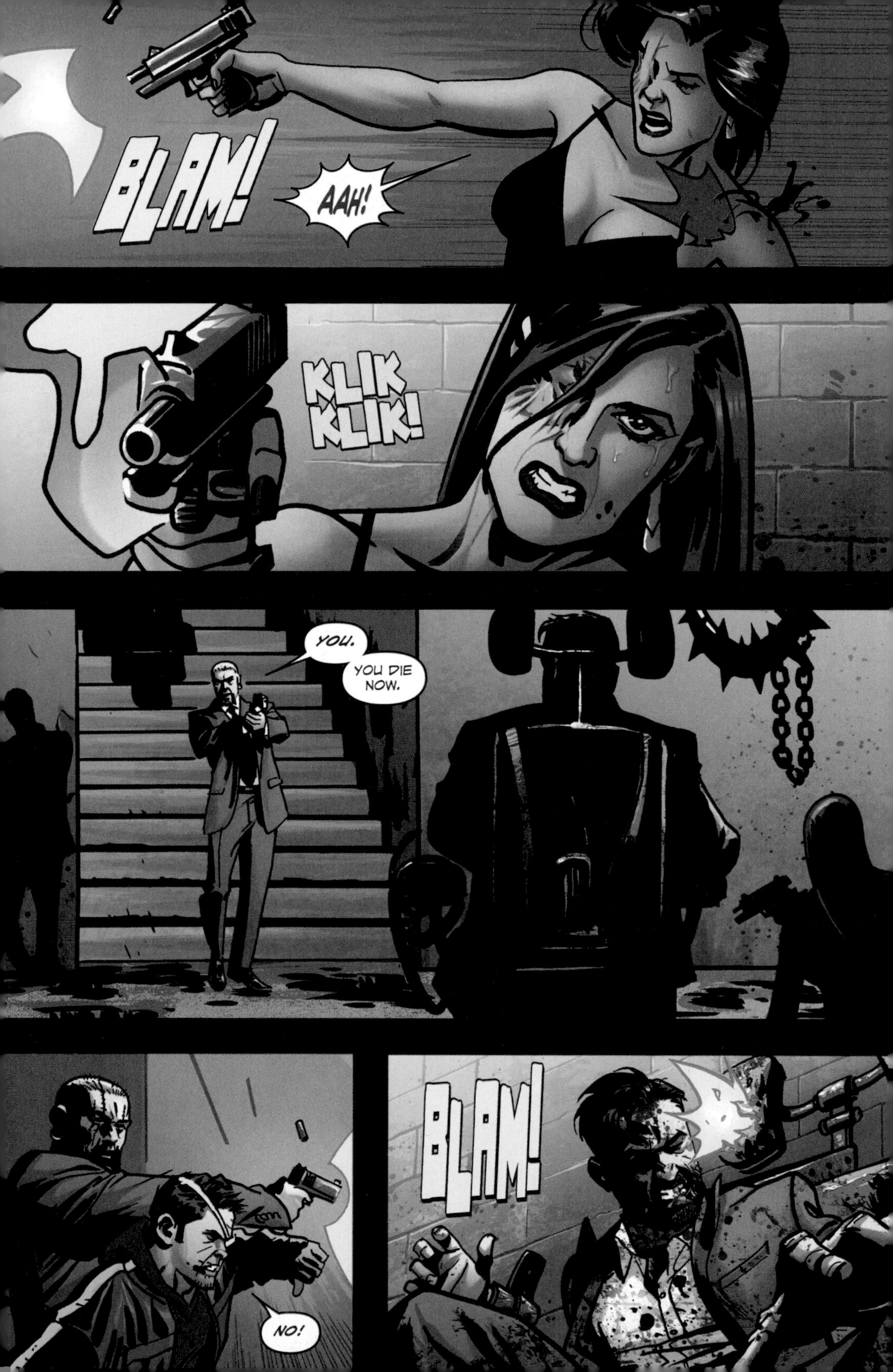
BLAM!
AAH!
KLIK KLIK!
YOU.
YOU DIE NOW.
NO!
BLAM!

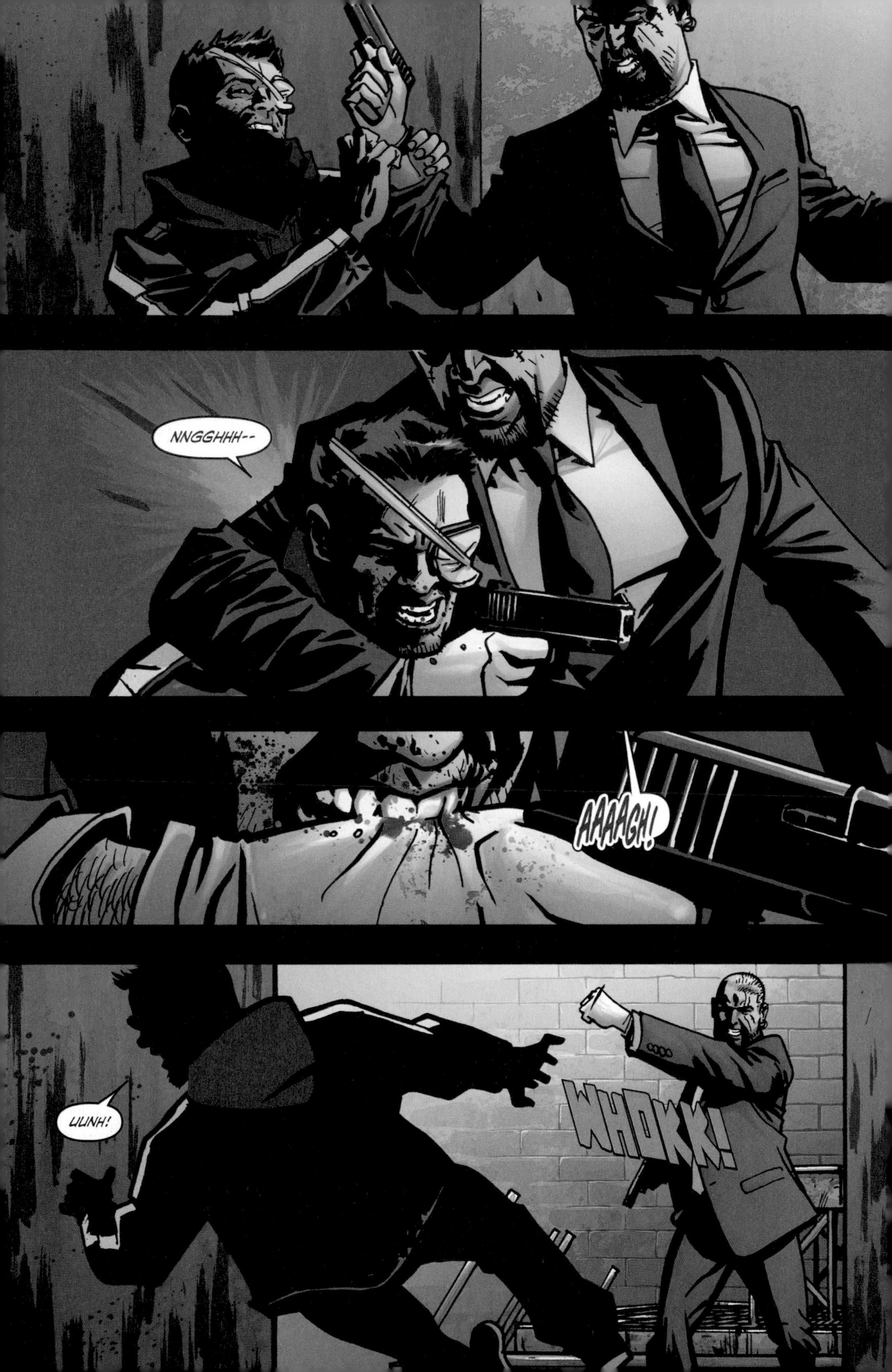
NNGGHHH--
AAAAGH!
UUNH!
WHOKK!

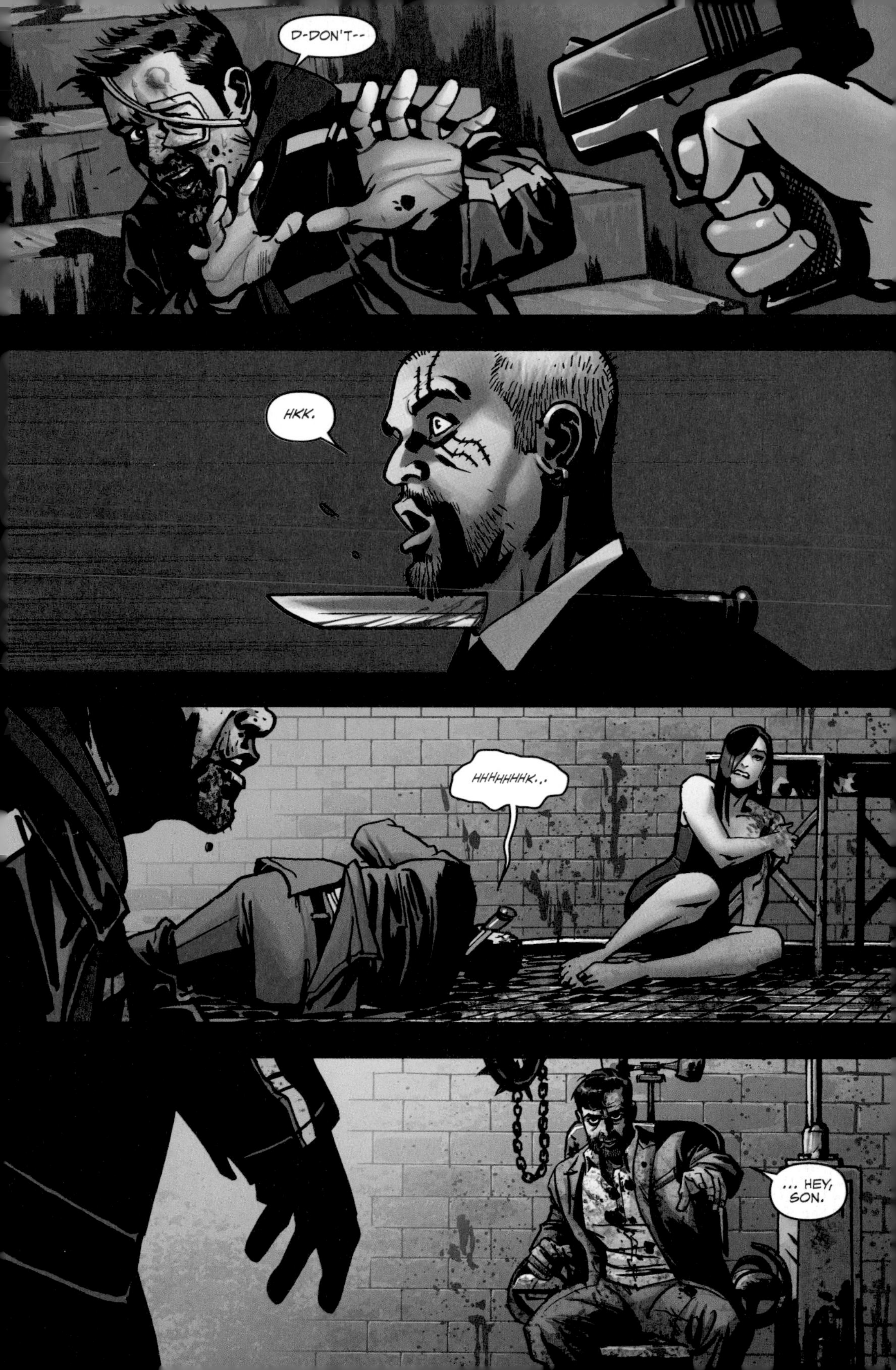
D-DON'T--
HKK.
HHHHHHHK...
... HEY, SON.

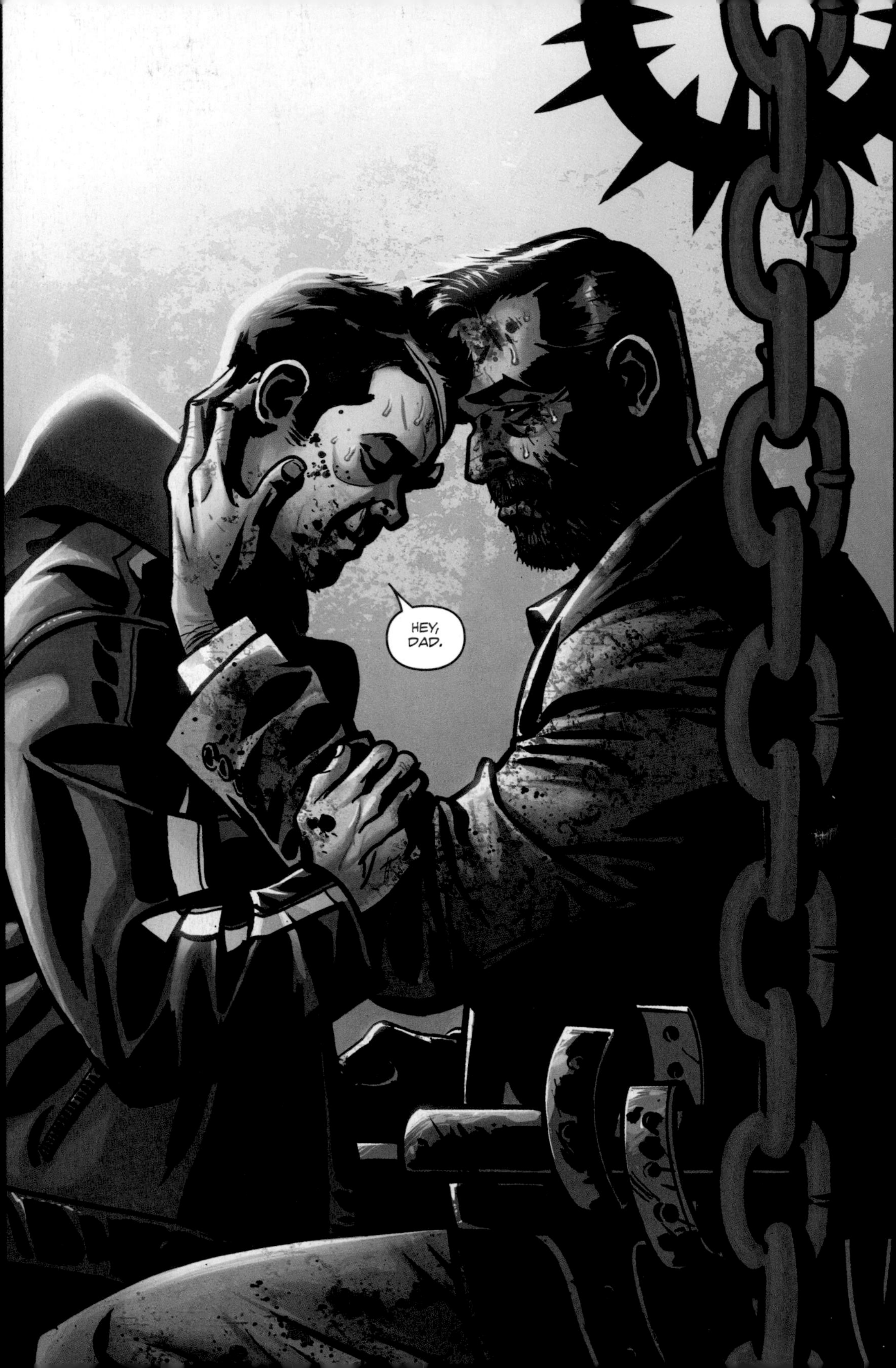
HEY, DAD.

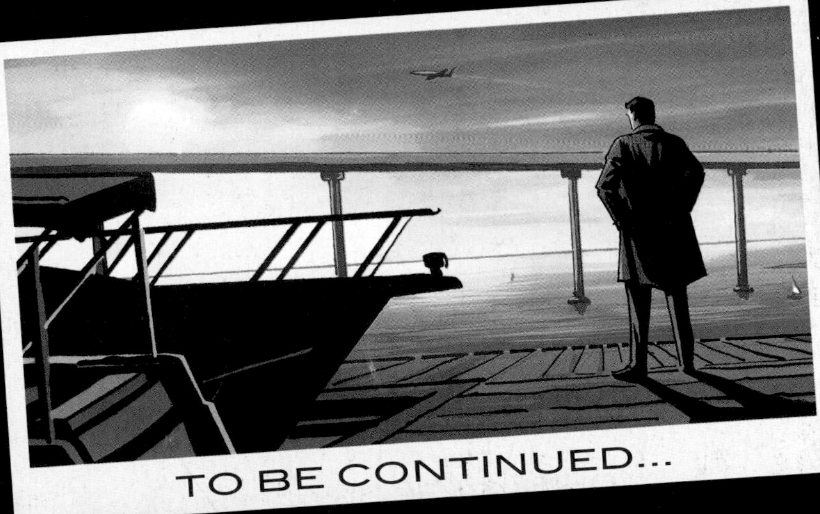

TO BE CONTINUED...

SKYBOUND INSIDER

Join the **Skybound Insider** program and get updates on all of Skybound's great content including **The Walking Dead**.

- Get a **monthly** newsletter
- **Invites** to members-only events
- **Sneak peeks** of new comics
- **Discounts** on merchandise at the Skybound and Walking Dead online stores.

Membership is **free** and it only takes a minute to sign up.

BECOME A SKYBOUND INSIDER TODAY!
insider.skybound.com

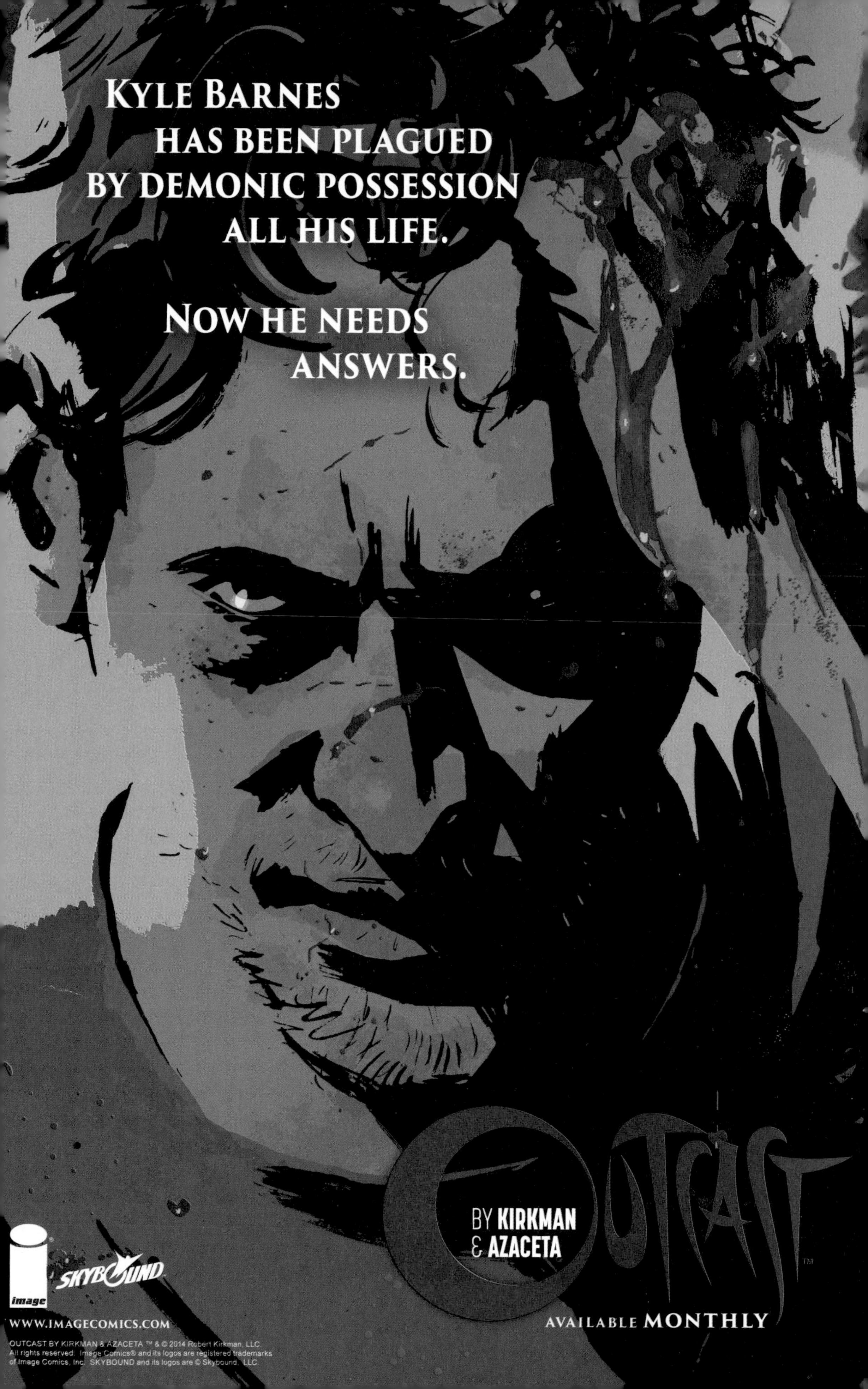
KYLE BARNES
HAS BEEN PLAGUED
BY DEMONIC POSSESSION
ALL HIS LIFE.
NOW HE NEEDS
ANSWERS.
OUTCAST
BY KIRKMAN
& AZACETA
AVAILABLE MONTHLY
image
SKYBOUND
WWW.IMAGECOMICS.COM
OUTCAST BY KIRKMAN & AZACETA ™ & © 2014 Robert Kirkman, LLC.
All rights reserved. Image Comics® and its logos are registered trademarks
of Image Comics, Inc. SKYBOUND and its logos are © Skybound, LLC.

FOR MORE OF THE WALKING DEAD

TRADEPAPERBACKS

ROBERT KIRKMAN TONY MOORE
THE WALKING DEAD
VOLUME 1
DAYS GONE BYE

VOL. 1: DAYS GONE BYE TP
ISBN: 978-1-58240-672-5
$14.99
VOL. 2: MILES BEHIND US TP
ISBN: 978-1-58240-775-3
$14.99
VOL. 3: SAFETY BEHIND BARS TP
ISBN: 978-1-58240-805-7
$14.99
VOL. 4: THE HEART'S DESIRE TP
ISBN: 978-1-58240-530-8
$14.99
VOL. 5: THE BEST DEFENSE TP
ISBN: 978-1-58240-612-1
$14.99
VOL. 6: THIS SORROWFUL LIFE TP
ISBN: 978-1-58240-684-8
$14.99
VOL. 7: THE CALM BEFORE TP
ISBN: 978-1-58240-828-6
$14.99
VOL. 8: MADE TO SUFFER TP
ISBN: 978-1-58240-883-5
$14.99
VOL. 9: HERE WE REMAIN TP
ISBN: 978-1-60706-022-2
$14.99
VOL. 10: WHAT WE BECOME TP
ISBN: 978-1-60706-075-8
$14.99
VOL. 11: FEAR THE HUNTERS TP
ISBN: 978-1-60706-181-6
$14.99
VOL. 12: LIFE AMONG THEM TP
ISBN: 978-1-60706-254-7
$14.99
VOL. 13: TOO FAR GONE TP
ISBN: 978-1-60706-329-2
$14.99
VOL. 14: NO WAY OUT TP
ISBN: 978-1-60706-392-6
$14.99
VOL. 15: WE FIND OURSELVES TP
ISBN: 978-1-60706-440-4
$14.99
VOL. 16: A LARGER WORLD TP
ISBN: 978-1-60706-559-3
$14.99
VOL. 17: SOMETHING TO FEAR TP
ISBN: 978-1-60706-615-6
$14.99
VOL. 18: WHAT COMES AFTER TP
ISBN: 978-1-60706-687-3
$14.99
VOL. 19: MARCH TO WAR TP
ISBN: 978-1-60706-818-1
$14.99
VOL. 20: ALL OUT WAR PART ONE TP
ISBN: 978-1-60706-882-2
$14.99
VOL. 21: ALL OUT WAR PART TWO TP
ISBN: 978-1-63215-030-1
$14.99
VOL. 1: SPANISH EDITION TP
ISBN: 978-1-60706-797-9
$14.99
VOL. 2: SPANISH EDITION TP
ISBN: 978-1-60706-845-7
$14.99
VOL. 3: SPANISH EDITION TP
ISBN: 978-1-60706-883-9
$14.99
VOL. 4: SPANISH EDITION TP
ISBN: 978-1-63215-035-6
$14.99

HARDCOVERS

THE WALKING DEAD
BOOK ONE
a continuing story of survival horror.

BOOK ONE HC
ISBN: 978-1-58240-619-0
$34.99
BOOK TWO HC
ISBN: 978-1-58240-698-5
$34.99
BOOK THREE HC
ISBN: 978-1-58240-825-5
$34.99
BOOK FOUR HC
ISBN: 978-1-60706-000-0
$34.99
BOOK FIVE HC
ISBN: 978-1-60706-171-7
$34.99
BOOK SIX HC
ISBN: 978-1-60706-327-8
$34.99
BOOK SEVEN HC
ISBN: 978-1-60706-439-8
$34.99
BOOK EIGHT HC
ISBN: 978-1-60706-593-7
$34.99
BOOK NINE HC
ISBN: 978-1-60706-798-6
$34.99
BOOK TEN HC
ISBN: 978-1-63215-034-9
$34.99

COMPENDIUMS

The ultimate edition of The New York Times bestseller!
THE WALKING DEAD
COMPENDIUM ONE
Robert Kirkman • Charlie Adlard • Tony Moore • Cliff Rathburn

COMPENDIUM TP, VOL. 1
ISBN: 978-1-60706-076-5
$59.99
COMPENDIUM TP, VOL. 2
ISBN: 978-1-60706-596-8
$59.99

SPECIALTY BOOKS

THE WALKING DEAD
THE COVERS

THE WALKING DEAD: THE COVERS, VOL. 1 HC
ISBN: 978-1-60706-002-4
$24.99
THE WALKING DEAD SURVIVORS' GUIDE
ISBN: 978-1-60706-458-9
$12.99
THE WALKING DEAD: ALL OUT WAR HC
ISBN: 978-1-60706-002-4
$24.99

OMNIBUS

THE WALKING DEAD

OMNIBUS, VOL. 1
ISBN: 978-1-60706-503-6
$100.00
OMNIBUS, VOL. 2
ISBN: 978-1-60706-515-9
$100.00
OMNIBUS, VOL. 3
ISBN: 978-1-60706-330-8
$100.00
OMNIBUS, VOL. 4
ISBN: 978-1-60706-616-3
$100.00
OMNIBUS, VOL. 5
ISBN: 978-1-63215-042-4
$100.00

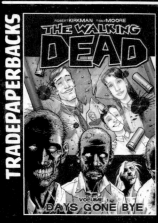

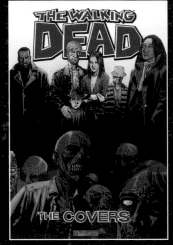

FOR MORE OF INVINCIBLE

TRADEPAPERBACKS

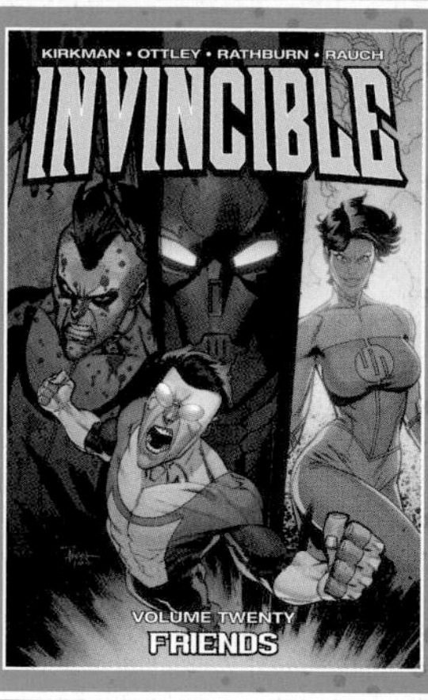
KIRKMAN • OTTLEY • RATHBURN • RAUCH
INVINCIBLE
VOLUME TWENTY
FRIENDS

VOL. 1: FAMILY MATTERS TP
ISBN: 978-1-58240-711-1
$12.99

VOL. 2: EIGHT IS ENOUGH TP
ISBN: 978-1-58240-347-2
$12.99

VOL. 3: PERFECT STRANGERS TP
ISBN: 978-1-58240-793-7
$12.99

VOL. 4: HEAD OF THE CLASS TP
ISBN: 978-1-58240-440-2
$14.95

VOL. 5: THE FACTS OF LIFE TP
ISBN: 978-1-58240-554-4
$14.99

VOL. 6: A DIFFERENT WORLD TP
ISBN: 978-1-58240-579-7
$14.99

VOL. 7: THREE'S COMPANY TP
ISBN: 978-1-58240-656-5
$14.99

VOL. 8: MY FAVORITE MARTIAN TP
ISBN: 978-1-58240-683-1
$14.99

VOL. 9: OUT OF THIS WORLD TP
ISBN: 978-1-58240-827-9
$14.99

VOL. 10: WHO'S THE BOSS TP
ISBN: 978-1-60706-013-0
$16.99

VOL. 11: HAPPY DAYS TP
ISBN: 978-1-60706-062-8
$16.99

VOL. 12: STILL STANDING TP
ISBN: 978-1-60706-166-3
$16.99

VOL. 13: GROWING PAINS TP
ISBN: 978-1-60706-251-6
$16.99

VOL. 14: THE VILTRUMITE WAR TP
ISBN: 978-1-60706-367-4
$19.99

VOL. 15: GET SMART TP
ISBN: 978-1-60706-498-5
$16.99

VOL. 16: FAMILY TIES TP
ISBN: 978-1-60706-579-1
$16.99

VOL. 17: WHAT'S HAPPENING TP
ISBN: 978-1-60706-662-0
$16.99

VOL. 18: DEATH OF EVERYONE TP
ISBN: 978-1-60706-762-7
$16.99

VOL. 19: THE WAR AT HOME TP
ISBN: 978-1-60706-856-3
$16.99

VOL. 20: FRIENDS TP
ISBN: 978-1-63215-043-1
$16.99

THE OFFICIAL HANDBOOK OF
THE INVINCIBLE UNIVERSE TP
ISBN: 978-1-58240-831-6
$12.99

INVINCIBLE PRESENTS,
VOL. 1: ATOM EVE & REX SPLODE TP
ISBN: 978-1-60706-255-4
$14.99

COMPLETE LIBRARY

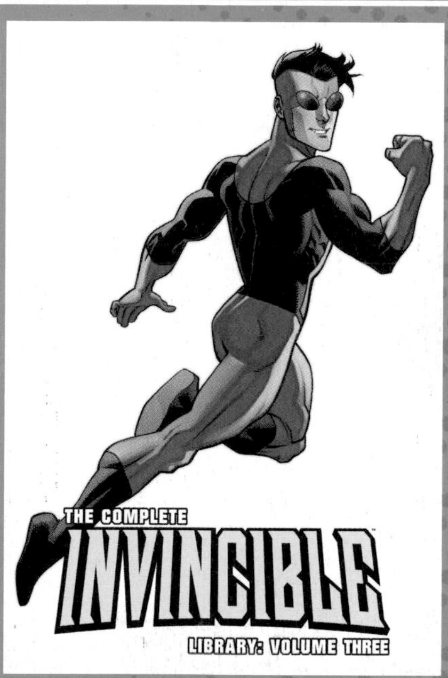
THE COMPLETE
INVINCIBLE
LIBRARY: VOLUME THREE

THE COMPLETE INVINCIBLE LIBRARY, VOL. 2 HC
ISBN: 978-1-60706-112-0
$125.00

THE COMPLETE INVINCIBLE LIBRARY, VOL. 3 HC
ISBN: 978-1-60706-421-3
$125.00

COMPENDIUMS

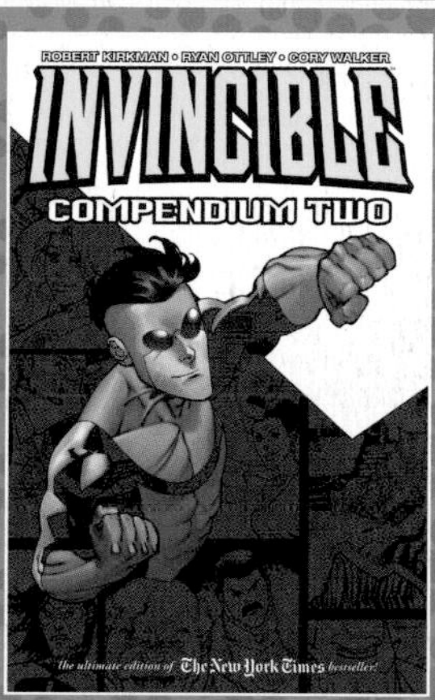
ROBERT KIRKMAN • RYAN OTTLEY • CORY WALKER
INVINCIBLE
COMPENDIUM TWO
the ultimate edition of The New York Times bestseller!

COMPENDIUM VOL. 1
ISBN: 978-1-60706-411-4
$64.99

COMPENDIUM VOL. 2
ISBN: 978-1-60706-772-6
$64.99

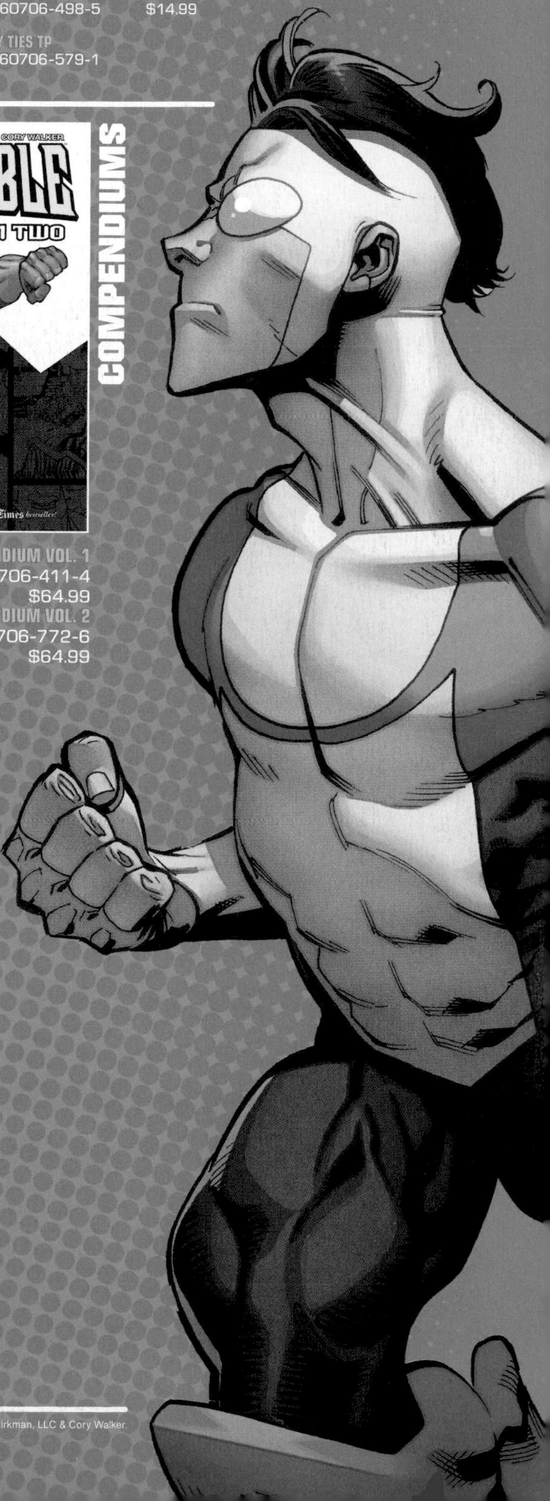

ULTIMATE COLLECTIONS

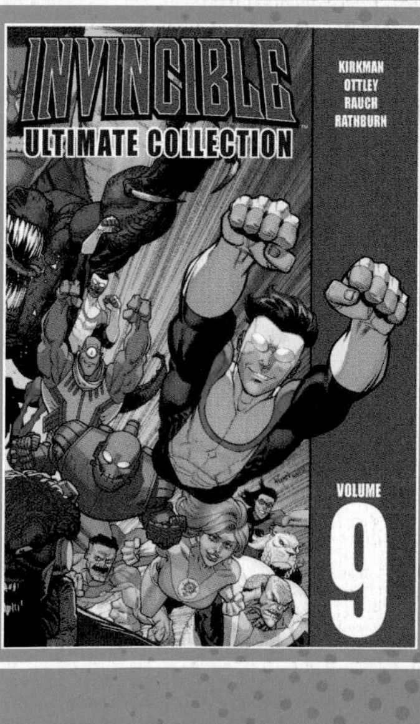
INVINCIBLE
ULTIMATE COLLECTION
KIRKMAN
OTTLEY
RAUCH
RATHBURN
VOLUME
9

ULTIMATE COLLECTION, VOL. 1 HC
ISBN 978-1-58240-500-1
$34.95

ULTIMATE COLLECTION, VOL. 2 HC
ISBN: 978-1-58240-594-0
$34.99

ULTIMATE COLLECTION, VOL. 3 HC
ISBN: 978-1-58240-763-0
$34.99

ULTIMATE COLLECTION, VOL. 4 HC
ISBN: 978-1-58240-989-4
$34.99

ULTIMATE COLLECTION, VOL. 5 HC
ISBN: 978-1-60706-116-8
$34.99

ULTIMATE COLLECTION, VOL. 6 HC
ISBN: 978-1-60706-360-5
$34.99

ULTIMATE COLLECTION, VOL. 7 HC
ISBN: 978-1-60706-509-8
$39.99

ULTIMATE COLLECTION, VOL. 8 HC
ISBN: 978-1-60706-680-4
$39.99

ULTIMATE COLLECTION, VOL. 9 HC
ISBN: 978-1-63215-032-5
$39.99

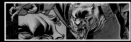

A Kalmus Classic Edition

George Frideric

HANDEL

JUDAS MACCABAEUS

An Oratorio

for Soli, Chorus and Orchestra

CHORAL SCORE

K 06206

Kalmus